IN THE POWER OF THE SPIRIT

SOIXANTE CINQ

Sermons de Iean Cal-
VIN SVR L'HARMONIE
OV CONCORDANCE DES TROIS
Euãgeliſtes, S.Matthieu, ſainct
Marc,& S.Luc.

RECVEILLIS FIDELE-
mẽt par feu M.Denys Ragueneau,à meſure
qu'on les preſchoit.

A GENEVE.
Imprimé par Conrad Badius,
M. D. LXII.

Title page of Calvin's *Soixante cinq sermons sur l'Harmonie ou Concordance des trois Evangelistes* (Geneva: Conrad Badius, 1562)

IN THE POWER OF THE SPIRIT

SERMONS ON MATTHEW, MARK & LUKE

John Calvin

Translated from the French of 1562

by

Robert White

THE BANNER OF TRUTH TRUST

THE BANNER OF TRUTH TRUST

Head Office
3 Murrayfield Road
Edinburgh, EH12 6EL
UK

North America Office
610 Alexander Spring Road
Carlisle, PA 17015
USA

banneroftruth.org

First Banner of Truth edition 2024

ISBN
Print: 978 1 80040 428 1
Epub: 978 1 80040 429 8

*

Typeset in 11/15 pt Adobe Caslon Pro at
The Banner of Truth Trust, Edinburgh

Printed in the USA by
Versa Press, Inc.,
East Peoria, IL

CONTENTS

'I have baptized you with water, but he will baptize you with the Holy Spirit' (Mark 1:8).

And when Jesus was baptized, he went up immediately from the water, and behold, the heavens were opened, and he saw the Spirit of God descending like a dove and alighting on him (Matt. 3:16).

Then Jesus was led by the Spirit into the wilderness to be tempted by the devil (Matt. 4:1).

And Jesus returned in the power of the Spirit into Galilee, and a report concerning him went out through all the surrounding country (Luke 4:14).

And there was given to him the book of the prophet Isaiah. He opened the book and found the place where it was written, 'The Spirit of the Lord is upon me, because he has anointed me to preach good news to the poor' (Luke 4:17-18).

INTRODUCTION

MODERN interest in Calvin's work as a preacher is of relatively recent date. The demand for the Reformer's sermons, either in their original printed form or in translation, which was much in evidence during his lifetime and for thirty years after his death, was not destined to last. For the next three centuries Calvin was known essentially as the author of one book, *The Institutes of the Christian Religion*, which for generations of readers provided the only point of entry into his thought and work. Nor was the situation greatly altered by the publication, between 1863 and 1900, of Calvin's collected works, including over 850 sermons on both Old and New Testament books.[1] At the beginning of the twentieth century, Emile Doumergue, in his lengthy study of Calvin's life and times, was one of the few to recognize the value of the sermons for an understanding of the Reformer's theology.[2] Sporadic attention was paid to Calvin's preaching in the interwar years in Germany, but it was not until the immediate post-war period that English-speakers were treated to the first serious account of Calvin as preacher, and to a number of new translations, the first in almost four hundred years.[33] Interest in Calvin's homiletic works may be said to have

[1] G. Baum, E. Cunitz and E. Reuss (eds.), *Calvini opera quae supersunt omnia*, 59 vols (Brunswick and Berlin: C.A. Schwetschke & Son, 1863–1900). Hereafter cited as *CO*. The sermons are variously placed between *CO* 23 and 58.

[2] Emile Doumergue, *Jean Calvin, les hommes et les choses de son temps*, 7 vols. (Lausanne/Neuilly: G. Bridel/La Cause, 1899–1927), Vol. IV, Parts 2 to 7.

[3] Notable publications were those of T.H.L. Parker, *The Oracles of God: An Introduction to the Preaching of John Calvin* (London: Lutterworth, 1947), and Leroy Nixon, *John Calvin, Expository Preacher* (Grand Rapids: Eerdmans, 1950). To Parker and Nixon

been decisively rekindled in our own time by the publication, in the *Supplementa calviniana* series, of hundreds of manuscript sermons held by various European libraries, and which reveal, if proof were needed, Calvin's skill as a biblical expositor and his passion as preacher and pastor.[4]

Of the sermons which Calvin preached in the course of his long ministry in Geneva (1536–38, 1541–64), over 2,300 were recorded in shorthand, transcribed and kept initially in manuscript form, with a view, perhaps, to eventual publication. Of those which were recorded, some 1,640 have survived, most of which are available in print.

The sermons translated here belong to a series on the Synoptic Gospels, titled *Soixante cinq sermons sur l'Harmonie ou Concordance des trois Evangelistes, S. Matthieu, S. Marc et S. Luc*, published in Geneva by Conrad Badius in January 1562. A pirated edition appeared that same year in Lyons, to be followed by a second—authorized—Genevan edition of 1590.[5] Calvin's sixty-five sermons cover a comparatively small portion of the three Gospels. Denis Raguenier, Calvin's stenographer, died in the winter of 1560–61. Subsequent sermons on the Synoptics went unrecorded, with the result that although the preacher continued his exposition for three more years, his words are lost to us.

With the exception of his sermons on the Book of Acts, all of the Reformer's New Testament sermons were preceded by a published commentary. Calvin's commentary on *A Harmony of the Three Evangelists* appeared in 1555. In it, as in the sermons, the Gospel texts were arranged in the form of a harmony or

---

we also owe independent translations of Calvin's sermons on Isaiah 53, and to Nixon selected sermons on Job and on other New Testament texts.

[4] *Supplementa calviniana: Sermons inédits de Jean Calvin* (Neukirchen-Vluyn: Neukirchener Verlag, 1961 ff., 12 vols. to date). An historical survey of studies on Calvin's work as preacher is provided by Richard Stauffer, *Dieu, la création et la providence dans la prédication de Calvin* (Bern: Peter Lang, 1978), pp. 309-18.

[5] For bibliographical details, see Rodolphe Peter and Jean-François Gilmont, *Bibliotheca calviniana*, 3 vols. (Geneva: Droz, 1991–2000), II:953-60.

conflated narrative, a device borrowed from Martin Bucer, whose *Expositions on the Gospels of St Matthew, St Mark and St Luke* were first published in 1527. Calvin freely acknowledges his debt to Bucer in the 'Outline' which prefaces his commentary, and he claims him as his model.[6] When the time came to begin his pulpit exposition of the Gospels, the preacher was thoroughly in command of his material.

While none of the *Soixante cinq sermons* is dated, external evidence suggests that the whole series was delivered between July 1559 and November 1560. All are Sunday sermons, since Calvin's weekday sermons were reserved for Old Testament texts; but whereas his earlier practice was to preach twice on Sundays, ill health now restricted him to one Sunday service a week—a considerable commitment nevertheless, given that his voice was not strong and that the sermon was rarely less than one hour in duration.

* * *

Calvin begins his Synoptic sermons with the birth and infancy narratives of Matthew and Luke and concludes with the Beatitudes (Matt. 5:1-11; Luke 6:20-26).[7] Between these two poles lie major events of Jesus' initial ministry in Galilee. The prophetic work of John the Baptist, Jesus' baptism in the Jordan, his temptation in the wilderness, his ministry of teaching and healing and his calling of the first disciples—it is with these elements that the preacher is concerned.

With the exception of five verses which Matthew assigns to a later chapter (Matt. 8:14-18), all of Calvin's texts belong to

[6] 'Outline', *Commentary on the Synoptic Gospels, CO* 45:1-4. The same outline prefaces the *Soixante cinq sermons* (CO 46:iv-vii).

[7] See our earlier translations: Calvin, *Sermons on the Beatitudes* (Edinburgh: Banner of Truth Trust, 2006); Calvin, *Songs of the Nativity* (Edinburgh: Banner of Truth Trust, 2008).

the early chapters of the Synoptic Gospels: Matthew 3:1–4:25, Mark 1:1-39, Luke 3:1–5:11. Generally speaking, it is Matthew's chronology which the Reformer follows, except where material unique to Mark and/or Luke requires a change of direction. In expounding his texts he gives equal weight to each of his sources, considering an event attested by only one Evangelist to be as credible and noteworthy as one attested by all three. He is not unaware of what was later to be called the Synoptic problem, but he regards it as a false issue. All three Evangelists, he holds, worked independently of each other, 'setting out to record faithfully the things of which they were sure and certain, but according to God's providence which directed everything. So too the Holy Spirit, despite their differing approaches, nevertheless prompted them to agree fully about what mattered most.'[8] Our estimate of the Gospels depends, in Calvin's view, not on our ability to arrange their varied data to our satisfaction, but, in the words of Ned B. Stonehouse, 'on the unity which they possess as trustworthy witnesses to Christ'.[9]

In his sermons on the Synoptics, Calvin spends only as much time as is strictly necessary on the narrative itself. It is the doctrinal implications of his texts and their relevance to Christian living which occupy him most. Among the doctrines which engage his attention, three, cast in a thoroughly Trinitarian mould, are especially prominent: the Father's unerring ordering of events, so that all that happens conforms to his perfect will; the authority and power exercised by the Son, whose words and deeds reveal his divine majesty; and the guidance and enabling of the Holy Spirit, who both fills the Son and confirms the nature of his calling.[10]

[8] 'Outline', *Soixante cinq sermons* (*CO* 46:vi).

[9] *Paul before the Areopagus and Other New Testament Studies* (London: Tyndale Press, 1957), pp. 126-27.

[10] While all three Synoptists record the Baptist's prophecy of the Spirit's advent, his descent at the time of Jesus' baptism and his presence with Jesus in the wilderness, Luke

The Evangelists depict a series of unremitting conflicts in which God's grace confronts the demonic forces of temptation, ignorance, unbelief, suffering and disease. While the outcome of these conflicts is not in doubt, since God is sovereign and since Satan acts solely by God's leave, Jesus is acknowledged as the Christ only by the unclean spirits, who speak partly out of fear and partly in derision. Acclaimed, like John the Baptist, as a prophet and, unlike John, as a miracle-worker, he arouses astonishment and even awe, but finds acceptance only among a nucleus of disciples who leave all to follow him. The world's Redeemer is for the time being unacknowledged; the Messianic secret remains as yet hidden.

Just as striking as the doctrinal import of these passages, are the spiritual and ethical challenges which the preacher throws out to his congregation. As in all of Calvin's preaching, the hearers are called on to confront not only the fact of their finitude—an effort requiring only a modicum of honesty—but their moral defilement, their iniquity, their want of righteousness, their estrangement from the God who made them and who from birth has amply supplied their needs. They, like their father Adam, have proved rebellious and ungrateful.

It is not surprising, then, if these sermons often sound the note of judgment. It could hardly be otherwise, given that the first of our sermons begins with the Baptist's call to repent, a call repeated by Jesus himself and given greater urgency by the threat of impending wrath (Matt. 3:7; Luke 3:7). We must therefore, says the preacher, learn to humble ourselves under the mighty hand of God, and to see ourselves as vile, habitual offenders, deserving only death. We dare not trifle with God. Genuine repentance consists in the determination to put sin behind us,

adds two significant details: it is in 'the power of the Spirit' that Jesus is said to begin his Galilean ministry (4:14), and it is the same Spirit, foretold by Isaiah (Isa. 61:1-2), whom Jesus, in the Nazareth synagogue, claims to rest upon him (4:18).

to deny ourselves and to give ourselves in obedience to God. It is measured not by the strength of our remorse but by the depth of our shame and self-condemnation. Yet with the call to repentance comes also the possibility of redress. John preaches a baptism of repentance for the forgiveness of sins (Mark 1:4; Luke 3:3). We cannot absolve ourselves: that is the Father's prerogative and the prerogative of Jesus Christ his Son. Simon Peter, Calvin claims, was both right and wrong to ask Jesus to depart from him (Luke 5:8). He was right because his sinfulness was an offence to the one who stood before him; but he was wrong because he could not admit the idea of pardoning grace. 'What are sinners to do,' comments Calvin, 'except ask our Lord Jesus Christ to have mercy on them? He did not come into the world for those who were holy; he came to heal the sick … Knowing this, we can say, in contrast to Peter, "Lord, I am a wretched sinner. I am therefore here to ask you to make me your own, to dwell even in me, and to clothe me with yourself."'[11]

The obverse of judgment is thus acceptance, deliverance from guilt, the remission of sins. It is this that makes the gospel 'good news to the poor' (Luke 4:18). The first words which Mark attributes to Jesus are the dual call to repent and believe the gospel (Mark 1:15). Repentance and faith go hand in hand; they are necessary to conversion. They constitute, says Calvin, the sum total of the gospel. The good news consists in the proclamation of an end to our estrangement, in our reconciliation to God and in his adoption of us as his children. It is all a work of mercy. 'God,' declares the preacher, 'sets his goodness before us without waiting for us to seek him out; he forestalls us with such exceptional grace that we cannot grasp even a hundredth part of it.'[12] What we do grasp, we grasp by faith. The author of the *Institutes* defines faith succinctly as 'a firm and certain knowledge of God's

[11] Sermon 15.
[12] Sermon 10.

goodwill toward us, founded on the free promise given to us in Jesus Christ.'[13] In his Synoptic sermons, he expands his definition thus: 'Faith means knowing that God is willing to bury all our transgressions, and that he chooses not to reckon with us as our judge but will accept us as righteous, because our stains have been washed by the blood of his Son. Moreover, what we cannot do for ourselves, he will do by the grace of his Holy Spirit. Since we are incapable of changing ourselves, he himself will change us.'[14]

Few of Calvin's sermons fail to celebrate God's grace in Christ, and the Holy Spirit's work of renewal which, given our stubbornness, is the work of a lifetime. Christians never cease to be scholars in God's school. It is thus no accident that these sermons are peppered with appeals to learn, note, observe, grasp and remember the lessons which they convey, and that Jesus Christ is constantly represented as the church's *maistre* and *docteur*, its teacher and instructor. Only as we apply and practise what we have learned can we be said to profit from God's word and to grow in faith. How, then, is growth to be measured?

It is measured, first, by the genuineness of our love of, and delight in, the gospel, which Calvin describes as a priceless treasure and as the key which opens the door by which we come to God. With every proclamation of the gospel, God is said to meet us 'face to face'; the act of proclamation is in the truest sense a theophany.[15] Our growth is measured also by our determination to live according to God's will, to shoulder the yoke he places on us and to accept both his rebuke and his correction.[16] Among the lessons we need to learn, the hardest perhaps is patience in adversity, and readiness to bear the trials which test our powers of endurance, powers which are not native to us but

[13] *Inst.* III.2.7.

[14] Sermon 10.

[15] Sermons 1, 4, 7, 11, 13, 16.

[16] Sermon 4.

which are given by the Holy Spirit who strengthens and cleanses even as he sieves and winnows us. 'God makes us good grain, where once we were only chaff, straw and dust.'[17] And since the Christian life cannot be lived without conflict, because, in the preacher's words, 'we end one fight only to begin another', we must make Jesus Christ our mirror and model, taking God's word to be our shield and, like Christ, looking for deliverance to the Father, who reckons us as his children and who loves us in the Beloved.[18] And when, finally, we find ourselves assailed by doubt and by despair, when we are conscious only of our faithlessness and fruitlessness, what else can we do but cast ourselves on the grace and mercy of God, who 'keeps us walking when we cannot fly, and who, when we cannot walk, lets us at least creep forward'?[19] Above and beyond all this, we must let God be God; we must bow before his majesty and acknowledge his right to rule us. It is the mark of the spiritually dead to believe that they have God in their pocket or, in Calvin's phrase, 'up their sleeve'. To lay down the law to him is to tempt him, to put him on trial. 'God's promise not to fail us should suffice.'[20]

* * *

The present volume comprises eighteen sermons; they are numbered in the original edition 41-42 and 45-60.[21] To the best of my knowledge they have not before been translated into English, despite the extraordinary diligence of Calvin's Elizabethan translators. The first four sermons bear on the message and ministry of John the Baptist, the remainder on Jesus'

[17] Sermon 4.
[18] Sermon 6.
[19] Sermon 2.
[20] Sermon 8.
[21] The Badius edition reverses the order of Sermons 40 and 41, both of which treat the same text; it numbers Sermon 41 as 40. *CO* retains the numbering of the Badius edition.

baptism, temptation, preaching and works of healing in Galilee. The Evangelists' grand theme is the proclamation of the reign of God and its arrival in the person of Jesus, Son of God, whose word and works attest its power and reality. He speaks with authority, on God's behalf, promising forgiveness to those who repent of their sins; his healings and exorcisms demonstrate that God is returning order to a world characterized by disorder and distress. Satan, the 'strong man', is being despoiled by one who is stronger than he.

This translation is based on the text established by Baum, Cunitz and Reuss,[22] but has been extensively compared with that of the Badius edition of 1562. Paragraph divisions have been introduced and punctuation modernized. Scripture references have been moved from the margins into the main body of the text, and have been corrected and supplemented when necessary. When Calvin cites or, as frequently happens, paraphrases the biblical text, I translate the text as given. The short extempore prayer which immediately followed each sermon, and which was omitted by the editors of *CO*, has been restored. Sermon titles are my own, and I have added a small number of explanatory notes.

I wish, finally, to thank the trustees of The Banner of Truth Trust for their willingness to publish, and am especially grateful to the Trust's staff for their generous help, advice and support.

ROBERT WHITE
1 February, 2024
Sydney

[22] *CO* 46:487-500, 513-26, 551-760.

PRAYER BEFORE THE SERMON[1]

Let us call upon our good God and Father, beseeching him, since all fullness of wisdom and light is found in him, mercifully to enlighten us by his Holy Spirit in the true understanding of his word, and to give us grace to receive it in true fear and humility. May we be taught by his word to place our trust only in him and to serve and honour him as we ought, so that we may glorify his holy name in all our living and edify our neighbour by our good example, rendering to God the love and the obedience which faithful servants owe their masters, and children, their parents, since it has pleased him graciously to receive us among the number of his servants and children.

[1] The Genevan liturgy of 1542 allowed, in the Sunday services, for a prayer of illumination to be said by the minister immediately before the sermon, but prescribed no set form of words. Calvin's practice was to use a prayer which he had already employed in the French church of Strasbourg, and which was modelled on Bucer's German liturgy. Text in *CO* 23:741–42.

I

GOD'S KINGDOM PROCLAIMED

In those days John the Baptist came, preaching in the wilderness of Judaea, [2]and saying, 'Repent, for the kingdom of heaven is at hand.' [3]For this is he of whom the prophet Isaiah spoke, saying, 'The voice of one crying in the wilderness: Prepare the way of the Lord, make his paths straight' (Matt. 3:1-3).

The beginning of the gospel of Jesus Christ, the Son of God. [2]As it is written in the prophets, 'Behold, I send my messenger before your face, who will prepare your way before you; [3]the voice of one crying in the wilderness: Prepare the way of the Lord, make his paths smooth' (Mark 1:1-3).

In the fifteenth year of the reign of Tiberius Caesar, when Pontius Pilate was governor of Judaea, Herod, tetrarch of Galilee, his brother Philip, tetrarch of the region of Ituraea and Trachonitis, and Lysanias, tetrarch of Abilene, [2]and when Annas and Caiaphas were high priests, the word of God was given to John the son of Zechariah in the wilderness (Luke 3:1-2).

WE declared previously that what was said in the prophet Isaiah was confirmed and fulfilled by John the Baptist.[1]

[1] The reference is to Isa. 40:3-5 ('a voice crying in the wilderness'), a passage which

For at that time everything was in a sad and sorry state. The poor church was so disfigured that it seemed impossible to raise it up again. In a word, all was hopeless. There was no semblance of order even in the priesthood. We see that although Caiaphas was the high priest, Annas, his father-in-law, enjoyed both the rank and everything else that belonged to the priestly office. The law stated that whoever was the high priest would remain in his post until death. That, however, had all been overturned. Indeed, we know that at that time the lot of the Jews was as wretched as could be. It was as if they had been abandoned by God and were doomed to be forever cursed, viewed by all men with horror.

No one, therefore, could have ever imagined that the Saviour who had been promised to them would have appeared. Nevertheless, John the Baptist preached in the wilderness, to show that God had truly said through Isaiah that, although he had long allowed his people to languish, he would speak again, and would even send his heralds throughout the wilderness. That is, although everything was in turmoil and although only ruins remained, he would not fail to restore all things by his power. This he had already announced.

We must notice now what was said by John the Baptist in the wilderness. The essence of what he taught and preached was this: '*Repent*,' or '*Mend your ways, for the kingdom of God is at hand*.' This was why he is said to have preached a baptism of repentance and remission of sins: these two things go together and have the same end in view. We will begin with what is said about the kingdom of God, and will then speak about repentance.

When Scripture speaks about the kingdom, it first of all makes clear that we are all excluded from the hope of the heavenly life. We are estranged from God, cut off from his grace and love. In short, the devil is rightly called the prince of this world (John

---

Calvin had expounded at length in his preceding sermon (Sermon 40 of the *Gospel Harmony*).

12:31), since he holds tyrannical sway over us. It is true that in Judaea God had shown himself to be king, and the people were called by Moses a kingdom of priests (Exod. 19:6). How then is it now said that the kingdom of God is drawing near, seeing that it had existed since the giving of the law? It is because all of God's promises depended on the coming of the Redeemer. For although the fathers of old had cause to rest in these promises, and although they had an opening from God to call upon him and had assurance of their salvation—they had the Spirit of adoption by which they held God to be their Father, so that with firm faith they looked to their heavenly inheritance—these things, as I said, were in abeyance. It was necessary for the fathers of old to fix their gaze on our Lord Jesus Christ, and to wait from afar for him to accomplish what had been said concerning him. That is why our Lord Jesus Christ declares that Abraham saw his day (John 8:56), for Abraham could not have tasted anything of God's goodness unless he had set his sights on that blessed seed of which he had been told (Gen. 13:16; 22:17-18).

It is with good reason, then, that Jesus Christ is said to have come to set up and establish the kingdom of God his Father, for he ratified the promises which had previously been made. He gave reality to the earlier symbols; he was the solid form and substance of what had been shadows. In a word, he possessed that entire perfection which the law lacked, as the apostle explains at greater length in the letter to the Hebrews (Heb. 7:11, 19; 8:7; 10:14).

In any case, what we see here is that until we are reconciled to God through his only-begotten Son, he disowns us and we have no relationship with him. Instead, there exists a state of deadly war. It was thus necessary for our Lord Jesus Christ to make peace between God and men, even those who, in Paul's words, were near (Eph. 2:17). What he means is that although God had called the Jews to himself and had shown and testified that he recognized them as his people, and although, compared with the Gentiles, they were privileged to be close to him, even so they still needed Jesus Christ to be their peace. As for the Gentiles, they were without God, without life and without hope, as Paul says in that same passage (Eph. 2:12). Even so, Jesus Christ came to reconcile them to God.

So this is what we need to remember: if Jesus Christ were to be taken from us, there would be so great a distance between God and us that we could not in any way draw near to him. He would even have to give us up and to regard us as his deadly enemies, since he is judge of all the world, and since we are poor, miserable sinners, having within us every iniquity and cause for condemnation. We should certainly lower our gaze when Scripture tells us how bad our plight was before our Lord Jesus Christ was revealed to us. Let us boast as much as we like: we do not deserve, says God, even to be reckoned as one of his creatures. He makes it clear that he is separated from us, and that as rotten limbs we are estranged from him. We are only an abomination in his sight. True, despite Satan and despite all unbelievers, God does not cease to reign both high and low, but not in the same way as is described here. God reigns when he determines all things by his providence. We, however, perceive nothing of his rule when we are rebellious to him, when anything is acceptable and when no one listens to his word which is the royal sceptre by which he has dominion over us. We perceive nothing when we are not so ruled by the Spirit that, being led into obedience, we allow him to live within us, while we ourselves cease to live any way we please, as is our nature.

God does not therefore reign in this manner except when the gospel is preached to us, and when our Lord Jesus Christ, who has been made God's deputy, directs us by his word and by his Holy Spirit. Accordingly, we read in the Psalm: 'God reigns (*or* will reign); let the isles or distant lands rejoice' (Psa. 97:1). Now it is most certain that God, as we have said, being the Creator of all the world, has never relinquished his authority. His power must therefore extend to every place. However, when his word is not proclaimed, he continues to rule but in a way which is hidden from us and which we cannot understand. On the other hand he has a way of ruling by which he regenerates and remakes us, so as to show that he is near us and that we in turn are one with him. That is what causes us to rejoice, as the Psalmist says. For when unbelievers serve God and are instruments of his power, because what they do does not come from an impulse of the will, humanly speaking they have no cause to be glad; but when God brings us into submission to himself so that we conform to his righteousness, we have reason to rejoice. This is what we daily ask for in the prayer which God's Son has taught us: 'Your kingdom come.'

All the confusion which we see in the world is set against that kingdom. We see first of all that the devil so mixes and muddles everything that God seems to be denied his rights and sovereignty. Then too, we see just how rebellious men are to him: all they want is to raise their horns against him, so as to try, if they can, to pitch God's majesty out of heaven and to tread it deliberately underfoot. We see, therefore, how the wicked and those who scorn God—the godless—seethe with such rage that God has no pre-eminence among those who do their best to dishonour him.

What of ourselves? While we may be keen in some degree to submit to God, and while we may show it by what we do, we are nevertheless driven by so many desires to rebel. There is so much antagonism, so many obstacles which prevent God's kingdom from quietly prevailing among us, that we need each and every day to plead: 'Your kingdom come.' In other words, may God begin with us. May he quell those evil desires which oppose his righteousness, and may he bring the wicked to heel either by remaking them or by shaming and crushing them. Even so, we must always come back to this truth, that the devil has dominion and tyranny over us until God through Jesus Christ establishes his seat. This he does when the gospel is proclaimed, and when God adds to it the power of his Holy Spirit, so that the teaching which comes from the mouths of men is not ineffective, but produces fruit—teaching which pierces our ears so that we hear what is said, and which turns our hearts which were of stone into hearts of flesh, making them pliable so that we behave according to God's command.

That, I say, is how God begins to reign, which is what John the Baptist says here: *The kingdom of God is drawing near*. Briefly put, we are taught two things which are highly useful to us. First, in order to bring us low and to destroy all pride and arrogance in us—since we are utterly lost—God abandons us, rejects and disowns us until such time as our Lord stretches out his hand to us. That is one point. From this we may infer a second point: the message of the gospel should be precious and pleasing to us, since through it God takes us into his care and acknowledges us to be his people, whereas before we were his enemies. He desires to dwell among us and wishes us to come to him in person, to appear before him and to offer him the homage of our bodies and souls, which is our due. When, therefore, we see that the gospel brings us so great and priceless a blessing, how ungrateful would we be if we were not so thrilled as to seek this treasure out? And when it is given to us, should anything stop us from wanting it, so that we forget everything else? Should not the vanities of this world and all its blandishments be as nothing to us in comparison? So much for this second point.

Accordingly, John the Baptist, having announced that the grace of God was near at hand, draws from it the exhortation set here before us: '*Repent, therefore!*' As long as we are far removed from God, not one of us is unhappy. We are so immersed in our filth and uncleanness that it never occurs to us to bewail our faults or to stop enjoying them. We are, so to speak, bewitched by Satan, until light comes from the gospel to reveal our degradation. A man afflicted by vermin will continue to wallow in the dirt, but once awakened he will recognize his problem and look for a way out. Thus those who are black with dirt and grime, and who are badly sullied and stained, forget all about it while it is dark, but when light comes they feel ashamed. It is the same with us. That is why this conclusion is drawn: 'Since the kingdom of God is near, be sure to repent.'

Now John did not mean that we have to anticipate God's grace by our repentance. God comes to us of his own free will. He fulfils indeed what is said elsewhere in Isaiah: 'He was found by those who did not seek him, saying to those who did not ask of him, "Here am I, here am I"' (Isa. 65:1). Hence God is always the first to begin. If he were to wait until we were disposed to receive his grace, and until we of our own volition sought him out, alas, we would perish a hundred thousand times, and we would remain lost before ever help arrived. It was necessary for God to take pity on us when we were so dazzled that in our misery we could scarcely see a thing, and when the devil both owned and blinded us so that we despised all integrity and righteousness. Thus, in rescuing us from hell's deep pit, God had to come and seek us just as we were, and to extend his infinite mercy to us. Nevertheless we are unable to receive the grace held out to us in our Lord Jesus Christ unless we acknowledge our sins. For we must always notice something which we will see directly, that he came to give light to the wretchedly blind, to set the captives free and to heal the sick (Luke 4:18). If we do not feel our afflictions, we will never think anything of the physician nor of the remedies which he might bring.

Repentance must thus be joined to faith, which is why we read elsewhere in Isaiah that the Redeemer will come from

Zion, to save those in the house of Jacob who turn from their transgressions (Isa. 59:20). What the prophet means by these words is that those who are incapable of correction should not hope for any mercy from God: rather, they must feel that he is their judge. However, as for poor sinners who are troubled by sorrow and who know that they are lost—these are called to receive the salvation which God offers them when they turn from their iniquities.

Here, then, is the sum of John the Baptist's preaching. First, he proclaims that the kingdom of God is drawing near, for John was in a sense an intermediary between the prophets and our Lord Jesus Christ. Because the gospel is, so to speak, the means by which God's kingdom is established, Scripture says that it is near, inasmuch as it was then that God stretched out his arms to call to salvation those who were lost, to call to life those who were in death, and to make those who were his enemies, his children. He chose, that is, to adopt those who before were cut off from him like rotten limbs, so that they should be heirs of his kingdom. That is why it is said that men must repent, and be moved by such awareness of their misery that they humble themselves before God, so hating the evil within them that they are led to yield to God's righteousness. In the same way Paul, in urging believers to be renewed for God's service so that it is acceptable to him, seeks to impart a strong sense of feeling to his teaching when he exhorts them—challenges them, as it were—'by the mercies of God', by the most tender affection with which God was pleased to call us to salvation (Rom. 12:1).

It is certain that if we had a single drop of common sense, if we were not absolutely mindless, and even though our hearts are impossibly hard, we ought to be touched by the fact that God has disclosed to us his innermost self in order to show how much he pities us, and how much he loves us in the person of his Son. For what are we to think when, as our Lord Jesus Christ was being crucified, his side was laid open, as if to reveal his very heart? Should we be neither moved nor touched when our Lord invites us so winningly to himself and gives us such a pledge of his love? Notice, then, that there is nothing which should more drive and inflame us to come to God than when he comes to us with such sweetness, and when he meets us with his unmerited grace so that we do not perish. And although in ourselves we are already condemned and dying, he nevertheless is willing to pull us out of the pit in which he finds us.

To help us better understand these things, we should realize that these words contain all that the gospel teaches. For what commission does our Lord give his apostles when he sends them forth? 'Go,' he says, 'and preach repentance and the remission of sins' (Luke 24:47). Understand, therefore, that when mention is made of John the Baptist, it is not that he taught something quite different. He began by being a herald of the gospel, although, as we will later see, his work was not as full and complete as that of the apostles. They were preferred to him. Scripture in fact records that the least of those who preach the gospel will be judged to be greater than he was (Matt. 11:11), for, as I said, he stood midway between the prophets and the apostles. However that be, the substance of his preaching was not different; and since these two points contain the entire message of the gospel, we ought to pay attention to what is briefly taught here.

When Matthew tells us that John preached a baptism of repentance, and when Luke adds, 'for the remission of sins', they were simply stating what had already been said, that the kingdom of God was near, and that men should therefore repent. We turn, then, to an explanation of repentance and faith. I do not propose to discuss everything which might be said; my aim is to make it easier to understand these things.

Two things are necessary if we are to be saved. First, we should know that God is willing to bury our faults, so that they will not prevent us from being acceptable to him, since our Lord Jesus Christ is our peace. Through him we have been reconciled. He offered a sacrifice by which God was appeased; he shed his blood in order to make us clean by washing our spots and stains away; he rendered full obedience to God his Father, so that our trespasses might not be imputed to us. That is how, in our Lord Jesus Christ, we have complete assurance that God is willing to receive us and to reckon us as his children, even though we are not worthy to be acknowledged as his creatures, or to be counted as worms, insects or the least of the world's vermin!

Faith grasps something else in Jesus Christ: he brings to us the Spirit of renewal. When we examine all our thoughts, motives and affections, we are certain to find nothing but evil and wilfulness. Hypocrites flatter themselves; they hide in the midst of their darkness and seek to be thought of as just; they try with all their might to conceal their iniquities. This is an evil which is found more or less in everyone, but it does us no good: God condemns us, and as we have seen we are already estranged from him. Now if he is the source of all goodness, what will be left to us if we are cut off from his kingdom and if he refuses to have any dealings with us? So faith, in the first place, accepts and receives the grace which God has given to us in his only-begotten Son. He chooses to blot out the remembrance of our sins, and to welcome us so that, miserable sinners though we are, he nevertheless regards us with favour. Not that he loves sin or endorses it: he wipes it away through the work of our Lord Jesus Christ. The fact is that we must accept the free gift of God's Spirit in order to be renewed, so that we cease to follow our natural corruption and are stripped of our evil thoughts and affections. In short, we are so changed and remade that God controls us and lives within us.

The real object of faith is our Lord Jesus Christ. Until we have him to point the way, it is impossible for us to believe in God.

As we said before, the distance is much too great, and we would faint a hundred thousand times before we got close to half-way along the road, if Jesus Christ did not forestall us so as to lead and guide us to God his Father. He is the true object of faith. That is, just as those who shoot with a gun or with a bow have a target, so faith's true target is Jesus Christ. That is why he said to his disciples: 'Do you believe in God? Believe also in me' (John 14:1)—indicating that this is the path to which we must keep.

Consider, however, on what terms Jesus Christ is given to us, and what it is he brings us. According to Paul, he is given to us for wisdom, righteousness, sanctification and redemption (1 Cor. 1:30). We are in darkness, poor and blind; yet here we have Jesus Christ who is given to us for wisdom, as much as to say that we should be content with the message of the gospel. We ought not to let our thoughts drift, since being curious we are always itching to know. It is with the simple gospel that we should stop. Paul also says that Jesus Christ is given to us for redemption. That is, God has redeemed us from everlasting death, which Jesus Christ accomplished when he paid the price. Next it is said that he is given to us for righteousness and sanctification. What does the term 'righteousness' imply? It is as Paul declares in the fifth chapter of Second Corinthians: 'he was made sin for us' (2 Cor. 5:21). In other words he himself bore the condemnation for our sins: he who was innocent, he who was beyond reproach, chose to bear all our iniquities. Our righteousness, says Paul, comes from the fact that we are accepted as righteous, for God takes no account of our lack of worth and of the many offences of which we are guilty. To this Paul adds sanctification, which means the gracious gift of the Holy Spirit.

I was right, therefore, when I said that faith not only understands that God is full of pity and that he desires to show mercy, but that he wishes at the same time to govern us, and to correct the corruption of our nature, so that his Spirit leads us into all righteousness. Now if it is Jesus Christ who brings us both these things, our faith must look to him, or else fancy will lead us astray.

This, then, is the point I make. When mention is made of God's kingdom and when faith too is spoken of, we are taught that, while we were estranged from God, cut off from him and in the deepest hell, God drew near to us. We should not doubt that our sins are forgiven since our Lord Jesus Christ has obtained absolution for us. Further, God declares that he will not leave us always captive to our evil appetites, nor will he permit the devil to harass us now here, now there, planting his foot upon our throat and exercising his tyranny over us. This is what faith is all about. Repentance, on the other hand, means that when poor sinners realize how awful it is to have God as their judge, despairing of themselves and confessing that they are doomed and lost, they seek one thing only: to yield and to be made new. That is the meaning of repentance.

The papists use the word 'repentance', but faith itself is wholly swept away. They seek God, but aimlessly, at random. Moreover they would always leave us in a state of doubt, shifting back and forth. They claim that it is presumptuous for a man to say that God loves him and is favourable to him. Why so? Because, they say, we do not know if we are worthy of him. Such is faith according to the papists: not knowing if we deserve to be loved by God, we remain confused, lurching to one side or another; opinion is all that we have. Faith, on the contrary, is assurance of a very different kind. They twitter endlessly on about repentance: the word falls glibly from the lips of priests and canting hypocrites, but it is no more than a money-trap. What is it they say? 'You must confess.' That is one thing. So already out of greed and self-interest they stretch their nets. Then satisfaction must be made, and satisfaction requires atonement to be made by means of Masses, pilgrimages, offerings, anniversaries, charitable foundations—this and that—and by oblations. We see, then, how they have completely stifled faith, and have so distorted repentance that no one can tell the difference between black and white.

We should therefore pay all the more attention to this doctrine, for it is the mark of our salvation, as we explained when we cited various parts of Scripture. Repentance implies something much higher than the papists imagine. Although they speak about contrition and attrition, it is all a game. Their only object is to leave poor consciences beset by scruples, so that people respectfully kowtow, go to confession and breathe into the priest's ear. It is rather like the man who, having drunk his fill of wine, disgorges from his bloated belly half a bucketful of muck! It is enough if the papists come and chirp about their sins in the priest's ear. Satisfaction consists in the form of self-redemption; everything passes through their hands. It is not that they are called to know themselves as they really are, that is, as men entirely under the curse. Far from it! There is free will, good intentions, acts of preparation and the means, too, of earning merit. The result is that Jesus Christ has simply opened the door, so that we may enter in by ourselves and in our own righteousness.

Besides the works of satisfaction which we spoke about, there are works of super-satisfaction, attracting merits which they can flaunt and boast about.[2] God may indeed sprinkle a little water on them, but the greater part of salvation is ascribed to men. When repentance is in view, the papists are thus a long way off from starting at the correct end. Instead, they build everything back to front, and they set out to spite God by exalting man.

How then does Scripture speak about repentance? It says that we should be so utterly crushed as to be filled with fear

[2] The preacher here alludes to the Roman Catholic doctrine of works of supererogation, acts such as fasting, pilgrimage and almsgiving, done over and above what the law and gospel strictly require, and to which special merit attached.

and despair, knowing that in God's sight we are irremediably damned, and that we behave as those whom Isaiah describes in the passage we treated last Sunday.[3] Scripture, in referring to the voice crying in the wilderness, proclaims that all of man's glory and dignity are merely as grass or a flower. When God's Spirit blows, everything withers and vigour departs (Isa. 40:6-8). What then remains? That the word of God should endure forever, and that we should see his salvation which comes from his mercy. This is not something which we have obtained or for which we can claim praise.

Repentance, as is clear from all of this, means first of all that we are nothing in ourselves, having no hope, troubled and distraught, and that we are wretched creatures, lost and damned.

It is here that repentance begins. Furthermore we must hate the sin and evil within us, and when we realize that we are God's enemies, we should abhor our wickedness which so offends our God and which provokes his wrath against us. Do we therefore hate and despise our evil nature? Then we must seek to give God our obedience and to submit to him, so that we make every impulse conform to his holy commandments and fight against every temptation to do wrong. From these things come the fruits of repentance, of which more will be said when we deal with the preaching of John the Baptist. That, in short, is what we have to grasp concerning repentance.

Accordingly, since God has declared that he will reign among us, and since the gospel, which is called his royal sceptre, is preached to us, and since he invites us so sweetly, let us not be like wild beasts and kick out against him when all he asks is to win us for salvation. Since, then, he shows himself so merciful toward us, let us be stirred up to repentance. That is, let us look

[3] In his thirty-ninth sermon on the *Gospel Harmony*, Calvin had cited Isa. 65:2, which speaks of Israel as 'a rebellious people, who walk in a way which is not good, following their own devices.'

within and carefully examine our entire life. When we see that there is only evil in it, let us be ashamed, and being ashamed let us learn to seek God, to place ourselves in his hands and under his control. Let us pray that when he sends us the word of reconciliation, we do not prefer to perish in our filth instead of turning back to him. May we not be so ungrateful that we fail to accept the medicine which he freely gives; may we resolve to be brought to repentance through faith. And as we receive Jesus Christ who is given to us for wisdom, for righteousness and for the remission of sins, may we lay hold of these things so that our life may testify that we are truly penitent—and that not merely for a day.

For as we will explain later and in more detail, repentance is not just an initial act by which we come to believe in Jesus Christ. Because there is always a residue of sin in us, and because we will never be wholly rid of our evil desires, repentance must, in a sense, be renewed each day. We must practise it continually; we must strive for it throughout our lives. We must remember this each and every day, so that we walk in the light of God's truth. There we see the depravity within us, so that we feel ashamed, and detesting what we see, we delight to be united with our God and to cling to him. That after all is his goal for us, as he says through Moses: 'What do I require of you, O Israel, but that you cleave to me, serve me and honour me as your only God?' (Deut. 10:12.)

Let us think of this, then, if we would benefit from the gospel and from all the sermons which we come to hear. May Scripture be profitable to us for salvation. Let us, I say, reflect on these two things. Let us not be like those who gad about and lose their way. Let us always have a target and a firm direction. Let us learn to be obedient, and having tasted God's grace may we grow in our knowledge of it until we are replete. And inasmuch as we grieve for our sins and are moved by true zeal to come to

God and to yield to his righteousness, we may be certain that we have profited from the gospel, since we possess our Lord Jesus Christ. He is the treasure of our salvation; in him all fullness of blessing is found.

Now let us cast ourselves down before the majesty of our good God, acknowledging our faults and praying that he may help us more and more to hate them. May we strive to commit ourselves wholly to him. May his word be so powerful that it uncovers all the evils, rebellion and hypocrisy hidden in us; and may he so remake us that we seek, in all honesty and sincerity, to glorify his holy name.

2

JOHN THE BAPTIZER

Now John wore a garment of camel's hair and a belt of leather around his waist, and his food was locusts and wild honey. [5]There came to him people from Jerusalem and from all Judaea, and from all the region around the Jordan, [6]and they were baptized by him in the Jordan, confessing their sins (Matt. 3:4-6).

John was baptizing in the wilderness, and was preaching a baptism of repentance for the remission of sins. [5]And the whole country of Judaea and the people of Jerusalem went out to him, and all were baptized by him in the river Jordan, confessing their sins. [6]Now John was clothed in camel's hair and had a belt of leather around his waist; and he ate locusts and wild honey (Mark 1:4-6).

And he came into the region around the Jordan, preaching a baptism of repentance for the remission of sins. [4]As it is written in the book of the words of the prophet Isaiah: 'The voice of him who cries in the wilderness, "Prepare the way of the Lord, make smooth his paths. [5]Every valley will be filled, and every mountain and hill laid low; the crooked will be made straight, and the rough places smooth; [6]and all flesh will see the salvation of God"' (Luke 3:3-6).

IN THE POWER OF THE SPIRIT

WE have already seen what is meant by the words 'the kingdom of God', and why, because it is near, we must repent. God cannot rule within us unless we are changed, for by nature we are only evil and rebellious. Even what seems to us virtue is detestable vice, and whatever has the appearance and name of wisdom is merely futile in God's sight. For the rest, when God accepts us by grace and counts us as his children, when we are called to the hope of the heavenly life, since God looks with favour upon us, it is only right that we should want to be united with him, which we can only do by denying self.

It remains for us now to explain what is said to us here, following what we have already learned about the baptism practised by John. Baptism signified the forgiveness of sins and the hope of eternal life. Accompanying it was the exhortation that we should turn to God. That is one point. There is another, for Scripture expressly says that *John came preaching baptism*, in order to show that the external sign is nothing in itself unless it is joined to teaching. Let us learn then that when we are baptized, two things are set before us: God welcomes us provided that, on the one hand, we are reconciled to him by his free goodness, since he chooses to bury our faults and to reckon us as righteous, for we have been washed and cleansed by the blood of Jesus Christ; and on the other hand, that we are made new, since he wills to make of us a temple in which he is purely served and worshipped. We must therefore have done with the corruptions which prevent God's name from being honoured, and which stop us dedicating ourselves in obedience to his service.

This is a point worth noting, for most people do not know why they have been baptized. Thus the sacrament which should be a pledge of salvation to them serves to condemn them twice over, because they profane it by their mindlessness and trample underfoot so priceless a treasure. True, some indeed will babble that baptism stands for the remission of sins and repentance, but they know nothing about what we said before, that is, what repentance means and how it is that we are reconciled to God. Accordingly, we ought carefully to remember this lesson and not think that we have learnt it straight away. Even if we were to spend the rest of our life rehearsing the point, it would be rare indeed if we finally got so far as to know why we are baptized, the efficacy of the sign, its proper use, the purpose of its institution and the fruit it brings us!

Now what we must understand is that John's baptism was no different from that of our Lord Jesus Christ, which we presently practise in the church. For when we speak about the sacraments, we must not waste our time on things that are visible. We have to know why they were instituted and what it is they represent. John's baptism relied on the same promises as the baptism which we use today. We conclude, then, that there is no difference. Attend, however, to what the verse says: 'John came preaching baptism.' This makes it clear that John did not misuse the sign which God had committed to him, as do those who have no teaching to offer the church by which it can be built up. John baptized, but he also showed why, so that his was no petty ritual, devoid of both purpose and usefulness.

We will understand this better if we think of the corruptions which have existed, and which still exist, in popery. They baptize, but how is it done? Do they offer instruction? The promises contained in baptism, the fruit and efficacy of the sign—are these explained? Not a bit! It is nothing but wizardry, as if a sorcerer were to appear to cast his spells. A priest mumbles prayers and performs so many monkey-tricks as is horrible to relate![1]

Notice that when God gave us the sacraments, it was not so that he should stand before us mute. He stamped them with his

[1] See further *Inst.* IV.15.19. There Calvin describes the Roman Catholic rite of baptism as a 'farce', arguing that its ceremonial accretions, such as the use of spittle, salt and consecrated oil (chrism), bring the sacrament into contempt.

own mark, so that we should know why he gave them to us. It is like a coin which cannot be used unless it has gone through the die. And the die identifies what coin it is, what it is worth and how it is to be used. Thus God's mark must be stamped upon the sacraments, and his mark is his word. It has been well said that the sacraments are words made visible.[2] So when what is contained in holy Scripture is preached to us, we take it in with our ears, but because of our ignorance and infirmity God adds another help. He wills that our eyes as well as our ears should receive instruction, and that every sense, as it were, should be reserved for him.

If our ears are open so that they hear, while our eyes are fixed elsewhere on many vain things, whatever is said drifts away. For this reason our Lord is not content to teach us orally; he wants us to grasp visibly what he teaches us, by means of signs. Hence, in baptism, we see water and we understand that we are truly washed and cleansed of all our uncleanness. And as baptism is administered on the authority of our Lord Jesus Christ, we realize that his office is to make us clean. This is not something we have in ourselves, and so we conclude that we are wholly unclean and corrupt until God takes a hand. Then too we recall that the Holy Spirit is likened to living water, and that there is nothing in us—no, not one drop of life—unless the Lord Jesus quickens us by his grace.

Baptism must therefore be preached. That is, it is not enough for water to be poured out without anyone knowing why: the use to which the sign is put and the benefit it confers must be explained to us. We must understand that God wants to show us visibly, so to speak, that it is his work to wash us; and as he has done this through his only Son, he wants it applied to us, so that we should be cleansed and our souls washed by the blood of our

[2] The saying is found in Augustine, *The Gospel of John* 80.3; *Against Faustus* 19.16. Calvin cites him to this effect in *Inst.* IV.14.6.

Lord Jesus Christ. It is the secret power of the Holy Spirit which accomplishes this, but the sign is added, as we said, because of our ignorance. We need to be led gradually, step by step, rung by rung, as it were, of the ladder that brings us up higher and takes us beyond our reach, for this is how God calls us. That, in sum, is what we need to know about the baptism preached by John for the forgiveness of sins.

The Evangelists record that John the Baptist was a man of austere life, being *clothed with camel's hair*—that is, his robe was made of coarse woollen cloth—*and his waist was girt with a leather belt; he ate locusts and wild honey*. This is said in order to show that our Lord sought to move those who at that time had grown hard and dull of mind. The Jews were loud in their boast that the God who had chosen and adopted them was the Creator of heaven and earth, that he had taken them under his protection and would cause the kingdom of David to prosper, thus finally redeeming them as he had promised. Many such boasts were to be heard, yet it was something of a miracle that anyone was expecting the kingdom of God, as was said earlier of Simeon and Anna (Luke 2:25-38). The people had sunk so low that they rode roughshod over the law and despised the prophets.

How terrible it was when we too, living through times of superstition, saw Scripture treated merely as a relic! In Judaea in those times no one knew anything of the message of salvation. Hypocrites, it is true, pretended to be informed and clever, but everything was perverted and corrupt. Accordingly, God had to use an external sign to move those who had turned away from him and who had gone totally astray. That was why John the Baptist led so austere a life and why, as we have seen, he preached in the wilderness, in order to show how desperate things were, and how the truth of the gospel was meant to create a new world and to rectify a state of utter confusion. It was necessary, then, that his manner of dress should mirror this.

Not that John's holiness was bound up with the clothes he wore or with his belt of leather! People are always obsessed by nonsense of this kind: it means practically nothing to God. Paul therefore says that what pertains to the body scarcely aids the salvation of our souls (1 Tim. 4:8). Naturally there are some things about the body which are beneficial to us, but whatever we do externally can never lead us to perfection, nor even bring us close. We ought not to think, then, that John's holiness lay chiefly in the fact that he ate wild honey, locusts and grass-hoppers (which are a kind of insect). Even so there was some point to it. It was not, either, that he lived like a hermit. That is how the papists see him, as a man withdrawn who shunned the company of everyone. In fact, they were not content to make for him a robe of camel's hair, as we read here: they dressed him completely in animal-fashion, imagining camel's hair to be no more than animal skin! Such is wisdom among the papists! If we said that this is a stupid mistake on the part of painters and sculptors, well and good. But have their scholars so forgotten themselves that they fail to see that 'hair' does not mean 'skin'? Besides, they place the head of a calf or sheep between his legs, which shows us that in popery things are so muddled that the devil makes sport of these poor blind souls. He makes them look ridiculous even in the eyes of children, so that they deserve to be mocked by all. Clearly, God has deprived these wretches of all sense and reason, for they have turned away from the simplicity of his word.

John the Baptist did not, therefore, adopt an austere manner of life because he was a hermit. He was, however, in the wilderness, which is why he lived in harmony with it. If he had lived in towns he might have lived as others do. God, however, chose, as I said, to work this way so that those who had grown drowsy should think harder about the change they ought to make, remembering that God was looking with mercy on his church. This too is why

Jesus Christ upbraids the Jews for not allowing God to win them over by any means at all. 'John came,' he says, 'neither eating nor drinking' (Matt. 11:18). (Of course John both ate and drank, but what is meant is that he fed on grasshoppers, wild honey and running water, not on bread and wine.) 'Did it,' our Lord continues, 'do you any good? No! You used him falsely, and making him your excuse you tried to conceal my name and power. Here I am, living among you. I drink wine and eat as everyone else does, so as to be closer to you. Yet here I am, God's Son, in whom all fullness of majesty dwells. I am a brother and comrade to you, yet you will not be moved. So whatever approach God takes, you prove to be wild beasts, impossible to correct. No one can tame you in the slightest.' At this point he introduces a metaphor. 'If I sing one tune,' he says, 'some may be moved; if another, others may be more affected. What then? Nothing works with you!' What he means is this: 'Whether God sings or is mute, whether he does exactly as you want in order to draw you to him, you show that by nature you are wilful and wicked. God is wasting his time when he appeals to you as he does.'[3]

We see from this that John the Baptist is not to be admired because he refrained from every pleasure, otherwise he might be preferred to Jesus Christ who, as I said, lived the common life. John did this for the sake of others, in order to prepare everyone to receive the imminent gift of grace. So when John with his strange ways makes his appearance, it is so that all may be led to attend with utmost care to the message which he brings on God's behalf. This also is why, in that same text (Matt. 11:18), Jesus Christ declares that those who are finely dressed are in the courts of rulers, whereas God chose to send an embassy in the wilderness in order to save the Jews. There he raised up a man who had not a shred of splendour or anything else. However, we see in John the Baptist that God displayed his majesty much

[3] A very free, extended paraphrase of Matt. 11:16-19 and Luke 7:31-35.

more clearly than if John had enjoyed honour and esteem among men.

John, in fact, was unknown, and although he was the son of a priest of the chief order which entered the sanctuary (Luke 1:5), he nevertheless removed to a far-off place. God appeared to have denied him all honour and rank. Yet his task was to prepare the way for our Lord Jesus Christ and to make things ready for him. God sought therefore in every way to reveal his power in John. And although he is no longer alive in the world, it should be profitable for us to know not only that God in those days rebuked the Jews for their ingratitude, but that now too he has cause to do the same to us if we remain unmoved by John's message, and if we fail to receive it reverently so that we are led to Jesus Christ and fix our eyes on him.

Think of the grace God shows us when he is pleased to consider our infirmity and when he forgets nothing that is good for us; when he condescends to us in the smallest things so as to win us over; when he keeps us walking even if we cannot fly; and when we cannot walk he lets us at least creep forward! In the same way as we carry infants in our arms, God is willing to carry and guide us. That is how he treats us. So woe to us twice over if we are not teachable and meek enough to yield to him, seeing that he stoops so low and overlooks nothing which is to our advantage. There is a parallel here with Paul, who writes to the Galatians: 'Brothers, be as I am, for I am like you' (Gal. 4:12). With these words Paul shows that he wants only to be as they are. Not that he pretends not to see their faults, for as he says, if he sought to please men he would no longer be a servant of Jesus Christ (Gal. 1:10). His aim was to show that he had no wish to treat them harshly but wanted to win them over by every means possible. Now if Paul, God's servant, thought ill of the Galatians for not obeying God whom they knew to be kind and forgiving, what shall we say when God in his majesty condescends to us, wishing, as I said, to draw us to himself and to win us over with all the helps which he knows are suited to our nature? This is what we should remember when Scripture speaks of John's food and drink.

That John did not withdraw from human company is obvious from the fact that *people came from the whole region of Judaea and were baptized in the Jordan.* The Jordan is mentioned because the mode of baptism was by total immersion in water, as the word implies. True, today we do not plunge those we baptize into water, but we should not waste so much time on unimportant matters or quarrel about such things. The normal mode of baptism, considered as a symbol, was immersion in water, representing the total cleansing which should take place in us. To be renewed in obedience to God, we must not, as I have said, be reborn only in part. From the top of our head to the soles of our feet we must be wholly remade, since in God's eyes there is nothing but filth and rottenness in us. Moreover, the aim of baptism is to show that we must die to ourselves and to the world and must, so to speak, rise again, so that God may live in us. This was more clearly expressed when people were fully immersed in water.

That is why Christ is said to have withdrawn to a well-watered region, so that baptism might be more easily administered. However, I say again that we should not so concern ourselves with things of small importance that we stir up arguments on that account. It is enough if baptism is performed in the way required, and that it demonstrates to us that from our mother's womb we are corrupt and abhorrent in God's sight until he makes us thoroughly clean. All we need to know is where our cleansing may be found and from whom it comes—through the blood of our Lord Jesus Christ. We need also to know that we must die to self, which is why water is poured over the head, as if the child who is being baptized has been placed in a river to die. We need finally to know how this comes about, and how, by his Holy Spirit, God imparts his grace to us. When these things are explained to us, we should be content. This is what baptism entails.

Scripture goes on to say that *those who were baptized by John confessed their sins*—and rightly so, for every sacrament involves a mutual pact or accord between God and us. When men draw up a contract with each other, both parties are present: each states his terms and each answers for himself. If one is selling and the other buying, there is the matter of a sale price. Both sides arrive at a clear deal, so that as one accepts certain responsibilities, so does the other. God in his infinite goodness does the very same thing, testifying to his fatherly love by means of the sacraments. There he enters into a contract with us, and we with him, and although he can owe us nothing, he willingly accepts to be duty-bound toward us, and makes himself our debtor, so to speak.

So far as baptism is concerned, God testifies that our sins are forgiven, as if to say that he will no longer take account of them. He remits them to us, thus abandoning his rights, for by his sentence we are guilty of eternal death until, through his unmerited generosity, he absolves us. Thus he binds himself to us, promising to accept us and sealing his promise by the power of his Holy Spirit, through whom he also gives us new birth, so that all that belongs to our corrupt flesh and nature might be mortified and destroyed. Such is the obligation which God, for his part, assumes. We, for our part, must understand that we have what is called a mutual or reciprocal obligation. Just as God accepts us as his children, we solemnly declare that we acknowledge him as our Father. Just as he cleanses and purifies us, so we declare that we accept the cleansing that he gives in and through Jesus Christ. And just as he promises to bring us to new birth by the grace of his Holy Spirit, so we declare that we are ready to deny ourselves and to give ourselves to him.

Scripture tells us, then, that those who came to be baptized by John confessed their sins. Why was that? We already stated that John preached baptism, explaining the purpose of the sign and affirming that God was ready to receive us in his mercy. For how could I possibly understand that God will not impute my faults to me if I am unaware of them? Indeed, if I think of myself as righteous, I have no need of a remedy. Only when I know that my sins have made me God's enemy, only when I seek after him that he may mercifully blot out and bury my offences—only then will my baptism be confirmed and allow me to share in its benefits. It was thus necessary for those who were being baptized to confess their faults, for they had come looking for absolution. As I said, unless they confessed their debt, knowing themselves to be wretched and guilty sinners, baptism was useless to them. So much for that point.

What we notice here is that those who were baptized were already of adult age. For just as circumcision began with Abraham and was given by God to him and to his family, so it is with baptism. Adults had to participate in baptism so that they might be gathered into the church by the word purely preached, since in John's day there was confusion everywhere. True, the Jews were circumcised, and for that reason they were said to be near to God (Eph. 2:17). Everything among them, however, was in disarray, so that God had to institute a new sign in order to bring the church together. He began, then, with adults, and with those who were able to understand the teaching presented to them. They were brought into the church, and at the same time God joined their offspring to them. Those whom the Evangelists describe had to acknowledge their sins in order to have access to baptism; God could only absolve them if they recognized their guilt.

Now the papists are utterly stupid in trying to prove their practice of confession from this text. By citing the word 'confess', they think that they have won the day. Have they? If I confess that I have done wrong, does it mean that I have to go and breathe into a priest's ear and receive absolution from him, having related all my sins without exception, in order to be reconciled as if by magic and sorcery? What does the pope's law say about confession? That we must detail all our faults. Can we detail even a hundredth part of them? This is the way to cast poor souls into the deepest hell! For there is no one with an ounce of common sense who, on examining himself and totting up his sins, can even get half-way to full confession: he is bound to fail as soon as he begins. Yet here is the pope seeking to bind unhappy souls by this law, which is calculated to drive them to despair.

It is further commanded that everyone should confess once a year.[4] For popish confession to take place, baptism would therefore have to be repeated. Thus the papists would have to become Anabaptists and be baptized all over again—yes, year in and year out.[5] Now the Evangelists relate that those who came to John to be baptized confessed their sins, but it is not said that each person had to repeat his confession, nor is this said of baptism. Yet the papists insist that it be done every year. This, as we said, would also apply to baptism, which is the height of absurdity and a blasphemy against God. Moreover they have tied God's grace to their practice of confession, so that instead of being called through Jesus Christ to purity and righteousness before God, we are told by the pope: 'No, the door to heaven is closed to you if you do not confess all your sins each year, or at least

[4] The practice of confession at least once a year was made mandatory by the Fourth Lateran Council of 1215.

[5] The Anabaptists refused to recognize the validity of infant baptism which they held to be 'the chief abomination of the pope'. They required those who were newly converted to be re-baptized on profession of faith. Calvin, along with the other mainstream Reformers, regarded infant baptism as a covenant ordinance and therefore as the norm, and since the sacrament depended on God's promise, not on man's performance, he accepted the Roman Catholic rite as sufficient, despite its manifest flaws. Cf. *Inst.* IV.2.11 and 15.16.

intend to do so should sudden death forestall you.' Those are his very words.

We see, then, just how silly it is to cite this text and to use it in this way. Of course they have to find some false pretext for their lies by perverting Scripture. It is shameful of them to exert such tyranny over the church, to construct laws and statutes, to demand obedience under pain of mortal sin and to take such awful liberties when Scripture gives them no excuse. Nevertheless God exposes their insolence, by showing them to be forgers who falsify his word which he intends for our salvation, but which they turn to ruin and damnation.

It would be a waste of time to combat these rascals any further. Let it suffice that the Evangelists record that those who presented themselves for baptism which God had again ordained, came confessing their wretchedness and their transgressions. For here is the key which opens for us the door to the church and to the kingdom of heaven: the knowledge that God accepts us although we are totally unworthy of him. Our worth consists in this, that being utterly struck down we seek our salvation in him, since we ourselves are damned.

So turning from the folly of these hypocrites, let us remember that in order to enjoy both baptism and the Supper, there must be a mutual accord between God and us. We were baptized as infants, and most of us were sullied by the papists' foul perversions. Because our Lord, however, now declares by this sign that he reckons us as his and as heirs of his kingdom, the truth of baptism remains eternal and will be effective for us if we continue to use it as we should. That is, we should daily acknowledge our faults and sigh to God, conscious that we were poor lost creatures when he took us to himself, and that our salvation is grounded in his simple mercy. Yet now that we have reached the age of discretion, as it is called, we have continually ignored baptism's promise of the forgiveness of sins, and have plunged back into perdition. Having been washed by God, we have returned to the mire and rottenness from which he took us. We have not ceased to provoke his wrath both night and day and in countless ways. It is only right, then, that we daily learn the true use of baptism and that we boast before God that we are righteous. Of course we are not, but we are by imputation, for the blood of our Lord Jesus Christ answers for us. He is the cleansing and the satisfaction which release us from all our debts.

So knowing the priceless blessing which God has given us through being reconciled to us, and through desiring to be our Father instead of our judge, we should understand that he would have us struggle daily against the sins which remain in our nature. They have not yet been uprooted, nor will they be until we are stripped of our flesh. We will always be held captive, dragging our bonds about with us as long as we live in this world. All the days of our lives we must therefore practise what we are told here, confessing our sins before God—not into the ear of a priest!—and confessing them where necessary before men, thus rightly humbling ourselves and showing that God alone deserves all the praise.

Now what I have said about baptism applies also, for similar reasons, to the Lord's Supper. When the table is set up and made ready for us, and when there we hear God's promises that under the symbols of bread and wine Jesus Christ offers us his body and blood, let us come like poor hungry souls, knowing that we need food and that Jesus Christ must give it to us. This is not food that we will find on earth; it will not benefit the imperishable life of our souls. As Paul says, 'Food is for the stomach, and the stomach for food, but God will destroy both' (1 Cor. 6:13). When, however, it is a question of the spiritual life, Jesus Christ must show that it his work, and only his, to feed us. Thus when we draw near to the Supper we should be clear that there is no life in us, so that we seek in Jesus Christ what he has promised we will find in him. Let us not come to the Supper as mindless beasts, as some do. Why come at all? 'For God's honour.' Yes, but is God honoured when dogs eat at his table, and especially when both dogs and pigs thrust their snouts into the body and blood of Jesus Christ? How is that honouring to God? Instead it is an intolerable sacrilege!

Consider how timely all this is, given that we are to receive our Lord Jesus Christ's Supper next Sunday.[6] If for the rest of our lives we did nothing but prepare ourselves for it, we would never really succeed. Even so we should try our hardest, and let each of us in our small way strive to that end. So the time is near when we will receive the pledge by which Jesus Christ truly shows that he is our life, and that he did not spare himself but willingly surrendered to death. Even today he does not spare himself, but desires to be the bread of life for our sake. Each day he gives himself and renews the gift which he made once and for all. When we see, then, that Jesus Christ for his part binds himself to us and sweetly invites us to come to him, let us, for our part, give ourselves to him, that he may live in us and that we may no longer be addicted to our evil desires. Let us endeavour instead to give ourselves to him so that we become his own possession. May he in all peace have his way with us, and may we show in actual fact that we are united with him. For he has called us in order to make us members of his body, provided that he is our Head and that we receive all fullness of blessing from him.

Now let us cast ourselves down before the majesty of our good God, acknowledging our faults and asking him so to make us feel them that we cease to have any pleasure in them. May we try more and

[6] The Lord's Supper was celebrated in Geneva four times yearly, at Easter, Pentecost, the first Sunday in September and the Sunday nearest Christmas. Advance notice of the sacrament was required to be given, as here. Calvin's outspoken reference to 'dogs and pigs' reflects his constant concern that the sacrament should not be profaned by the worldly and impenitent.

more to rid ourselves of them, until we draw closer to, or arrive at, the righteousness to which he calls us. And all the while may he uphold us, that we may yet be privileged to claim him as our Father, despite the many flaws and failings which so impede and hinder us.

3

ONE MIGHTIER THAN I

'Truly I baptize you with water for repentance, but he who is com-
ing after me is mightier than I, whose shoes I am not worthy to car-
ry; he will baptize you with the Holy Spirit and with fire. [12]*He has*
his fan in his hand, and he will clear his threshing floor and gather
his wheat into the granary; but he will burn the chaff with a fire
which never goes out' (Matt. 3:11-12).

And he preached, saying, 'After me comes he who is mightier than I,
the strap of whose sandals I am not worthy to stoop down and untie.
[8]*Truly I have baptized you with water, but he will baptize you with*
the Holy Spirit' (Mark 1:7-8).

Tax gatherers also came to him to be baptized, and said to him,
'Teacher, what shall we do?' [13]*And he said to them, 'Demand no*
more than is appointed you.' [14]*Soldiers also asked him, 'What shall*
we do?' And he said to them, 'Trouble no one and do no violence, and
be content with your wages.' [15]*As the people were waiting, and all*
were thinking in their hearts whether he was not the Christ, [16]*John*
answered and said to them all, 'Truly I baptize you with water; but
he who is mightier than I is coming, the strap of whose sandals I am
not worthy to untie; he will baptize you with the Holy Spirit and
with fire' (Luke 3:12-16).

THERE is a general rule to which we are all subject and which is the same for all. But since God invariably lays down how each person should order his life, every individual should follow the vocation to which he is called. Not all have the same situation in life, so a general rule cannot be made for everyone. If a man does not have children, he will not have to preach as a father does when he has to control the children who have been given to him. If a child has no father or mother, he cannot be told to obey either of them, humbly to submit to them or to come to their aid: that would be superfluous. And what would be the point of telling a recluse, a stay-at-home, to become a magistrate, a king, a ruler or an officer of the law?

What we must notice then is that once God's law has been set before us, teaching us in general what he requires of all the faithful, we should each consider the work to which we have been individually called. A person living privately in his own house should reflect that God demands that he instruct his children and his servants for whom he is accountable; he should live peaceably with his wife and should support her. Likewise a person who has official duties should think of what is required of him, and of what is entailed by the office in which God has placed him.

Thus it is that John the Baptist not only laid down a general rule for all without exception, but when *tax gatherers and soldiers came to him*, he told them what was specific to their calling. Tax gatherers and soldiers were especially mentioned, to show that through our Lord Jesus Christ the door to life stands open to all. For if there are people in the world who are dissolute and from whom very little can be hoped, it is soldiers who allow themselves much licence and who live unruly and reckless lives. Since they sell themselves for hard cash and bargain with their lives, one might suppose that they were half animal. A man would have to strip away all kindness when, instead of managing his household and engaging in honest and lawful toil, he turns and takes his pay from whoever offers him more. And on what terms? That he kill or murder, or that he be killed himself! Many are driven by greed, being people who would snatch as much as they can, instead of being content with what God provides and using it to live peacefully at home.

The same is true of tax collectors. Those who are tax farmers and who go around collecting dues and taxes show, so to speak, that they are hardened and bold as brass. Neither the hatred nor the reproaches they receive worry them. A man would find it hard to continue in such work without getting into arguments and being greatly stung by criticism. Anyone who had some honesty would certainly prefer not to touch one penny or farthing than to hear such abuse as is heaped on them, for they are reviled and slandered by all. People like this must often, as I said, have lost all sense of shame, and be past caring whether they have friends or enemies.

Consequently John the Baptist is said to have instructed both soldiers and tax gatherers concerning their duty. Now I said earlier that Luke wanted to show that all would be received into repentance, and that God is ready to accept all who yield to him, whatever their station. This, I meant to say, was on one condition—that the work we do is not condemned by God's word. To be sure it is no fit occupation to keep brothels, alehouses and similar things: popish priests and monks cannot deny that such is their occupation! When Scripture uses the word 'vocation', it warns us that no manner of life is good or acceptable unless God is its author. 'Vocation' means 'calling', and 'calling' implies that God beckons to us, saying to each of us, 'I want you to live in such-and-such a way.' So that is what 'occupation' means: we are not to engage in things that God condemns in his word.

It was very difficult in those days, as I said before, for soldiers to remain uncorrupted amid so much turmoil. When they went to war it was for pay. This they did for almost all their lives, or else for the intervals of time when they left home and roamed about, or else manned garrisons if they were not moving around the countryside. Nevertheless their occupation itself was not open to reproach. Similarly tax collectors are necessary in order to bring in levies and taxes. In the matter of war, it is true, we must always wish that God will not allow us to be forced to take up arms against our enemies; but just as magistrates have their officers of the law to execute justice, so also they have soldiers in time of need to give them armed assistance. Thus war in itself cannot be condemned, as long as we are not led by self-interest, greed, envy or spite, or set out to attack our neighbours when they wish to live in peace. It may be that we are unjustly harassed, or that some ruler might come who seeks to attack the freedom of a city which he judges to be strategically placed. Although he bears the title 'ruler', because he is misusing his authority we must regard him as a thief, so that it is lawful to take up arms, in the same way as justice is done to a robber or to some other offender. I therefore repeat that since, in cases like this, God allows war, soldiers are necessary.[1]

As for tax collectors, we see from Paul that magistrates, kings and rulers must demand taxes, and that we must pay them in all good conscience (Rom. 13:5-7). Yet there is something here we need to note: those who inflate the price of taxes, levies and duties prove that they seek to rob all and sundry and they think that everything is allowed them. Now everyone repeats the

[1] For most of Calvin's lifetime, and well beyond, Geneva faced military threats from France in the west and Savoy in the south. The city's alliance with its more powerful neighbour, Bern, was a partial safeguard, but did not obviate the need for vigilance and self-defence. In discussing the issue of armed conflict, the preacher accepts the idea of a 'just' war waged in response to unprovoked aggression. His argument should also be seen as a reply to the Anabaptists' rejection of war or military service in any form: these they denounced as 'unchristian and devilish weapons of force' (Art. 4, The Schleitheim Confession, 1527). See further Willem Balke, *Calvin and the Anabaptist Radicals*, tr. William Heynen (Grand Rapids: Wm. B. Eerdmans, 1981), pp. 282-89.

proverb about cheating on taxes, and because many would like if possible to get out of paying their dues, when they defraud the public they simply shrug it off, refusing to see that this is theft twice over. For rulers and magistrates receive taxes and dues in order to maintain the social fabric, and since such moneys are put to this use, those who soil their hands with fraud commit sacrilege of a sort. Dishonest tax collectors pillage on every hand and grow hard in their craft and cunning; they take even more liberties and use their claws and nails to rake in as much as they can. That is why John the Baptist warns them not to trouble anyone, and says the same to the soldiers, telling them to be content with their wages.

In sum, we are reminded here that while God in Jesus Christ stretches out his arms to welcome those who take refuge in his mercy, and excludes none, nevertheless those who are in some dangerous occupation which offers the opportunity to do wrong, must be on their guard. In the same way magistrates should reflect on how difficult their office is. It is the same for ministers of God's word when they fail in their duty to God and men, to whom they are accountable. They have less excuse than others: their public responsibilities should serve as so many goads impelling them to do their duty much better. Merchants too should recall that they have greater opportunities for false dealing, for cheating and for doing wrong. They should tell themselves, 'Well now, since today this occupation is beset by so many ills, and since I am walking among thorns, I must look more closely to myself.' Tradespeople in turn should reflect, 'Well, we have so much to do with vanities, luxuries and frivolity, we should cut back on the frills as much as we can.' Yet however hard we try, we will never succeed, because nowadays licentiousness is rife in every walk of life.

For the rest, let each of us, according to our occupation, think hard about ourselves, so that we avoid defiling ourselves by the many evils and villainies which are so popular today. And when it comes to choosing our occupation, let us make sure that we do not deliberately put God to the test, and let us not get tangled up in such a mess as will finally destroy us.

Think, for example, of a man who has to choose some way of earning a living, or of a father who seeks to choose a certain style of life for his children. They must take care not to be so fond of gain that they forget the essential thing. 'Oh,' we say, as we pitch our children about, 'here's a nice, well-paid job. I'll put him there.' Yet we do not see that Satan's nets are stretched and that we are pushing our children to destruction. Fathers give the matter no thought. Why? Because the devil has put a blindfold over their eyes, so that they are like a greedy bottomless pit: their only concern is to make their children rich. In effect they cast them straight into hell, their sole thought being that they should be rich like the others, opulent, doing important deals. They do not consider that great harm will come of it, and that in many ways God will be sorely offended.

We should thus be mindful of the message we are given here, so that when we are in dangerous occupations which may end up badly, we look all the more to God, watchful lest we are led astray or deceived, or lest the devil trick us on the pretext that everyone is doing it—everyone, that is, who leads a similar kind of life and has similar responsibilities. So when we have to choose, let us make sure that we apply ourselves to things that are useful and approved by God, for there are many dangers and many ways for us to fall into sin. Even so, no one should be excluded from the hope of salvation, for, as we see, John the Baptist welcomed tax gatherers and soldiers. Let us not be so severe that we shut out those we consider somehow dubious. We should help them to see that God is ready and prepared to forgive their offences, as long as they turn back to him with all their hearts.

Next all three Evangelists record these words of John the

Baptist: '*I baptize you with water, but after me there comes one who is greater and more excellent; he will baptize with the Holy Spirit and with fire.*' Luke explains the context of this saying: *Many were waiting to see if John the Baptist was the Christ.* For although at that time only a handful of people were truly awaiting God's kingdom, as was said before, the ordinary people, while devoid of godliness and being in a sense degenerate—they did not know the God who had adopted them as his own—felt great distress, and had heard the common rumour that the time had come for the Redeemer to appear. We also know how troubled Herod had been to learn that wise men had come from the east to worship the king who had been born in Judaea (Matt. 2:3-8). That was why people were waiting to see whether John the Baptist was the Christ. It was a well-known theme in both the law and the prophets that God would send a Redeemer, and time had reached a critical turning point. The nation, too, could bear it no longer: God must come to its aid, or else it would completely collapse. This accounts for why it was thought that John might be the Christ. The people saw an almost angelic holiness in him, together with other wonders. And when he baptized, he brought about a type of renewal.

Now when God gave his law, it was not so that it might be changed, for he had said at the same time that it should be kept with nothing either added or subtracted (Deut. 4:2; 12:32). Here then was a complete change of events: either John the Baptist was the Redeemer, or the time of restoration had perhaps come, with John heralding the advent of our Lord Jesus Christ. Already people were obsessed by the idea that John might be the Redeemer. John therefore protests that *after me comes one who is preferred to me*—one who is greater, as is more fully stated in the first chapter of John (John 1:15).

Notice, first of all, that John the Baptist wants one thing only, to advance the glory of our Lord Jesus Christ, and to exalt him so high that all might look to him. In the same way our Lord declares that he will be raised on high, just as the serpent was lifted up in the wilderness (John 3:14). That also is why Scripture likens him to a banner (Psa. 60:4; Isa. 13:2). Such was John the Baptist's purpose. He was instrumental in making Jesus Christ known, so that all might cleave to him and abide with him. It is further said in another verse: 'He must increase, and I decrease' (John 3:30). There John compares himself with the person of God's Son, declaring that he must be brought low. Now John was famous, and could not avoid being admired and spoken about. Yet all that, he says, is temporary: he must fade away so that Jesus Christ should have the honour which is his due.

There is a rule here for those charged and entrusted with bearing the message of the gospel. They must not be motivated by vanity and pride so that they seek men's esteem or look for their applause; they must not be thought of as clever, learned, eloquent or anything else, nor should they set out to acquire that reputation. All must be brought low, or no man will ever be diligently employed in God's service. Let him forget himself and not seek for any sort of recognition. That is the lesson for ministers here.

This message, however, is profitable for the whole body of the church. It allows us to distinguish between those who truly serve God and those who are only out for themselves. It should thus be much easier for us to accept what we are taught here, to be built up and to be strengthened more and more. Note, then, that when it is a question of recognizing pastors who are sound, and of distinguishing them from those who merely bear the title, we have this touchstone. A sure test is when a man does not seek his own glory or have any wish to advance himself, but wants the Son of God to be worshipped and us to bow the knee before him. He is a man who leads by example. Whoever sets out to exalt Jesus Christ, making him his teacher, is the one we should accept without fail. Conversely, if a man is full of wind, is seen to use flowery language and wants only to be idolized; if he cares little whether Jesus Christ is honoured as he deserves and does not mind how ruinous things are, provided he is appreciated and, as it were, worshipped—we may always conclude that such a man has nothing of God in him, and that he is a hireling, not a shepherd. This is something else to bear in mind when the example of John the Baptist is set before us.

Concerning him who is to come, John plainly says that *he is not worthy to untie the strap of his sandals*. Mark puts it differently: *he is not worthy to stoop before him*, or to kiss the ground where his feet have trodden. These expressions mean that every creature is, so to speak, reduced to nothing, so that our Lord Jesus Christ should have his rights, with none of them being taken from him.

Now among pastors some distinctions may exist, given that God distributes his gifts as he chooses, and not in equal measure. One might be more outstanding than another, yet all must obey their calling so that it is Jesus Christ they serve. Each pastor must also recognize the others as his brethren, with no rivalry or envy among them; and the lowliest should be considered great and honourable, since he serves God and his church. That is how it is with those who teach the people. In the case, however, of our Lord Jesus Christ, every being on earth must be brought low, and he must be exalted—he alone! That we should assign him a partner is out of the question: his church can have only one Head and one King, to whom all must do homage. This is the first thing to remember when John the Baptist is heard to say that he is not worthy to untie the strap of Jesus Christ's sandals. It is as if he meant to say that, in comparison, there is nothing in him, as we saw already when John declares that he must decrease, and the other increase.

Here is a truth which is highly useful to us, for we can never stop ourselves going to extremes. When God confers outstanding gifts on some, we are seized with awe and wonder, and we at once make idols of those who are instruments of God's glory. At any rate, when God works in this way through us, his poor creatures, and when he displays the power of his Holy Spirit in weak and worthless vessels, he certainly does not intend to forfeit what is his by right. It is so that his power may be all the more clearly exhibited among us here below, and that we may be roused to honour him and to bless his name.

We, however, do everything back to front. As soon as we see someone whom God has endowed more generously than others with the gifts of his Spirit, he becomes an idol. We stand amazed, unable to restrain ourselves. Thus, many people like this forget themselves, are quite carried away and no longer acknowledge their own condition or anything else. This is how everything is spoiled, which is why we should practise what we are taught here all the more. For where is the teacher, however clever, who can set himself above John the Baptist? Nevertheless we know what John solemnly declared: he was as nothing, and nothing should prevent Jesus Christ from being exalted, so that all might look to him.

As we are all aware, it was failure to obey this truth which led popery into such a maze that this proverb which is on all their lips is fulfilled: 'No one can tell Christ from his apostles.'[2] So their own mouths condemn them, and God saw to it that they had no other judges but themselves. Experience shows that this is how it is among them. However many male and female saints they have, all are idols whom they worship. They make them advocates with God, and finally they make them God himself! They will as readily say 'Our Father' before a statuette of St Agatha or St Catherine as before the crucifix. It should

[2] The saying is cited a number of times by Calvin in his sermons. The form sometimes varies: 'No one can pick God out from among the crowd' (*CO* 46:746); 'No one can tell God from the apostles' (*CO* 48:599).

have been an irrevocable edict for them that Jesus Christ bore the mark of God his Father, that he alone is the light of the world, he alone is the way, and that the heavenly Father desires to be honoured in and through his only Son. To him we must give obedience.

It is essential, therefore, that we know that God means to defend his honour and will not have anyone steal one drop of it in order to assign it to some created being. We must also know in what way the Lord Jesus Christ has been given to us, so that we have no excuse for thinking that God is too remote from us and too hidden by his majesty. Rather, he has revealed himself to us in his living image. This is a basic principle to be grasped, but because men knew nothing of it, the devil muddled everything, and Jesus Christ was, we might say, buried, instead of being raised to full pre-eminence. So let us learn what we are taught here, that when we compare Jesus Christ with every other creature—be it the angels of heaven—all must be brought low, and he alone exalted.

It is true, however, that in him we still count for something—for a great deal, in fact! Even so, this must not obscure his honour, as we will see in more detail later on. John the Baptist tells us here that he is not worthy to kiss the ground on which Jesus Christ has walked. Nevertheless John remains an heir of the kingdom of heaven; he continues to be more than a prophet, and Jesus Christ declares him to be such (Matt. 11:9; Luke 7:26). So John is most honourable in rank. It is our Lord Jesus Christ who gives him that rank, and demands that it be recognized. Yet when all is said and done, John did nothing which would have diminished the honour of God's Son, so that what was properly his should not be lost to him, but should remain intact.

Although God wants his servants to be honoured and the gifts he has placed in them to be valued and acknowledged, they must nevertheless be willing to be blotted out so that men may look to our Lord Jesus Christ. Also, we should treat those who are greatly endowed with the Spirit's gifts as if they were ours. As Scripture says, 'All are yours, whether Peter or Paul; and you belong to Jesus Christ alone' (1 Cor. 3:22-23). We must keep returning to this truth. Paul had no wish to see his work reviled, yet he ends up identifying with the faithful and seeking to serve them, otherwise he could not serve God (1 Cor. 4:15). Even so, his wish is that all should be Christ's. Here is a lesson worth remembering. We belong to the Son of God; all that concerns our salvation is to be sought in him. Moreover we must make wise use of those who are sent to us on God's behalf; we should regard them as ours.

We turn now to John the Baptist's words as we find them in Scripture: 'I will baptize you with water, but he who comes after me will baptize you with the Holy Spirit and with fire.' Undoubtedly what John sought here was to anticipate an objection which might be brought against him, as is more clearly revealed in the Gospel of John (John 1:19-22). There the story is told of the scribes and especially the Pharisees who, seeing that John would not accept the honour and noble title of Messiah or Redeemer, came and rebuked him: 'What's this? The role you have assumed is not lawful. You introduce something new into the church: you bring in baptism! You have got to be the Redeemer, or else you should be punished as a deceiver and false prophet.' We well understand how serious was the temptation facing John. For when men are attracted and enticed by the prospect of honour, it is very hard for them to resist; and human nature is so prone to ambition and arrogance that there is no one who does not presume to make that his aim, out of pride. This applies all the more when pressures come from elsewhere: there are very few who retain their self-control, and who think to themselves: 'I know myself. I do not want to be more than what God has appointed for me.'

It is as I said: by nature we are inclined to other things, so it was a rude shock for John the Baptist when he was flattered and applauded, and when the scribes and even the Pharisees, who were then most influential, came to pay him homage. 'Look,' they said. 'You are the world's Redeemer, and the King promised from the dawn of time.' Nevertheless John remained firm as a rock in the face of this temptation. There was, however, an even greater trial, the threat that he might be judged a false prophet and be stoned, unless he accepted the role of Messiah. So both his honour and his life were at stake. Yet he resisted everything, in every way.

John's example deserves our close attention. First, when there are things which really attract us, and when the devil seeks to dazzle our eyes by suggesting that we might rise to a place of honour, let us be prepared, so that we do not entertain his flatteries and greedily drink them in. That is one point. It is not enough to be content with our lot in life, to flutter aimlessly about or to seek success. When opportunities arise we should hold firm, humble ourselves and remain as we are, lowly. Even in matters of life and death we must resist all of Satan's wiles, should he try to inflate our sense of ambition. Not only did John the Baptist have to refuse and despise the false honours attributed to him, he had to be equipped to face abuse and denigration, on the grounds that he was thought to be a deceiver.

Now that is worse than death. There are many, we know, who would prefer to endure death and disgrace in men's eyes, than to suffer blame as if they were guilty. That is why Paul, when urging believers and especially ministers of the word to be steadfast, writes: 'We suffer persecution; indeed we are defamed' (1 Cor. 4:12-13). He regards this as the greatest evil. Thus John was not only obliged to reject the honour which the devil was offering him through his servants; he had also to scorn his own life, to forget himself and to suffer stoning. In the third place he had to run the risk of being disgraced in the sight of all, of being condemned as a false prophet, a deceiver who had upset the church by seeking to assail the law of Moses, and as an apostate who had changed and corrupted everything. It was to all this, I say, that John the Baptist had to submit, placing his own life in danger.

We see, then, how greatly God strengthened him in his hour of need. His example is set before us so that, when we feel like making much of ourselves in the world's eyes, we may learn to renounce all such things. There are certainly many people who would be most welcome if they chose to deny Jesus Christ. On some of them honours and titles would be heaped, and benefices on others. Well then, we must be armed against the temptations of Satan so that we do not fail. Let us prefer to be poor, despised and mocked, than to do anything to obscure the honour of our Lord Jesus Christ. Are we resolved, then, to walk humbly? Would we rather be in God's house—yes, in the smallest corner—and be singled out for scorn, than have all the world's wealth and all its honours? Have we, I ask, got that far? And that is not all. Supposing we were to be sacrificed and to have to answer with our lives, we must take a second step, following John's example. Although the world should heap abuse and invective on us, although we might be torn, as it were, to pieces—just as everywhere we are called heretics, dogs, renegades, troublers of Christendom—we must swallow all these insults. Why? In order that Jesus Christ may be glorified in us. When we have fought under his banner and defended his right to supremacy; when we have brought all in obedience to him and have finished our race, then all the abuse we have suffered will be changed into honour, and we will share in the crown of glory prepared for all who did not seek their own good, but sought to glorify the Lord of hosts, in and through his only Son.

Now let us cast ourselves down before the majesty of our good God, acknowledging our faults and praying that he may be pleased to touch us more and more, and to open our eyes that we might clearly see what we are like. By this means may we be led to humility, seeking to live for him alone and to bring others to him. May we endeavour to move further along our path, so that our whole life may testify that we are willing to obey him and to have him rule over us in peace. May he uphold us in all our infirmities, and more and more correct them until, cleaving to him, we attain that fullness of blessing which is to know that he is all in all.

4

WITH THE SPIRIT AND WITH FIRE

'Truly I baptize you with water for repentance, but he who is coming after me is mightier than I, whose shoes I am not worthy to carry; he will baptize you with the Holy Spirit and with fire. [12]*He has his winnowing fan in his hand, and he will clear his threshing floor and gather his wheat into the granary; but he will burn the chaff with a fire which never goes out'* (Matt. 3:11-12).

And he preached, saying, 'After me comes he who is mightier than I, the strap of whose sandals I am not worthy to stoop down and untie. [8]*Truly I have baptized you with water, but he will baptize you with the Holy Spirit'* (Mark 1:7-8).

John answered and said to them all, 'Truly I baptize you with water; but he who is mightier than I is coming, the strap of whose sandals I am not worthy to untie; he will baptize you with the Holy Spirit and with fire. [17]*His fan is in his hand, to clear his threshing floor and to gather the wheat into his granary, but he will thoroughly burn the chaff with a fire that never goes out.'* [18]*Thus he proclaimed good news to the people, exhorting them also concerning many other things* (Luke 3:16-18).

WE have seen that John the Baptist could not be induced, either by empty flattery or by the fear of death, to exalt himself instead of our Lord Jesus Christ. He remained in the place where God had put him, declaring that all honour must be given to God's Son, and that he alone should be supreme in the church. All creatures were as nothing compared with him and with the eminence which is his. In short, he should be acknowledged as the church's Head and Teacher. Ministers and preachers of the gospel should be under his feet, so that they may serve him and never usurp his headship.

It remains for us now to see how he replied to the accusation which had been brought against him, for those intent on putting him in the place of our Lord Jesus Christ had criticized him, saying that he should only baptize if he were the world's promised Redeemer. They therefore asked for evidence. What was its source? At this point John excused himself, affirming that *he baptized with water, but that he who was coming after him*—he who possessed all majesty—*would baptize with the Holy Spirit.* This was John's way of saying that he took nothing away from our Lord Jesus Christ or from the office given to him by God his Father. Although ministers have the task of baptizing, as to its power it is Jesus Christ alone who baptizes. We administer the external sign as we are commanded to do, but Jesus Christ always reserves for himself the privilege of giving effect to baptism, so that its entire fruit depends on him and on his grace. That, in brief, was John's intention.

A false explanation of all this has been given, as if the sacrament which we have today in the Christian church is not the same as John's.[1] It is not a question here of the sacrament itself, but only of those who ministered it. It is quite certain that no

[1] Both Chrysostom and Augustine drew a distinction between John's baptism and Christ's. Cf. *Inst.* IV.15.7. Similarly, the Council of Trent in its decree on the sacraments (March 1547) condemned those who held the two baptisms to be identical (On Baptism, canon 1).

difference exists between the two; that is, that the baptism entrusted to John was exactly like the one we have, and which we still observe today. For sacraments derive their value from God and from his word, of which they are, in a sense, seals.

The sacrament indeed is nothing in itself. If we baptize without showing why, and without explaining the promise which is given there, baptism would be merely a monkey-trick, just as there are really no sacraments in popery. They are mere rubbish, with mumblings and magic spells and suchlike. I am speaking of the papists themselves, for they have not been able to abolish baptism itself which was instituted by our Lord Jesus Christ.[2] Even so, they have trodden it underfoot and profaned it. Hence, if we want to know what John's baptism was like, we must look to what it was he taught, which was no different. He baptized, as we have already seen, for repentance, and as evidence of the remission of sins. We, today, have nothing more than this. Moreover we know that our Lord Jesus Christ willed to become one with us in baptism, and demonstrated the unity which we have with him, as members have with their Head. Now who was it who baptized our Lord Jesus Christ? So if the baptism which Jesus received was meant to show that we have part and portion of all his benefits, that he lives in us and that we are joined to him by an unbreakable bond, it follows that there is no difference between the baptism which we receive and John's.

This is the point to which we must come: a distinction is made here between our Lord Jesus Christ, and John the Baptist along with everyone else. As is said in John's Gospel, once Jesus Christ began to reveal himself to the world, he baptized many more people than John—not Jesus Christ himself, John adds, but his disciples (John 4:1-2). So our Lord baptizes, but not with his own hands so far as the outward sign is concerned. Yet baptism

[2] On the preservation of baptism in the Roman Church as a valid gospel ordinance, see *Inst.* IV.2.11, and see above, p. 28, note 5.

is attributed to him because he is its author, and it is he who gives it full efficacy; his disciples meanwhile perform the duties appointed to them. In sum, what the Evangelist tells us with his own lips should today be applied to all who baptize: we minister only the external sign, while the power belongs to our Lord Jesus Christ.

When we speak of the sacraments, we say that baptism is the washing of our souls, that it signifies the heavenly life, that it is an earnest of our adoption and ushers us into the church of God, so that we are reckoned to be his children. As to the Lord's Supper, we say that it testifies that we are made partakers of Jesus Christ, that his body is the bread which feeds our souls, that his blood is our drink, and that in him we have everything pertaining to our salvation. That is what we say—that is what we should say—about the sacraments. Why so? Because when we speak this way, on the one side is Jesus Christ, and on the other side is the minister. Both are joined together: the minister applies the water, and our Lord Jesus Christ fulfils his promise. Their purpose is not to disappoint us by offering us useless symbols. This is no comedy. What is shown to us outwardly, Jesus Christ fulfils in truth, inwardly. Thus when we speak about the sacraments, our Lord Jesus Christ is included in them as their author; he is there the moment they are introduced. Baptism and the Supper are not things invented by the mind of man. Thus Jesus Christ ensures that the sacraments are not pointless, but that they benefit us, so that we may receive the truth and substance of what is set before us.

When we speak about the minister, that is, about what is strictly his, we say that he is nothing. It is as Paul says: 'He who plants and he who waters are nothing' (1 Cor. 3:7). That is how ministers are humbled, if we consider only what is theirs; the Son of God keeps everything for himself, and rightly so. Therefore when we read here that 'John baptized with water', this is true of all ministers and pastors of the church. They baptize, and not without effect, since what they do is sanctioned by God; it is not pointless. Baptism is indeed the pledge which we have that the blood of Jesus Christ is our washing, that we are renewed by the power of his Holy Spirit and brought into the church as heirs of the heavenly kingdom. All this is true of the baptism which we administer. Why is that? Because our Lord Jesus Christ acknowledges us, for we do what he has commanded us to do, and in acknowledging us he displays the power of his Holy Spirit so that the sacrament is not given in vain. In the Supper not only bread and wine are offered. Our Lord Jesus Christ, who has commanded this rite, is present to ensure that we truly share in his body and blood, that we live in him and he in us.

Nevertheless, the ministry of men must not obscure the praise of our Lord Jesus Christ, and the minister must never put himself in the Master's place. The minister is mere dross: to muddle the two is out of the question. We must recognize the things which belong to the Son of God, and those that belong to men. Men must know that they have only the outward sign, and that it is Jesus Christ who plays the chief—indeed the total—part, as to the efficacy and substance of the sacraments. This is something we need to bear in mind.[3]

Consequently, when today we present children for baptism, we should value the visible sign, since it is not something hatched in men's heads. Our Lord Jesus Christ sought to strengthen us in our ignorance by providing this help, so we ought to value the sign. How do we do that? By not doubting that God has placed his mark upon us, so that we are counted as heirs of his kingdom and as members of the church. Nor should we doubt

[3] The preacher's comment that, in himself, the minister is 'nothing', and the distinction which he makes between outward sign and inner substance, should be seen in relation to the Roman Catholic belief that the correct celebration of the sacrament by the duly ordained priest is sufficient, *ex opere operato*, to confer grace. The doctrine was specifically upheld by the Council of Trent in its decree on the sacraments (canon 8).

that our children also are made partakers of grace, so that our Lord may clothe them with his righteousness, may cleanse them by his blood and may renew them by his Holy Spirit. We must not doubt these things unless we want to stop God working by his Holy Spirit, and Jesus Christ fulfilling what he intended the sign to represent.[4]

As long as our thanklessness provides no obstacle, it is certain that the sacrament will be neither empty nor useless. However, we must lift our eyes higher than created things, and we must not think that the man who pours water onto the infant's head has the Holy Spirit up his sleeve, that he is dispensing the blood of our Lord Jesus Christ or that he possesses anything which belongs to the eternal salvation of souls. We must realize that our Lord Jesus Christ is not separate from his ordinance, and that he works in such a way that the Holy Spirit acts jointly with the hand of him who is his minister. What belongs to Jesus Christ is thus reserved for him alone; it is not given to created beings, and he is not robbed of his honour or authority. Nevertheless, we acknowledge the things which he has entrusted to those chosen to be ministers of his church.

This is something we need to grasp. At the same time, however, these words teach us that the work of men is nothing in itself, but that it is the Holy Spirit, given by our Lord Jesus Christ, who does everything. No, men do not have him at their command, to dispose of him as they wish. Admittedly, our verse says nothing about the blood of Jesus Christ which was shed to cleanse us of our spots and stains. It is nevertheless presupposed by the word

[4] Calvin's position has been well summarized by Pierre Ch. Marcel: 'The children of believing parents are baptized by reason of the fact that they are children of the covenant and, as such, heirs of *all* the promises made by God at the institution of this covenant, included in which are the promises of the remission of sins and of the Holy Spirit for their regeneration and sanctification … [God] requires that in due course they should accept these gifts by faith, and he promises that through the operation of the Holy Spirit these gifts will become a living reality in their life.' (*The Biblical Doctrine of Infant Baptism*, tr. Philip E. Hughes, London: James Clarke, 1953, p. 198.)

'Spirit'. Why? Although, to be pure and clean in God's sight, we must seek refuge wholly in the blood of Jesus Christ, we must also know how we come to share in such a blessing. It is only, as Peter says, as our souls are sprinkled by the Holy Spirit with the blood shed once and for all (1 Pet. 1:2). The fact that Jesus Christ destined his blood for our spiritual washing would not have availed us if, as we have seen, the Holy Spirit had not been at work. For unbelievers remain in their defilement; in God's eyes they are full of corruption and are abhorrent to him. Why? Because they have not been washed and cleansed. Again, why is that? Because the Holy Spirit has not done his work in them.

It is with good reason, then, that Scripture speaks of the fruit and efficacy of baptism, and of the benefits we receive from it. It all comes back to the Holy Spirit, for while the substance belongs to Jesus Christ, it would be useless to us, as we said, unless imparted to us by the Holy Spirit's power and grace. Salvation cannot, then, be tied to water which is a fleeting and perishable thing. That would be to make an idol of it, as the papists do. They have done their best to pervert baptism so that it is only filth and corruption; they have turned it into a thing of magic and witchcraft. No further proof is needed to convict them than this: all sound doctrine has been banished. Yet they fancy that three drops of water are enough to ward off the devil and to constrain God. In popery baptismal water has been made an idol, and chrism more so, together with spittle, salt and all their other nonsense. They have little regard for the water itself, compared with the piffling trifles they have added in. At any rate, all this outward spectacle is meant to dazzle the eyes of the illiterate, so that they cannot be brought to Jesus Christ by baptism.[5]

What we learn here is that the visible sign which is set before us should serve as a ladder to take us higher, and to help us see

[5] See above, page 19, note 1.

that what baptism symbolizes is to be found in the person of God's Son. And everything has to be imparted to us through the Holy Spirit. Here, then, is the first thing to remember: we must distinguish the material signs which we have in the sacraments from the truth and substance which are in Jesus Christ alone. We must also understand how our Lord freely bestows his benefits on us, how we may draw upon his fullness and how, although we may err and fail, he graciously and generously supplies our needs—namely by his Holy Spirit, through whom he grants us all that he has received, all that God his Father has given him. For the Spirit enlightens us so that we may know Jesus Christ as he has been given to us. He also seals in our hearts the certainty of what he promises us in the gospel. He renews and sprinkles us in order to cleanse us of our filth and corruption. Our Lord Jesus Christ avails us as long as we partake of his Holy Spirit.

We must add one further point. It is Jesus Christ who gives us his Holy Spirit: so it is from him that we must ask for the Spirit. Every time we think of our baptism, we should turn to him who instituted it and pray to him into whom we were baptized, that we may have more than the water only, and that he may prove to us that the water is truly what it represents, an earnest, so to speak, of the reality of his Holy Spirit. This is how we should pray each day to Jesus Christ, asking that he may fulfil in us what is symbolized once and for all in baptism. The same must be done for the children who are daily brought by their parents and godparents. We must pray that, when come of age, they may know that they should take refuge wholly in Jesus Christ, and may honour him by confessing that it is for him alone to give effect to the visible sign. That is how we ought to put this teaching into practice.

Now what we said about baptism should also be applied to the Supper. Accordingly, when we come to our Lord's table, let us ask him in prayer to make us partakers of his body and blood, and that, when we take a small portion of bread and drink three drops of wine, it may not be an empty, trivial gesture. May we come instead to receive from him what he offers us, and may we always receive it through the power of his Holy Spirit.

When it is said that *he will baptize with the Holy Spirit and with fire*, this is not meant to imply two different things. The word 'fire' is something like a title given to the Holy Spirit. Sometimes he is also called 'water'. Not water in a physical sense: this is a figurative way of speaking. Thus, when Scripture says that the Holy Spirit acts as water does on us, it does so for two reasons. We read in Isaiah: 'You who are thirsty, come to the waters, and I will fully satisfy you' (Isa. 55:1). John in his Gospel shows what the verse means, for there our Lord declares that this was fulfilled in his very person (John 7:37). Here is confirmation of the point we made a moment ago, that Jesus Christ alone gives the Holy Spirit. When, therefore, the Holy Spirit is spoken of as water, it is because we are barren; we are parched and famished wretches who faint unless we receive strength and substance from the Holy Spirit. That is one reason why the Spirit is called 'water'.

Another reason is found in Ezekiel, where the prophet says, 'I will pour pure, clean water upon you, and you will be cleansed' (Ezek. 36:25). What he means is that we are all defiled and utterly rotten before God, and that the only way we can be made clean is for God to wash us with pure water. We cannot in our own strength remove the dirt and defilement which makes us abominable in God's sight. He must do it for us. How? Through his Holy Spirit. For these two reasons, then, the Holy Spirit is called 'water'.

The same may be said of the Spirit when, as here, he is called 'fire'. Just as fire consumes all the dross and cleanses all that is foul, this same work is done by the Holy Spirit in respect of our souls. In us there is only sin until we receive cleansing from him. What are all our feelings and desires if not filth and vileness? We cannot, as I said, cleanse ourselves; God must work in us with power. That is why the Holy Spirit is fire. We must go back into the oven when God chooses to make us new.[6] It is as if we were made to pass through the furnace. True, if he were to cleanse us severely, nothing would be left of us; we would be completely consumed, as we read in Isaiah (Isa. 66:15-16). However, he cleanses us in such a way that, although by nature we are totally corrupt and full of iniquity, rebellious and evil, God finds a means which far exceeds our every thought, so that in bringing us through the furnace he draws forth solid gold and good, pure silver.

Now there is not an ounce of gold or silver in us! We should be totally consumed! When gold and silver are passed through the flames, although they contain much dross and waste which appear to be useless metals, solid gold and silver are drawn off from them. It is not the same with us. There is nothing good in us, yet God puts it in us, so that he brings gold and silver forth from what is only dung and rottenness. In this way the Holy Spirit is the furnace who purifies all the defilement in our souls, with the result that we are reckoned to be pure and clean in God's sight. First, then, as we hear all this, let us learn to humble ourselves and to understand that from God's unmerited goodness we receive all that belongs to our salvation, inasmuch as he has generously bestowed on us, in Jesus Christ, all fullness of blessing. This is what should lead us to humility. In the second place, let us learn to glorify the Son of God with praise and thanksgiving, and let us revere his power as he deserves. Thirdly, if we want our baptism to be effective and useful for our salvation, let us allow ourselves to pass through the furnace, so that God may transform and consume all our iniquity. May he cause

[6] 'Back into the oven': French has *recuits*, 're-cooked'. Calvin employs the same metaphor in his Pentecost sermon on Acts 2:1-4 (*CO* 48:629, 633).

the flame to burn us, as it were, for it is certain that we will never be remade and dedicated to God's service unless force is applied.

It is thus as if we passed through fire. It is no easy thing for men to enter into themselves, to take all their feelings and passions captive, and especially to tread all reason underfoot and to acknowledge that God must rule them, and that they themselves are powerless. Much conflict comes as a result. We do not think it strange, then, that Scripture likens the renewal of God's children to a fire which burns and devours everything. Without force, as I said, and until we are inwardly constrained, we cannot be made to please God.

For the rest, John the Baptist adds that *Jesus Christ has a fan in his hand, to cleanse his threshing floor and to disperse the chaff, that it may be burned in a fire that will never go out, while the good grain will be put into the granary.* There is no doubt that with these words John sought to threaten those who were hardened and who might have despised the grace offered to them in our Lord Jesus Christ. For there are many who are happy and complacent in their sins—people who spurn God's kindness, worldly people, dogs and swine. Those who are not so cut to the quick that they condemn themselves or despair of their wickedness and misery, will surely scorn God and have no taste for the heavenly blessings about which they hear in the gospel. Therefore many remain mindless, although the message is dinned into their ears that they were not made to dwell forever in this world, to live well and to indulge in every iniquity. They were created in order to honour God as their Father, so that he might receive them as his children into eternal life. What then? Nothing of this means anything to them: they want only to err and stray and do wrong, to be like pigs at their trough. And why? Because, as I said, they are mindless, having no feeling for God's judgment. They have no idea that they will be called to account; indeed they promise themselves that they will go unpunished, which is why they press on regardless and carry on as usual. There are others who are full of pride and arrogance, such as we see among the great of this world. They are indifferent to the news that God is reconciled to us through his Son. How many there are who are drunk on wealth and honours, and who despise God and the unfathomable goodness which he has shown, and which he daily shows us, in our Lord Jesus Christ!

As a result, when the gospel is preached there are very few who do not turn a deaf ear, refusing all that is offered to them. Such people must thus be woken up: they need a spur to prick them and to remind them of the vengeance prepared for all who do not deign to receive Jesus Christ in all humility. Accordingly, John the Baptist adds here the threats which we have heard. Earlier he had said that he bore witness to the remission of sins, and to God's will to rule the world and to gather the people to himself. He therefore invited all poor sinners to the hope of eternal life. He set before them the God of all pity who was ready to receive them in mercy. That is what he proclaimed. Yet, on seeing that many simply blocked their ears, as we said, he makes it clear that they will know God as judge if they refuse to come and find in him all fatherly sweetness and love. And when they will not accept the benefits which Jesus Christ brings, he tells them that retribution too will not be found wanting.

This is why Paul says that we have a sword with which to visit God's vengeance on those who will not yield and humble themselves (cf. 2 Cor. 10:4-6). For the gospel implies that all loftiness in this world will be brought low and that we will be put to shame, since we have nothing of which to boast, except in God. Well then, there are some who are so false that they cannot accept the message of salvation which is laid before them; and there are others who, as I have said, are like dogs, caring nothing for the heavenly inheritance. In a word, they defy God. Besides these there are hypocrites who are bursting with foolish presumption, and who fancy that God is very much in their debt. Now Paul insists that those who will not yield to the doctrine we proclaim will be made to feel that it is a sword which will mortally pierce them, and that God's vengeance is at hand, ready to be exercised against all disobedience on the last day.

Paul, to be sure, includes this terrifying detail in the gospel, but he does so in order to frighten those who are ungrateful to God, who are rebels and who are so senseless that they cannot be made to see their need and sickness. However, concerning the faithful, Paul adds, 'This will be when your obedience is complete' (2 Cor. 10:6). He thus demonstrates that the primary aim of the gospel is not to scare us but to draw us with free and willing hearts to our God, and to dispose us to obey him, so that we become his and so that he may peaceably have his way with us. When all this has come to pass, the unbelieving and the rebellious will see fulfilled all the threats that have been made against them. That too is why our Lord Jesus Christ says, 'Whatever you loose on earth will be loosed in heaven, and whatever you bind on earth will be bound in heaven' (Matt. 18:18). In the first place, we loose: that is, in calling poor sinners to Jesus Christ, we release them as from the depths of hell, from bondage to sin and from God's curse which rests upon them. That is how we loose. Our Lord Jesus Christ is daily set before us, so that we might know how, through him, we have the victory over Satan, sin and death. Conversely, we also bind, for those who refuse to be delivered by the work and grace of God's Son must be doubly bound: the devil takes possession of them so that no other remedy exists. Their sickness is quite incurable; already they are condemned.[7]

[7] Matt. 18:18 was fundamental to Calvin's understanding of discipline in the church and of the duty of pastoral care. To 'loose' is simply to attest, in God's name, the forgiveness of sins to the penitent; to 'bind' is to announce God's judgment on the impenitent and, if necessary, to exclude them from Christian fellowship 'until they mend their ways'. Cf. *Inst.* IV.11.1-2.

That, then, is how God works in the gospel. Such is John's meaning when he speaks of the fan in Christ's hand. Now what is said is not to be confined to the short period of time when John the Baptist preached on earth. His words concern the general nature and use of the gospel. It is as if the promise were made that, when God holds out his arms to welcome us, he will be favourable to us if we seek him with true repentance, and if we place our hope of salvation in Jesus Christ and in the mercy he has brought us. Having that promise, we must not be slow or sluggish. Let us appreciate this blessing, and in all humility and reverence thank our God for graciously looking upon such poor and wretched creatures and for treating us so generously. Let us also come as hungry souls, conscious of what misery there is within us until our Lord Jesus Christ in his goodness comes to our aid.

If, however, this is not how we feel, it will certainly cost us dear to have listened to the gospel while remaining indifferent, deaf to what God wishes to say to us. For since the gospel is the key which opens the kingdom of heaven to us, since it is God's power of salvation for all who believe (Rom. 1:16), since it is the sceptre of our Lord Jesus Christ by which he shows himself to be our king, it is also our very communion with Jesus Christ, as Paul writes in the first chapter of First Corinthians (1 Cor. 1:9), so that while we possess him, he has full dominion over us. The gospel has all these powers and uses, but if we remain wallowing in our filth and obsessed by earthly things, and if we are not consciously moved so that we come in obedience to God—ah! we will discover that the gospel is a fan. What will it do? It will separate out the chaff, throw it onto the dung heap and burn it with fire—a fire which will never go out!

To understand the image properly, observe that the gospel is like a fan in two ways. I am not referring to the wind which blows, but to a fan which winnows, or to a sieve, which many think is the better sense.

The gospel serves, then, as a fan or sieve in two ways, for this is how it should work in each of us. Why? Because we cannot be regarded as good grain, fit to be stored in the granary, until we have been cleansed of the chaff within us. Strictly speaking, chaff is what we are, but God makes good grain of us by putting in us the seed of life. So there you have good grain. Even so, the good grain which God has sown in us by the power of his Holy Spirit is covered with chaff, straw and dust, and with much dirt; it must therefore be cleansed. Thus when we come to hear the sermon, we must each say to ourselves, 'Alas, God has put a little goodness in me, some good grain. Nevertheless that little bit of goodness is full of filth and corruption, so what goodness there is would soon be choked, and would never be of use but only serve to condemn me, if God did not cleanse it by his Holy Spirit. God must fan and sieve me; he must make me clean of all the dross, for as long as he leaves me as I am, I am corrupt and defiled.' Let us not, then, remain mixed up and muddled, but when the gospel calls to us, it is as if God were shining a light to uncover what is hidden.

We are only too happy to cloak ourselves in hypocrisy, so that evil continues to fester but is not seen. Indeed we do not care to examine ourselves, but prefer to throw our sins behind our backs and think of them no more. God, however, uses his gospel like a fan or sieve, and makes sure that, like it or not, we are forced to perceive our faults and wretchedness. That is how each of us must daily be winnowed.

There is, however, a second way in which we are fanned or sieved. It is when God separates the good from the bad, and when the faithful know that they are good grain, while hypocrites must think of themselves as chaff. Admittedly, this is not something obvious to the eye, for nowadays there are many who mingle among us in the church, and who even thrust themselves far forward, but who despise God and have not one drop of piety in them.

However that be, the gospel is never preached in vain. Believers already sense the efficacy and power of what is preached to them—that is, they are able to find comfort in God, to rejoice in him and to call upon him freely, not doubting that he will answer them, since they are his children. They have his fatherly love sealed in their hearts by the Holy Spirit. That, therefore, is how the faithful are winnowed, separated, that is, from the chaff. On the other hand, however much unbelievers gnash their teeth and lash out at God, or however mindless and bewitched they may be, they nevertheless feel a certain remorse within—secret, unseen twinges. And although they do not know their source, bewildered, they already feel the fire of God's wrath: not as they will feel it at the judgment day, but the fire is lit, and although it lurks beneath the ashes, it will surely eat away and gradually devour them.

This is the second way in which Jesus Christ winnows and sifts his church. The gospel reveals to all the faithful who accept it humbly, with pure and willing hearts, that before God and his angels they are counted as good grain, which is reserved for the heavenly life. To the unbelieving, to scorners of God and to hypocrites, it reveals that they are being eaten away from within; they already feel God's wrath, and cannot avoid the condemnation that God is now their judge, and that Jesus Christ is sifting and winnowing them, and driving them onto the dung heap. This is what we need to understand.

We are now easily able to make sense of this verse. As long as we are sweetly and kindly invited to receive the grace of our Lord Jesus Christ, as long as we do not despise it but give ourselves wholly to God and so feel the Spirit's fire that we thrill at the thought of these heavenly blessings, we must resolve to walk through this world, no longer wrapped in all its vanities or addicted to them. That is what we must do.

We should fear, therefore, lest God exact the retribution which is set before us here. The gospel is of necessity a fan to disperse the chaff far and wide. It is a fact of course that, although we may be true children of God, he must winnow and sieve us, as we said. That our Lord should cleanse and purify us is something to be desired. Let us take care, however, that we are not winnowed like the hypocrites and despisers of God, thrown as rubbish onto the dung heap and burned with a fire that will never go out. Let us fear this condemnation, and let us learn to make the most of God's kindness, which he daily displays to us by calling us to the hope of life. He does not willingly act as judge toward us, provided we accept him as he offers himself to us, as Father and Saviour. Let us make sure, then, that the coming of Jesus Christ does not end in ruin for us, but let us receive him as Saviour and Redeemer, for that is how he daily presents himself to us. For his part he will put forth his power which was revealed for all time, in order that we, being baptized in his name, may feel the reality and effect of the visible sign. By his Holy Spirit we are renewed, and through that same Spirit he leads us on until he removes us from this world's vanity and lusts, and fully conforms us to his righteousness.

Now let us cast ourselves down before the majesty of our good God, acknowledging our faults and begging him so to make us feel them that we renounce them all. May he uphold us in our weaknesses, and although there is still much in us deserving of rebuke, may we not cease to be pleasing to him, until at length he brings us to that perfection to which he calls us.

5

MY SON, MY BELOVED

Then Jesus came from Galilee to the Jordan to John, to be baptized by him. [14]*John would have restrained him, saying, 'I need to be baptized by you, and do you come to me?'* [15]*But Jesus answered him, 'Let it be so now; for it is fitting for us to fulfil all righteousness.' Then he let him have his way.* [16]*And when Jesus was baptized, he went up immediately from the water. And behold, the heavens opened, and he saw the Spirit of God descending like a dove and settling on him;* [17]*and with that, a voice from heaven, saying 'This is my beloved Son, with whom I am well pleased'* (Matt. 3:13-17).

In those days Jesus came from Nazareth of Galilee and was baptized by John in the Jordan. [10]*And when he came up out of the water, immediately he saw the heavens rent and the Spirit descending on him like a dove.* [11]*Then there was a voice from heaven, saying, 'You are my beloved Son; with you I am well pleased'* (Mark 1:9-11).

And it happened that, as he was baptizing all the people, Jesus also was baptized and was praying, when the heavens opened, [22]*and the Holy Spirit descended on him in bodily form, as a dove, and there was a voice from heaven, saying, 'You are my beloved Son; with you I am well pleased.'* [23]*Jesus himself had now reached the age of about thirty, being the son, so it was thought, of Joseph, the son of Heli* (Luke 3:21-23).

IN the light of what was said previously about the use and nature of baptism, it is certain that the Son of God had no need to be baptized, for the sacrament as we described it signified repentance and the remission of sins. It is not in this class that we might place our Lord Jesus Christ: he was always united in perfect righteousness with God his Father. He did not need to be converted or to change his ways, not as we do who have to be renewed because we are totally corrupt. Nor was there any fault in him for which he needed pardon: he was spotless, without blemish. This was why John the Baptist refused to baptize him—not, as some have imagined, because he held him in high honour, as though he were a great and eminent prophet. If he had done that, he would not have acknowledged the office to which God had appointed him; he would have wronged and injured God. For we know that when God calls someone and gives him responsibilities, everyone must yield. If John had thought that Jesus Christ was only a prophet, he would certainly have honoured God, the prophet's teacher, and would even have welcomed Jesus Christ into the ranks of those who were coming to obtain remission for their sins, and to be remade according to God's image.

When, therefore, he says, '*I need to be baptized by you, yet you come to me*', he means that Jesus Christ should forgo baptism, that for him it was personally unwarranted. Moreover if Jesus Christ had looked only to himself, baptism was quite superfluous; but because he was joined to us as the Head is joined to its members, that was why he was baptized, in order to show that although he was pure and clear of all transgression, and was entirely holy, he was nevertheless willing to accept condemnation for our sins, to bow to God's judgment and to pay the price for them, in order to deliver and absolve us from them. At the same time he sought to demonstrate that God's Spirit had been given to him, not for his own use but so that he might impart him to us. Thus the baptism which our Lord accepted was as a bond of the union we have with him, by which we share in all his benefits, and of his union with us, by which he takes our wretchedness upon himself and frees us from it. Not, as I have said, that he is tarnished by our blemishes: his purpose was to rid us of them in God's sight. It was necessary for him to take this burden on himself, and to bear it.

In a word, when today we are baptized, we should remember that this is what it means: all that our Lord Jesus Christ received from God his Father now belongs to us. Why? Because he shared, in common with us, the sacrament and visible sign, in order to show that he will not be parted from the members of his body, and that, since he desired nothing for himself, everything should be given to us. He wished also to demonstrate that he gladly accepts all our ills and misery so as to free us from them, for their weight would utterly crush us.

Thus when he answers John, saying, '*Let it be so for now, for all righteousness must be fulfilled*', we cannot doubt that he was mindful of God's command. For those who represent baptism as a meritorious work are far too frivolous, like those empty-heads in popery. Our Lord Jesus Christ was simply pointing out to John that it was useless to argue about whether he should be baptized by the hand of mortal man, or whether he was the one to call all to his baptism. It was enough that the Father in heaven had laid down this rule. In this way, our Lord sought to fulfil all righteousness.

It is important to remember here what he himself declared in the seventeenth chapter of John: he sanctified himself for the sake of all who are his (John 17:19). In saying this he meant that he had consecrated himself in all purity to God his Father, so that we, who are wholly defiled, and who indeed were putrid and unclean, should come to share in the holiness which he possessed in all its fullness. Now we might doubt this, if Jesus

Christ had not been united with us through this visible symbol and if he had not given us this pledge of that holy union which makes us partners and partakers of all his benefits. As it is, we need have no doubts, since our Lord is shown visibly to us, as it were. Furthermore, because God's Son submitted to the law to redeem us from its curse, he wished to prove that he was his Father's servant—and in that very nature which he took from us, in order to make us free.

Thus when he came into the temple to offer sacrifice along with others, he was claiming to come as a poor sinner, yet we know that he was free of all faults. As I said, he did not want his lot in life to be different or separate from ours. By offering sacrifice he placed himself in the ranks of sinners. Nevertheless, as we know, he himself was the sacrifice, or was destined to become it. By accepting baptism which serves to seal the remission of sins, and which is a pledge of our renewal by the Holy Spirit, Jesus Christ sought to show that if we receive him, it is for cleansing by his blood, which is the spiritual washing of our souls, and for new life in him. That life is given through the power of his Holy Spirit whom he received in all fullness, and whom he grants to all his faithful people according to the measure and portion which he knows is right for them.

Now when we see how low the Son of God stooped, should we not thrill to know the boundless kindness he has for us? He gave no thought to what was proper, but considered only what would benefit us and work for our salvation. Let us learn, therefore, to make the most of the baptism we receive, knowing that it is meant to unite us with Jesus Christ by an unbroken bond, so that he may support us in our weakness and sustain us by his power. Its purpose, in short, is to help us possess all the good things which have been given to him. For we receive God's grace only on the grounds that we draw deeply from him as from our source. It is clear, then, that if we were not members of our Lord

Jesus Christ, we would be cut off from every spiritual blessing. Accordingly, the Spirit of God is said by Isaiah to have rested on him (Isa. 61:1). For good reason this is ascribed uniquely to him, for we are warned that as long as we do not partake of him by faith, we are empty of all goodness, righteousness and holiness; only evil dwells in us. When the Evangelists therefore tell us that Jesus Christ came to be visibly baptized by John the Baptist, we are encouraged to make much of the baptism mentioned here.

At this point a question might be asked concerning the ignorance shown by John.[1] How could he be God's minister? We must have resolute faith if we are to discharge the duties which God has committed to us. If we go at things when beset by doubt, we are not serving God. There is, however, an easy answer. John was well aware of the purpose of the baptism entrusted to him. He had already explained what it was, and he knew that God had raised him to a position above both church and people. Nevertheless, it is not surprising that he was overcome with wonder when God's Son appeared in person, for he knew that Jesus Christ was the sum and substance of baptism. If we ask what baptism is in itself, the answer is 'nothing'. Can water cleanse our souls? It is a perishable thing, so can it bring the Holy Spirit down to us from heaven? Much less so! Baptism in itself is therefore nothing. As for our Lord Jesus Christ, however, he is its true substance, its fulfilment and its end, so that the sign is neither empty nor unavailing.

Consequently John the Baptist, knowing that our Lord possessed the substance of baptism in himself, is overwhelmed with joy when he sees him coming. His ignorance did not prevent him from being a minister of the sacrament, or others

[1] For Calvin, John's 'ignorance' lies in his failure to understand the necessity of Jesus' baptism, and in his inability to grasp the full meaning of the incarnation. Cf. his commentary on Matt. 3:14 (*CO* 45:125): 'John was mistaken, for he did not understand that it was for the sake of others that he [Jesus] sought baptism. So Christ tells him to consider what befits the servant whose role he had assumed.'

from receiving it at his hand. He knew that everyone else needed it and that it should benefit them. Concerning Jesus Christ, however, all had not yet been revealed to him. Indeed, if we had to be like the angels of heaven in order to serve God by preaching the gospel and ministering the sacraments, we would have to give up! We are all in some way imperfect, as we well know. Thus we may properly serve God, the salvation of believers and the edification of the whole church, even though God's secrets are not fully revealed to us. It is enough if we are able to proclaim his will purely, adding nothing of our own, and if we declare the true purpose of the sacraments and the fruit we get from them.

The main point of what we are told here is to describe what happened at the time of our Lord's baptism: *The heavens were opened, and the Holy Spirit appeared in the form of a dove* (or *pigeon)*; and thirdly, *the voice of the Father was heard, saying, 'This is my beloved Son, with whom I am well pleased.'* And Luke adds this special comment, *Jesus Christ had now reached the age of about thirty*, to show that until then he had lived as a private person, and had been, in a sense, hidden. For although at his birth, as was said earlier, he was declared to be the Son of God, although the angels had proclaimed it with praise and thanksgiving, and although the star had appeared with many other signs attesting our Lord's glory and majesty, he did not choose to make himself known until the time appointed by God. Prior to this he had not revealed himself. And although John the Baptist was filled with the Holy Spirit, he said nothing until the time that Jesus Christ had to be revealed to Israel, for so Luke writes (Luke 1:80). Our Lord too remained quiet. He knew the task to which he had been called and did not go beyond his bounds; he led a private life without wishing his glory to be known. As we saw previously, he was subject to Joseph and to his mother, and it is highly likely that he lived by the trade of carpentry, since that was the reproach brought against him (Matt. 13:55; Mark 6:3; Luke 4:22).[2]

All the more, then, should we be warned to walk in all humility, for to our way of thinking it would be strange for God, having sent his Son to be the Redeemer of the world, to keep him hidden at home for the space of thirty years. Here, however, all human reason must be humbled and must cease: we must worship God's marvellous counsel even though we cannot tell why he should act this way. In any case, we must always acknowledge the mercy which God has shown us, and the love which our Lord Jesus Christ bore us by living in the form and frame of a servant, in all poverty, having no sign of nobility about him. So when we see this, let us learn all the more to feel the flame of love for him, and according as he gives us cause to rest with sure faith upon his grace, may we, when we must suffer indifference or scorn, patiently endure our lowliness. Nor should we be ashamed to be made like him whom the angels of heaven worship, and before whom every knee must bow, as is said in the second chapter of Philippians (Phil. 2:10). There Paul writes that our Lord Jesus Christ not only humbled himself for our sake, in obedience to God his Father, but became as nothing, to the point of suffering a shameful and accursed death. Therefore the Father exalted him and gave him the very highest name, so that every human creature should tremble before his judgment seat (Phil. 2:6-11). Thus, when we want to be uplifted by God's hand, let us learn to be sincere and humble in our walk, as is shown by the example of our Head and King.

As to the words which we have read, it is not only useless but wrong to try to be clever and to question how the heavens were rent: that would have meant destruction for the whole wide

[2] Almost half of Calvin's sermons on the *Gospel Harmony* (Sermons 6–37) bear on Matthew and Luke's nativity and infancy narratives. A selection of sermons on Luke 1 and 2 may be found in Calvin, *Songs of the Nativity*, tr. Robert White (Edinburgh: Banner of Truth Trust, 2008).

world! Whatever happens outside our finite minds we must accept, recognizing that God's secrets are beyond our understanding. The Book of Job, in particular, teaches us that we will be utterly perplexed if we try to delve too deeply into nature's secrets. Not that it is unlawful to study them and to strive to know what is useful to us; but when all is said and done, we must consider that God seeks to transcend all human perceptions in small details of this kind. How much more, then, when he performs a miracle and means to astound us! To try to be smart and to accept only those things whose cause is known to us—would it not be like diminishing God's loftiness and infinite power, and reducing him to our small measure? It would be as if we tried to pull the sun down from the sky!

Let us be content, then, that John the Baptist saw something like an opening in the sky and gazed on things the human eye cannot see.[3] Moreover, supposing the heavens still opened, and that this was not only possible today but could actually happen, we know that our sight cannot reach so high, cannot rise above the circuits of the moon and sun and, going beyond the last planet, Saturn, pass beyond the firmament. Our gaze could not reach so far. God, however, who performs miracles in every sphere, gave to the Baptist a power he had not had before and which he later ceased to have, a power of vision granted to him on our behalf. Admittedly this strengthened his own faith, but his task was to act as God's herald, to proclaim this thing so that we today might know that Jesus Christ has been truly confirmed. If we do not most certainly hold him to be the true and only-begotten Son of God, are we not contradicting the Father who has issued his decree and whose voice has been heard? And are we not also contradicting the Spirit of truth who appeared so that we should be made quite certain of the glory of our Lord?

[3] The Baptist's vision of the Spirit's descent from heaven is recorded in John 1:32-34. The Synoptists focus solely on Jesus' vision of the Spirit.

Now in the first place we see how in the one essence of God there are three persons. Observe that this expression does not imply what we commonly take it to mean. We must not imagine that it is as if there were three people there. The word 'person' signifies a distinct quality, so that when we speak about God, although he is one, there is nevertheless the Father, the Son and the Holy Spirit, who are not divided. There is one essence, one majesty, one glory. We must, however, conceive of a distinction, but not in the way that we think. It should be sufficient to note that here is the Father who sends his Son for the redemption and salvation of the world. The Holy Spirit, for his part, also appears. Now Jesus Christ is God manifest in the flesh; it is absolutely certain that he is the same God whose voice was heard from heaven. As to his special quality, however, he is not the Father, even though he is the same God, along with his Father; but it is the Father's prerogative to bear that title. Hence the Father is not his Son, and the Holy Spirit is neither one nor the other. Even so we can see how this distinction leads us to unity, so that we worship one God only, and we rest in him.

Nevertheless, we do not cease to believe what we are taught in holy Scripture. It was necessary for the heavens to be rent at the baptism of Jesus Christ, so that we might know that, in uniting himself with us, he allowed at the same time those who were banished and excluded from God's kingdom to enter in, and this through the preaching of the gospel. For why had our Lord delayed his baptism for so long? Why did he choose to receive it at the age he had? It was because the sacraments must never be separated from the message of salvation. For who would cut a seal in half, or attach it to a blank sheet of paper? What would be the point of that? It would be useless. But when a seal is affixed to a letter or legal document, it authenticates it. So it is with baptism. If the message of the gospel is not combined with it, baptism will certainly have no effect. Without teaching it is profitless. It is as I said, a seal can have no value unless attached to a letter.

This, then, is what we need to remember. Before he preached the gospel, our Lord Jesus Christ was baptized. John the Baptist, however, had already begun and had prepared the way, and what he taught was nothing less than the gospel. Although it had not yet been perfectly fulfilled, he nevertheless declared: 'Behold the Lamb of God, who takes away the sin of the world' (John 1:29). These words contain the full sum of what is taught to us each day. Notice, then, that since the gospel is preached by virtue of our Lord's baptism, the heavens are opened to us—not in visible fashion, for it is enough that by faith we are able to gaze upon them, however hidden they are from our normal view. We ought to rejoice and be glad that we can defy Satan and even our own sins, which otherwise might lead us to shun God's presence, making it an object of terror to us. Whenever we reflect that the news of salvation did not reach us by accident or by the will of man, but that God wants us to hear him speaking in it; and whenever we accept all of it as coming from him, and that what issues from the mouths of men has the authority not of them but of him who is its source—if that is what we have, it is as if God were opening his kingdom to us, and stretching forth his hand, saying, 'Come and claim the heavenly inheritance. The door was indeed closed to you on account of the curse which lay upon Adam and all his line, but now my Son has made an opening for you.'

In the same way, John writes: 'The time is coming, and is very near, when heaven will open and when the angels of God will ascend and descend' (John 1:51). That is, whereas before there was a deadly divorce between God and men who were alienated from him and who were even his enemies, now there is access, a way in, and angels will come down to earth, busy in serving our salvation; they will ascend to heaven to bring our requests before

God and to attend him on our behalf; they are sent to supply our necessities, to guide us and to keep watch over us.

The heavens opened once in visible fashion. John the Baptist saw it, and he was bound to bear witness to everything which happened at that time. Today, all of this should serve to dispel our doubts. Although we deserve to be disowned and abandoned by God, he nevertheless grants us intimate access to himself. Why is this so? Because we have been baptized into Jesus Christ, who has obtained for us the priceless blessing and privilege of being received by him, and of having his angels among us to watch over our salvation, to defend us and to ascend on high for our sake—all in reference to him who is our Head. For angels are not meant to be worshipped, nor should we on that account make idols of them. Whatever good we get from them, and whatever service they perform, comes through our Lord Jesus Christ whose members they are, and to whom they are inferior, like us. That is one point.

Here we might ask how the Holy Spirit is said to have descended on Jesus Christ, since already, when he was born, and even more when he was conceived, he possessed him in all fullness. Now it was for our sake that this happened. Although Jesus Christ, being the Son of God manifest in the flesh, cannot be separated from his Holy Spirit, and although even from a human point of view he fully possessed him, the Holy Spirit descended on him in a different way. Why? Because it was more expedient for us, and in order to impart to us the grace he had received. Isaiah the prophet understood this when he introduces Jesus Christ to us, saying, 'The Spirit of God is upon me, for he has anointed me and sent me to proclaim the gospel to the poor, to give light to the blind and to free miserable captives' (Isa. 61:1).

Thus our Lord makes it very clear that the Spirit of God is upon him. Indeed he was always with him, even in that human nature with which he clothed himself in order to be our

Redeemer. Still, he received a fresh anointing when he was sent and when he had to preach the gospel. Here, then, was another way by which he received the Holy Spirit. This, I repeat, was only out of consideration for us, not for him.

We might note, however, that the word 'descend' is strictly inappropriate here, for the Holy Spirit is not confined to a given place. As God, his essence can only be infinite, filling both heaven and earth. He descended, however, in order to show us that he is willing to make his home in us. Scripture says that we are God's temples, because his Holy Spirit dwells in us, as Paul writes in the sixth chapter of First Corinthians (1 Cor. 6:19). However, because of our ignorance and our frailty of mind, we needed to know how the Holy Spirit descends to us, for we are far removed from him—I mean from his power and grace. Not that he does not fill all things with his being, but we are empty and bereft of him until, through our Lord Jesus Christ, he draws near. That is how we should think of his descent.

It is important also that we understand why the Spirit appeared in the form described here, 'the form of a dove or pigeon'. Earlier the title 'fire' had been ascribed to him, because he cleanses us from all our filth by burning it up. That is what fire does. We also said that he is called 'water' for the same reason. Why then, given that Jesus Christ was to baptize with fire, did he descend in the likeness of a dove?

It was not that God's Spirit was himself transformed: there is nothing changeable about him, as we know, no variation or shadow of turning (James 1:17). Still, it was not at all absurd of God to depict his majesty according to our capacity, now by one sign, now by another. Thus God often appeared to our fathers, but not always in the same way. He chose whatever signs he pleased, as was useful and opportune.

This, then, is what we have to remember. The dove which descended on our Lord Jesus Christ represented what manner of Spirit he was to receive. And what was that? We recall our Lord's words: he will come with such gentleness as not to make us afraid; his voice will not arouse such dread as to alienate and repel those who hear it; he will not break the frail reed or extinguish the candle end which burns with half a flame or emits only a wisp of smoke (Isa. 42:2-3). Such is the prophet's testimony to Jesus Christ. All of this had to be made clear by the Holy Spirit who descended on him. Now just as the Holy Spirit is called 'fire', because he consumes all our filth and mortifies our evil passions, cleansing us so that nothing earthly remains; and just as he is called 'water' because he washes and sprinkles us and satisfies us with all good things, so, when he descended on our Lord Jesus Christ, it was in the form of a dove. Why? To assure us that he did not receive the power of the Holy Spirit in order to thunder against us, to crush us and to disperse us far and wide, but to show himself kind and merciful toward us, to demonstrate how gently he invites and, as it were, entices us, so that when he comes to us it is to support us in our weakness. And although we are full of faults, he will not fail to welcome us as his members. He causes the crippled to walk, carrying them on his shoulders; he gives such light to the blind who are in darkness that he sustains them in their ignorance; he heals poor sick souls, correcting what feebleness remains in them; he frees the captives, welcoming those who drag their chains, however slow they are in coming to him. That, in sum, is what we should remember about this verse.

The Father therefore sets the Son before us to testify that we have easy access to him. He will be like a dove: there is nothing fearful about him to cause us dread. On the contrary, he wishes only to supply our wants, so that we may boldly approach him and seek in him all we need for our salvation. Now as we said, John the Baptist found confirmation here of his vocation, and Jesus Christ was, in human terms, armed and equipped for victory in every struggle. Nevertheless it is for our sake that this story has been written, so that we might know what kind of Christ the gospel proclaims to us. We are not to imagine that he possesses a fearsome majesty such as would drive us away; we are not to have such fear of him that we fail to come boldly to him. We ought indeed to fear him in order to reverence him, yet we should also be absolutely sure that he will be all that this sign shows him to be.

This is a principle common to all sacraments, which we do well to remember. Baptism reveals that water serves to lead us to the spiritual washing of our souls: we must be plunged deep into the water, as it were, in order to die to ourselves and to the world. Similarly in the Supper, the bread is a token that our souls are fed by the substance of our Lord Jesus Christ, and the wine is a sign to us that we taste and drink of him. Thus the sign described for us here attests our Lord's gentleness, kindness and mildness, which assure us that, because he is so well-disposed, we should not hesitate to come through him to the throne of God, knowing that it is no longer a throne of terror and strict justice, but a throne of grace, as the apostle says in Hebrews (Heb. 4:16).

For the rest, let us be clear that all who will not yield to Jesus Christ by accepting the gentleness and mercy which he offers, will finally, despite themselves, know him as their judge. For them there will be only bitterness, dread and the gnashing of teeth. As for us, however, may we, seeing that God's Son is so merciful and kind, be clothed in the spirit of meekness. Let us put off all pride and presumption; let us come obediently as doves to the dovecote, and let us consent to remain under his wings, for he is ready and willing. In this way we will not experience him as our judge whose glory fills us with dread. Rather, everything which constitutes his glory, loftiness and majesty will serve to fill us with joy, so that we, being under his protection, may assuredly defy Satan, death, and all our enemies.

Now let us cast ourselves down before the majesty of our good God, acknowledging our faults and begging him so to touch us that we may come to hate them more and more. May he open our eyes so that we, being ashamed of our wretchedness, may ask for forgiveness. May he be pleased to cleanse us each day until we are remade, and may we strive to glorify his holy name. May he uphold us in our weaknesses, and gradually correct them until he calls us to himself, so that we may come before his face spotless and without blame.

6

LED BY THE SPIRIT

And behold a voice from heaven, saying, 'This is my beloved Son, with whom I am well pleased.' [1]*Then Jesus was led by the Spirit into the wilderness to be tempted by the devil* (Matt. 13:17–4:1).

And a voice came from heaven, 'You are my beloved Son; with you I am well pleased.' [12]*The Spirit immediately drove him into the wilderness.* [13]*And he was in the wilderness forty days, tempted by Satan; and he was with wild beasts, and the angels served him* (Mark 1:11-13).

And a voice came from heaven, 'You are my beloved Son; with you I am well pleased.' [1]*And Jesus, filled with the Holy Spirit, departed from the Jordan, and was led by the Spirit* [2]*for forty days in the wilderness, tempted by the devil* (Luke 3:22; 4:1-2).

EARLIER we saw that the Holy Spirit appeared upon the Son of God in the form of a dove, in order to show that we have easy access to him. He always receives us with mercy and will treat us kindly and graciously, for he will not break the reed that is already crushed, nor will he snuff out the candle which is barely smoking (Isa. 42:3). We therefore have sure testimony that when we are united to him by faith, we are acceptable to God.

These two things are highly worth noting. First, that we should not fear to come to our Lord Jesus Christ, in whom there is nothing so dreadful as would terrify us. On the contrary he is like a dove, possessing all gentleness and kindness. True, his majesty will be terrible toward those who scorn his gospel and whom he will therefore judge. So let us not abuse his gentleness by despising the grace which he offers us today. When we come to him to seek the salvation provided for us, it is certain that we will not behold majesty so awful that it will repel us. We will be able to draw near, for he will prove to be exactly as he said he was in the prophet Isaiah—a verse we cited last Sunday—and as was confirmed by the sight of the Holy Spirit descending upon him in the form of a dove. That is the first point.

The second point is this. Once our Lord Jesus Christ has received us and accepted us as his members, we will have no cause at all to doubt that God the Father is favourable to us, and that we are so dear to him that our sins and offences will not prevent him from being merciful to us, and from reckoning us to be clean and holy. For when the voice from heaven was heard: '*This is my beloved Son, in whom I rest content*,' this was not said for the sake of God's Son alone, but for the sake of all who are united to him by faith. For why was our Lord said to be the beloved Son, if not because he had accepted both to be and to serve as the Mediator who would reconcile us to God his Father? For by nature we are all God's enemies, engaged in deadly warfare—something which should make the hairs of our head stand on end, and should so appal us that we should each reflect how abominable it is to be the enemies of him who created and formed us, and to have his curse upon us!

At any rate, we deserve to bring from our mother's womb nothing but defilement and iniquity, since we have been excluded from all goodness in our father Adam. God is righteous, and he cannot deny his righteousness. He must therefore hate us and regard us with abhorrence. That is our condition until our Lord Jesus Christ receives us to himself. It is then that we begin to be loved by God, for our sins are wiped out, because they have been cleansed by his shed blood which is our spiritual washing. In this way the warfare and hostility between God and us comes to an end—that is, when we are incorporated into Jesus Christ.

Now it was necessary that we should have clear testimony to this, in order to crush all our pride and to humble us. Let us, then, seek the remedy where we can find it, and let God's Son have the honour reserved for him. Accordingly he is the only one of whom it has been said, 'He is my beloved Son.' We are thus led to conclude that God's love and grace are revealed only because of Jesus Christ. For although the angels in heaven are pure and holy, and not like us who are tainted by the corruption of sin, this is the one and only way that they can be loved by God. That is why Jesus Christ is called the first-born of all creatures (Col. 1:15). In short, there is no one in heaven or earth, or any inanimate creature that God can love, save in relation to his only Son. Our Lord Jesus Christ is thus set over against everything else, as much as to say that when we have run up and down, high and low, we will find no reason for God to love anything at all unless Jesus Christ is pleasing to him. So when we see God's hate and vengeance everywhere displayed, and their mark evident in both heaven and earth, we have every cause to feel utterly dismayed.

Nevertheless, as I have said, we are not meant to remain fearful and distressed. There is a remedy which is fully prepared for us. This voice should today echo in our ears: the heavenly Father vows to us and seeks to give us full assurance that Jesus Christ is his beloved Son, in whom his heart rests. In other words, if we are partakers of God's Son, we need not fear. We will find the Father gracious to us because he has set his heart's affection on his only-begotten Son, so that we may be acceptable to him. Thus, in the first chapter of Ephesians, Paul first describes

God's undeserved election and his call to us in the gospel to become his children; he then declares that we who once were his enemies have been made acceptable to him in his beloved Son (Eph. 1:3-6).

This is the point we must therefore understand: our Lord Jesus Christ is an unerring and certain pledge of God's love to us, although in ourselves we fully deserve to be cast out and pursued indeed to destruction. As we will later see, the Father accorded another privilege to his Son, namely that we should hear him (Matt. 17:5; Mark 9:7; Luke 9:35). Here, however, he simply sought to show that as long as men dwell idly on their own affairs, they will only find unhappiness, the more so as they presume on their own strength and resources. Thinking to acquire grace and favour they retreat even further, and provoke God's wrath still more. We must therefore yield to our Lord Jesus Christ if we want God to look favourably upon us and to receive us in his mercy.

The words of this verse, then, show us how all of men's boasting is thrown down. They themselves can do nothing which will let them worm their way into God's love. Everything is excluded, for this is the contrast we need to grasp: unless Jesus Christ is the beloved, we are hated and abhorrent. God has good reason to detest us. His image in us has been, so to say, blotted out, and Satan has put his mark upon us. Whatever we have in ourselves spells only death in God's sight. We might of course think highly of ourselves, but it is merely vanity and lies, delusion and arrogance. Let us learn, then, to take our stand on God's irrevocable decree. Since his heart rests in our Lord Jesus Christ, let us also seek our soul's repose in him.

Next it is said that *Jesus Christ was led by the Spirit into the wilderness to be tempted by Satan, and he was tempted for forty days*. As we go on to explain this text, we will see that Jesus Christ finally underwent the most severe and difficult alarms.

Here, however, as fully as time allows, we want only to stress that in these verses our Lord begins, following his baptism, to engage in battles much harder than before. We might find this surprising, since through baptism God welcomes us into his household, takes us into his care and ushers us into his church. He hides us under his wings and assures us that he defends us by his power. If baptism thus brings us close to God and allows us to be counted among his household servants, how is it that the devil has greater access to us so as to fight against us and to trouble us? This would seem to be inconsistent.

Observe, however, that whenever men prepare to serve God, they must also be tested by conflict. For if we are like wayward beasts, and are so little restrained that we abandon ourselves to evil and unruliness of every kind, the devil will take no action. Why? Because he has unchallenged use of us. When, however, we are determined and zealous enough to give ourselves to God's service, the devil sees that his rule is perishing and disappearing. It is then that he engages in battle and flies into greater fury. So as men prepare to serve God they have to prepare for many struggles. As one of the ancients has said, 'My son, if you seek to serve God, prepare your soul for tribulation.' This, then, is the reckoning we must make if we do not want to go astray: the more we try to give God our obedience and to dedicate ourselves to his righteousness in all holiness, the more Satan will assail and attack us. In earlier times he would leave us in peace, seeing that we were engrossed in our futile affairs. God was nothing to us, and we had neither fear nor reverence for him.

So when our Lord touches us to the quick and graciously kindles in us the will and desire to honour and glorify him, we should not think it strange that we are troubled more than ever and begin to face many trials, or that the devil worries and torments us by one means or another. No, we should not think it strange. This is a rule common to all believers, as we have said.

Indeed, there is almost no one who has not had this experience. For as long as we are drowsy, as long as God has not made us so obedient to himself that we know that our goal is to honour him while living in the world—as long, then, as we continue to be drowsy, we do not think that the devil has any hold over us. This is because we cannot tell white from black; we amble along, as it were, like Brown's cows, but once our Lord opens our eyes, once we realize that for a time we have drifted away from him and must get back on our feet, once we really mean to submit wholly to his will, to abandon the world, to deny ourselves and to keep to the path of salvation—some of us will be tempted one way, and some another, by things which did not touch us before and against which we did not have to struggle.

Now this so much upsets us that we feel like giving up. We find ourselves thinking: 'Before, when I did not know anything about God, I was more self-assured and not so obsessed by fleshly appetites; but since then I have never been so troubled by uncertainty, impatience and the like. I'd do better to give it up.' There are many people who, I repeat, when under a little more pressure than they can bear—or so it seems to them—want to throw everything away. However, as I said before, experience tells us that God's service involves many struggles, and that in order to obey him we must learn to be good soldiers and to fight courageously against Satan and all the attacks he makes on us. Yet notice how our Lord Jesus Christ was equipped by baptism to withstand Satan, and that his faith triumphed over all the temptations which we will presently consider.

Luke in particular records that *he returned from the Jordan, full of the Holy Spirit*, indicating that God's gifts were increased in our Lord Jesus Christ when God's power was revealed in him. There is nothing strange about this, for although he was conceived by the Holy Spirit, in terms of human nature, as we have seen, he grew before God and men in wisdom and in every other gift (Luke 2:52). We should not be ashamed to confess that our Lord was like us, except for sin, as Scripture declares (Heb. 4:15). In this way he displayed the boundless treasures of his kindness and love toward us, by choosing to humble himself and by becoming as nothing, as Paul says (Phil. 2:7-8). Why did he humble himself this way? It was not from personal necessity: he willed it to be so. That it was an act of his good will gives us greater reason still to extol the mercy he has shown us; it does not detract in any way from his majesty or glory.

We see, then, Jesus Christ, who in his human nature was filled with the Holy Spirit. That is the first point. Then too, what this also does is assure us that he is the fount of all blessing, and that since we ourselves are parched it is from him that we must draw. In drawing from his fullness, we will be fully satisfied, as we saw earlier in some detail and as we will later see again. Remember, therefore, that the Son of God was summoned to do battle but was armed at the same time with heavenly power and equipped to overcome whatever Satan his adversary might attempt. Accordingly our Lord Jesus Christ, when honouring us by bringing us into his service, wills that we be soldiers and that, when attacked in many different ways, we keep fighting all our lives; he wills also to give us what we need. We ourselves are weak; in fact we are less than nothing, but when we receive power from on high, we are able to say with Paul that we can do all things through him who strengthens us (Phil. 4:13).

This is the lesson we must learn. God rightly wants us to do battle in order to test the steadfastness of our faith. At the same time he arms us, and it is he who fights together with us. Without him we can do nothing, as we are taught in the fifteenth chapter of John (John 15:5) and as is attested in baptism. For although water is nothing in itself, God works by his secret power so that the visible sign which he has appointed is not empty. It is not meant to dazzle our eyes or to be merely a symbol: its purpose is to fulfil all the promises that it contains. Sacraments are not lifeless paintings: joined to them is the power of the Holy Spirit, provided we do not obstruct it by our thanklessness. Let us not doubt, then, that since in baptism we are made new by the Holy Spirit, we have the resources we need to withstand every temptation,[1] and that, if now and then we are tossed about and if Satan contrives to do his work, he can achieve nothing, for he who fights for us and who defends our cause will always come out on top, and by his grace we will live.

Think in this respect of the awful blindness which exists in popery. They are not ashamed to spew forth the blasphemy that in baptism we only receive the remission of our sins, and that what they call the chrism of confirmation is required to equip us and to give us power against Satan. Hence through baptism we are merely half-Christian. Those are their very words.[2] This they have decreed in a Council, and in their insolence they have gone so far as to contradict God and to suppress baptism's clear and open testimonies to his grace. For the sacrament is not only called our new birth, but we are said to put off the old man and to put on the righteousness of our Lord Jesus Christ, being armed and equipped with the power of the Holy Spirit to resist all of Satan's attacks and even to overcome them (Rom. 6:4-8). Yet all of this means nothing to the papists, which is why they venture to contradict our Lord and his apostles. So in order to resist the devil and all his works, we must resort to the abomination of that foul oil they have invented, and with which they mark the forehead. Is not this an absolutely hateful blasphemy? Knowing, then, the dreadful abyss into which we too were plunged, we

[1] See above, pp. 54-56.

[2] In the Church of Rome, the sacrament of confirmation was administered by a bishop by the laying on of hands and anointing with holy oil (chrism). The sacrament was said to complete and perfect the rite of baptism, with further grace being added and the Holy Spirit being given for incorporation into Christ and for battle. Calvin dismisses the doctrine as 'a false promise of the devil' and 'a flagrant insult against baptism' (*Inst.* IV.19.8).

ought to exalt all the more the goodness of our God, now that we have learned the meaning of baptism and the fruit it brings us—victory over Satan.

Now although this life is one of combat, in which daily we have to endure alarms, our faith will remain triumphant to the end, for God will not leave us bereft of means and will not expose us to our enemies so that they can overcome us. He will be our shield which repels their blows; he will help us fortify ourselves and will make up for all that we lack. He will so strengthen us that our frailty will not prevent us from holding fast. That is something we should take to heart.

When Scripture relates that our Lord Jesus Christ was led by the Spirit into the wilderness to be tempted by the devil, we might think it strange that this should be said. It would seem that here God was exposing his only Son to Satan. In any event we must stick to what the Evangelists record, that his struggles did not come about without God's leading and appointment. In fact it was the Holy Spirit who led our Lord Jesus Christ, as if leading him by the hand, in order to engage him in the fight which he sustained for forty days. God must inevitably be willing for Satan to assail us, otherwise what kind of confidence could we have if, when we were troubled by Satan, God had no thought for us? What would we do? How impossibly perplexed would we be? We could not resolutely call upon God, fully trusting that he will answer and assist us. When, however, we learn that the devil can do nothing unless God allows him, and that God wills to try us—for we were created in order to be tested, our whole life being continually examined to see if we have a living root of obedience—when, therefore, we know that this is what God intends for us, that he controls everything and that the devil cannot come near unless God chooses to let him; when, I say, we are convinced of this, then we may come to God and say, 'Alas, Lord, you know how much we are assailed, and you know us much better than we know ourselves. You see that we are weak and that we would be vanquished from the very first. The merest puff of wind would knock us over a hundred times a day if you did not sustain us. Be pleased then, Lord, to strengthen us.' We can call upon him in full trust when convinced by holy Scripture that he rules and directs our steps, so that if Satan torments, vexes and stings us, and tries indeed to crush us, God is over all. Nothing happens purely by chance. It is his will that we should be assailed this way. That is one point.

Still more, however, should be said. The Spirit led our Lord Jesus Christ into the wilderness. Thus God not only wished him to be tested, but gave him his Holy Spirit as his leader and guide. Notice, then, that when God supplies us with his Holy Spirit, and when we have received a measure of power and steadfastness to honour him and to give ourselves to his service, we too will be led by God's Spirit to be tested by Satan. It is true that this will not be revealed to us with certainty, nor is it said that Jesus Christ himself knew that this was why he had come into the wilderness. This was perhaps hidden from him, since he was man, and his deity was not always on display. He was so led by the Spirit that we cannot say that what was to happen was revealed to him ahead of time. Likewise, we do not know how God intends to work in us, for our eyes are closed to many of the gifts which he apportions to us secretly and in ways we cannot understand.[3]

God works in us in two ways. Sometimes he will make us conscious of his gifts, and sometimes we will be unaware of them. At any rate we recognize them after the event, and we

[3] That Jesus was led by the Spirit into the wilderness does not imply that he was a reluctant or unresponsive actor. As Geerhardus Vos remarks, no such inference can be drawn from the Gospels: 'Mark's "drove him into the wilderness" is not meant by the Evangelist to be so understood, but only stresses the powerful action of the Spirit, to which Jesus responded with equal energy' (*Biblical Theology: Old and New Testaments*, Grand Rapids: Eerdmans, 1948, p. 358).

have cause to give him glory. Thus we need to petition God every day, that he may be pleased to guide us who are like poor blind souls. And although we scarcely see anything in front of us, we must ask him not to let us turn from the path, or to let Satan our adversary oppress us, whatever conflicts he allows us to meet and which he appoints for us. May he teach us instead that these attacks are meant to exercise our faith, and may they be a sure test that we do not serve him hypocritically, but that we would rather yield to him and face every conflict than be like straying cattle, completely at ease. So much for that point.

What the Evangelists tell us here is rather incredible; we cannot comprehend it. How was it possible for our Lord Jesus Christ to be tempted? Temptation implies a certain lack of trust. If we had no faults or weaknesses in ourselves, we would surely not be subject to temptation. Think of an angel in heaven: he could not be tempted to be unfaithful. Why? Because he sees God's face and shares in his glory, so is exempt from temptation of any kind. As for us, it is certain that when Satan attacks us it is because of our infirmities, because we are not perfect like the angels, because we are not privileged to pass through the world without being buffeted now and then. In our Lord Jesus Christ, however, we find a weakness which has no flaw. Temptation, it seems, was never something which was proper to him or which might naturally befall him.

In order to make up our minds on this point, we must note first of all that our Lord Jesus Christ, while being without spot or stain, was nevertheless subject to our weakness—a weakness, however, without any flaw. To understand this better we should go back to Adam's origins. Before Adam was deceived, so that he stumbled and drew all of us after him to perdition, he was already prone to temptation, as the facts proved. For he could not have been deceived if he had not been subject to temptation. Already, then, he was in some respects frail. Since he did not possess divine strength, his status and abilities were those of a man. He was unstable, too much so. Our father Adam was without fault at the time of his creation. God did not create him as we are born today. We bring with us the seed of all iniquity; we are full of unbelief and rebelliousness, full of all evil desires. Man, in short, is a sink of all depravity and rottenness, thanks to Adam's sin and fall. This was not so in the beginning, otherwise sin would have come from God. Man was created pure and holy; yet by nature he was still subject to temptation, even though he was without fault.

We ought therefore to distinguish between natural weakness, which has always existed in man, and weakness involving faults which arose from the fact of original sin. It was thus perfectly proper for our Lord Jesus Christ to have had a measure of weakness, since that had already been the case with Adam. True, our Lord could not suffer defeat. His position was different from that of Adam: Satan could not overcome him. Nevertheless he had to undergo these first conflicts. That is one point.

To make these things clearer, let us look at what we each experience in practice. Whenever we are tempted, there is certainly some great failing on our part. For example, we can be tempted by mistrust, so that we cannot turn to God in confidence that he will answer our requests. Faithlessness is a fault which is especially displeasing to God. We do indeed dishonour him, seeing that we cannot hold fast to his promise or rely completely on him. In this way we diminish God's power by our evil thoughts. We cannot, then, be tempted by mistrust without mortally offending God. Again, if we are tempted by ambition in order to advance ourselves, we cannot do it without feeling the itch to go beyond our station, as if to spite God. For what happens when someone desires greatness for himself, a place of rank and eminence? Alas, to begin with, we are merely earth and dust, full of uncleanness. We ought, so to speak, hide ourselves in the bowels of the earth rather than show ourselves! Again, where there is greed, unbelief is mixed in with it; nor will we be temperate or self-controlled when what we want is to swallow everything. Again, in cases of immorality, evil is even more apparent; and with drunkenness, there is such appalling senselessness that men forget themselves entirely: they are like swine or savage beasts.

It is clear, then, that in every temptation some fault is present. We know that this is so, and that at such a time the devil finds something rotten in us. It is rather like a high fever which takes hold of a man who, though strong in body, has been intemperate and has eaten food so that he builds up many harmful humours. They have festered within him for some time, but now they appear in an instant. So here is a hale and hearty man who, as I said, is immediately struck down by the slightest excess he commits. It is the same with us. Admittedly the analogy does not quite fit, but it does not have to. It is enough if there is some resemblance which throws light on what we are saying here. In any case, our experience is that even when God graciously repels the temptations which come to us in our idle thoughts, we are nevertheless tickled by them; they reach deep into our hearts and to some extent they influence us. This cannot occur without some failing on our part, which rightly merits condemnation.

Here we see how absurd the papists are, for in all their schools or synagogues they hold as an article of faith that when we are tempted by immorality, as long as we do not completely consent to it, we commit no sin. True, they would be forced to recognize this as a fault except for baptism, for they imagine that baptism changes the nature of things. So when, they say, a Turk feels the slightest temptation to drunkenness, debauchery, ambition or other such things, he sins; his fault is manifest; he is to be condemned. In a Christian, however, on the pretext of baptism they say there is no fault, simply a test of strength. Perhaps so, but we are told to love God not only with our heart but with all our mind, our feelings and our strength. It is no sign that we love God with all our heart, mind and feelings, when we see something and crave it apart from his command. No, I may not consent to the desire I feel within me, otherwise I would immediately have to think again. But if my eyes covet someone else's goods or crave some form of self-indulgence, it is certain that I no longer love God with all my mind, strength and feelings. The law itself convicts me, and is not transgression of the law a sin?

We see, therefore, how stupid these wretches are, how empty of all judgment and reason. Still today they fight for these things with desperate stubbornness, so that when gathered in council they ordain and decree that all of men's evil desires and appetites are not sin, and that they do not have to ask God for forgiveness, for that would be to offend against baptism. So when we see how the devil has plucked out their eyes, should we not prize all the more the goodness and mercy which God has shown us by rescuing us from such a mess?[4]

Scripture thus reveals that all temptations imply some flaw in us, and that God has cause enough to condemn us, even though we may not give our assent. Nothing like this, however, was true of our Lord Jesus Christ: he could be tempted while remaining blameless. There was no evil desire in him, yet he was human and therefore subject to temptation. Indeed he had to be, for otherwise what would become of us when we were tempted, given that we have no strength to resist our enemy—or enemies? For we fight not against flesh and blood, as Paul says—that is, against men like us—but against all the powers of the air and the principalities of this world which are ranged against us

[4] A marginal note in the Badius edition refers the reader to the decrees of the fifth session of the Council of Trent (June 1546). In its first decree, on original sin, the Council affirmed not only that the guilt of original sin is remitted by baptism, but that the baptized person, being regenerate, although having within him concupiscence or incentive to sin, does not commit sin if he does not consent to it. Hence the preacher's wry remark that 'baptism changes the nature of things'. See Calvin's further comment in *Acts of the Council of Trent with the Antidote* (1547), *CO* 7:420, 425–28.

(Eph. 6:12). If we say, 'Yes, of course, but God will help us,' that is true, and we must certainly turn to him for aid. But such is our weakness that we cannot rise so high unless we come to the Son of God. And when we see that he subjected himself to our infirmities in order to have pity and compassion on us and, as the apostle says, to assist us (Heb. 4:15)—when we see that our Lord fought the same battles as we do, we can be sure that we will overcome every attack which is made on us, and that victory is already ours. When we fight beneath his banner, we cannot doubt that he will lead us and will help us triumph over all that the devil devises against us. This is the way in which our Lord Jesus Christ was tempted, so that today, in all our temptations, we cannot doubt that he fought on our behalf, and that we are victorious in him.

Note, incidentally, that when we are told that he was tempted for forty days, the faithful should not prepare to go into battle only once, or expect to be given leave after they have withstood one attack or two. Let us bear these words in mind, although more will be said directly. We are taught that when God seeks to try our faith by leaving Satan free to trouble us, we end one fight only to begin another. Thus we press on. We should not be surprised when we see this, for the same happened to our Lord Jesus Christ. He is the model and mirror to whom we must be conformed. We are called, as Paul says in the eighth chapter of Romans, to be like Jesus Christ and to follow his example (Rom. 8:29). And what is that? Just as he led the way by patiently enduring much adversity and misery, we too must pass that way, following in his steps. And when we see that daily we must suffer fresh attacks, let us not lose heart, but let us go on to the very end, knowing that as our Lord was never abandoned by God his Father, but that the Holy Spirit so strengthened him that he received fullness of power in himself, so also he will impart as much of it to us as is needful for our salvation.

Now let us cast ourselves down before the majesty of our good God, acknowledging our faults and begging him to blot out all remembrance of them, so that they no longer count before him. May he so strengthen us by his grace that we, through his power, may steadfastly resist all of Satan's attacks, and scatter all the obstacles which he puts in our way.

7

STONES INTO BREAD

And when he had fasted forty days and forty nights, he was at last hungry. [3] *And the tempter drew near and said to him, 'If you are the Son of God, tell these stones to become bread.'* [4] *But he answered, saying, 'It is written, "Man shall not live by bread alone, but by every word that comes from the mouth of God"'* (Matt. 4:2-4).

And he ate nothing in those days, and when they were ended, he was hungry. [3] *The devil said to him, 'If you are the Son of God, tell these stones to become bread.'* [4] *And Jesus answered him, 'It is written, "Man shall not live by bread alone, but by every word of God"'* (Luke 4:2-4).

WE noticed previously that because the Son of God, after his baptism, was preparing to fulfil the task committed to him by God his Father, he suffered fiercer conflicts from Satan than before. In the light of this, we said that as each of us gets ready to serve God, we must also be armed in order to engage in many battles, for it is then that the devil does all he can to lead us astray. As long as we are not very zealous or willing to give ourselves to God, we are idle and Satan hardly bothers to trouble us. When, however, he sees that God is calling us, that the Holy Spirit dwells in us and that we for our part are ready to be used, it is then he fights mightily against us. We have also seen that we must be prepared not for one battle only, but for many, and not just for one day but for as long as God chooses. In the same way, our Lord Jesus Christ was beset by many temptations for the forty days during which he fasted in the wilderness.

Let us say something about the fasting which is mentioned here. We read that God's Son neither ate nor drank nor partook of anything *for forty days and forty nights*. We must consider why. It was doubtless because in this way God sought to ensure greatness and reverence for the message of the gospel. Thus when Moses wished to proclaim the law, he withdrew to the mountain where he too fasted for forty days and forty nights (Exod. 24:18). The same is said of Elijah, whom God had appointed to restore religion which had been perverted and almost destroyed by much idolatry and superstition (1 Kings 19:8). Now the reason why Moses fasted is obvious: it was so that the law would be received with greater humility, as coming from God. Moses did not live among men for forty days and forty nights. He was exempt from all human needs, so that no one could regard the law as having been brought by some frail being. This was more than if an angel had come down from heaven, otherwise there would have been no such miracle. Moses' fasting for forty days thus served to confer authority on the law.

Authority had also to be conferred on the gospel, inasmuch as God had chosen, when the gospel was proclaimed, to reveal himself to the world more fully and perfectly than before. We should recall the contrast which Paul makes in the third chapter of Second Corinthians: 'If the message,' he says, 'which brought death and condemnation was exalted, and if God gave it glory and majesty in men's eyes, what shall we say of the message of life and salvation which delivers us from the curse into which Adam's sin plunged us?' (cf. 2 Cor. 3:7-8). And if, as another passage says, the law brought by Moses, a servant, was honoured, what shall we say when the Son of God who is master of the house and who is far superior, comes in person, and is both witness and ambassador for God his Father? (Heb. 3:5-6).

We may now readily understand why our Lord Jesus Christ fasted for forty days. It was so that the gospel should be no less great than the law, and so that the Jews should not be able to say: 'What then? Must our ceremonies now be trampled underfoot and their use abolished, when so many miracles attended the proclamation of the law?' To prevent their making this objection, our Lord Jesus Christ affirms that if the law was given with heavenly force, the gospel is similarly given, as is obvious. In short, our Lord's fasting was a kind of seal to show that the gospel must not be received as if it came from men, and that God is its author.

From this we may easily gather how stupid it is to counterfeit the action of God's Son by fasting once a year in Lent, as it is called. This is not something which I attribute either to the pope or to his ministers, for before the papacy existed the devil had already established this superstition. Nor should this surprise us. Even in his own time, Paul declares that the Antichrist was already beginning to bury the foundations underground. He calls it the mystery of iniquity (2 Thess. 2:7). Abominations were not yet as conspicuous as they later became, but even so Antichrist had begun his reign, sowing trouble and confusion in the church, corrupting the purity of the gospel and changing the truth into a lie. People are thus mistaken when they think that they are following our Lord's example by fasting for forty days. One would have to abstain from food and drink for forty days and forty nights in order to conform to the practice of the Son of God. Do they do anything of the kind?

Before the papacy was introduced, people used to fast for Lent. True, there was no law which forbade the eating of meat on pain of mortal sin. Nevertheless, pious practices were such that men fasted one day a week, or two, or three, but on Sundays fasting was not allowed because it detracted from reverence for the day. So this superstition has existed for the last fourteen hundred years. Since that time, however, the papists have established a definite law concerning this. They have prohibited meat on Sundays as on other working days. Now what parallel or likeness is there between what our Lord Jesus Christ did and what these clowns have tried to counterfeit? Moreover, if it is a question of following the example of God's Son, they would need to fast only once in their life: he did not keep Lent twice. Over a period of thirty years he did not fast like this, and he did not return to fasting later. We should, then, be content with only one Lent in our lifetime!

There is another consideration which comes easily to mind. Here, under the law, are Solomon, David, and Hezekiah, and all the other kings, together with the holy prophets and very many of the faithful who were of such excellent holiness that they were like mirrors of angelic perfection in men's eyes. Did they ever follow Moses' example? Did Lent exist among the Jews? It all comes down to this: if these fools and rascals who want to keep Jesus Christ company in their fasting, thought that their devotions were superior to those of David, the prophets, the holy kings and the many faithful who served God in all purity of heart, they might have some vague excuse. They should, however, be ashamed to compare themselves with the holy patriarchs and prophets. So we see how farcical it is to try to establish some precedent, as if our Lord Jesus Christ had taught his disciples to abstain once a year, not only for forty days but on days which they were free to choose. Ever since that time it has turned out exactly as I said. There is tyranny such that the eating of meat is forbidden, and it is commanded on pain of mortal sin and eternal damnation that Lent should be kept. Thus, as time went on, the devil grew ever more brazen, as is his habit.[1]

I refrain from mentioning how the papists currently fast in imitation of our Lord Jesus Christ. They abstain from eating meat, but those with the resources never keep a better table than during Lent! Besides the delicacies and great variety of other foods, they drink until they are fit to burst, and on the eve of a fast they stock up on their edibles. 'For,' they say, 'tomorrow we will fast.' The next day, however: 'Look, we fasted yesterday, time now for our reward.' So much so that they seem to want to avenge themselves on God and to defy him, because he has forced them to fast for one day. Yet they have had more delicacies than ever, and since they do not eat meat in public—I am speaking about rulers, who punish their subjects with death if they eat a bit of fat in Lent!—they invariably eat meat in the privacy of their rooms. In short, everything is forgiven them as long as they are firm defenders of the Catholic faith. Is this not to make a mockery of God? But the worst, the most evil thing, apart from, as I said, this absurd tomfoolery, is that they blaspheme God and clearly wrong our Lord Jesus Christ.

Then too, they detract from the authority of the gospel. For here God did a most memorable miracle, but do men not obscure it when they try to copy the Son of God's example? In a way we cannot comprehend, and which is quite contrary to nature, he abstained from food and drink. God exempted him from the normal human lot. Will men then trample this miracle in the dust? Yet they try to mimic it, so as to mask the fact that there God displayed extraordinary power—something which should thrill us with wonder! Furthermore, here our Lord Jesus Christ shows himself to be the world's Redeemer, the messenger

[1] Note that Calvin's objection is not to fasting as such, which he will shortly defend as a helpful spiritual discipline, but to the superstition and hypocrisy to which it gives rise when imposed as a strict obligation on all the faithful. Cf. *Inst.* IV.12.15–21.

of God's high counsel, as Isaiah calls him (Isa. 9:6), the one who was sent to fulfil all prophecy. He is, in a word, the head of the angels and of every created thing. He fasts in order to give proof of his divine glory. Shall we then try to copy him? That would be to make ourselves the peers and partners of the Son of God, as if all who keep Lent could call themselves redeemers and assume the divinity which our Lord possesses!

Accordingly, they lessen the reverence that all should have for the gospel. The fact that our Lord Jesus Christ fasted before taking up the task of preaching shows that his message comes not from the world but from heaven. When we fast out of piety, claiming that we are following our Lord's example of abstinence and sobriety, what becomes of the seal vouchsafed to us concerning the message of salvation? We must understand that the popish practice of Lent involves not only superstition, foolishness and farce; it is a grievous offence against God and his only-begotten Son. In sum, it is a ruse of Satan, designed to destroy the certainty of our faith.

This is not, however, to condemn all fasting, which has been appointed for very different ends. To begin with, it is intended to keep us in check, to tame our flesh. Again, when our Lord warns us of the wrongs we have committed, when he beats the drum, as it were, in order to threaten us, then we will fast and confess that we are miserable offenders; we will admit our guilt and will ask him for mercy. Such is the purpose of fasting: to subdue our flesh, to lead us to pray to God (which is why fasting and prayer go together), and to make us confess our sins, as if we were dressed in mourning, just as formerly there was sackcloth and ashes and dust thrown on the head. The true use of fasting lies in these things; it has nothing to do with Lent.

We now see that, by fasting, our Lord Jesus Christ sought to exalt the gospel. Before taking up the office of prophet in order to make known his Father's will, the Son of God was willing to fast, so that we might be certain of what the gospel taught, and might know that it came from heaven. Let us take this truth to heart.

In the following verse, it is said that *the devil tempted him*. It is not that he began only then, as we said earlier, for Mark and Luke both stress that he fought continually for forty days, and that his later fights were the hardest and most difficult. This is how God deals with all his people. He does not deal with them in equal measure, yet this rule applies to all of us. When we are still immature and novices, so to speak, God does not try us so severely. He spares us. But once he toughens us up and corrects our weaknesses by strengthening us by his power so that we can fight more courageously, it is then that he treats us more severely, testing us according to the pattern which we see here in our Lord Jesus Christ.

It is thus right and proper that we should be told to conform to his example (John 13:15), not in each and every way but in all that pertains to God's service, to faith, endurance and the obedience we owe to God. In all these things, I repeat, we must conform to our Lord's example. Not, however, to his majesty (as shown by Scripture's record of his fasting): in that respect we cannot conform, otherwise we would have to raise the dead, heal the sick, give sight to the blind and make the lame walk. In short, we would have to transform men and change water into wine! Where would it end? Since the Son of God is set before us as an example and mirror of faith, obedience, endurance and so on, in these things we are meant to see that he has shown believers the way, so that we may follow in his steps. We should never doubt that the victory which he won, he won on our behalf, as he says in the sixteenth chapter of John: 'Be confident: I have overcome the world' (John 16:33). He does not say: 'Be confident: you will overcome.' What he says is this: 'Since I have overcome, rest assured that your faith, if it is grounded in me, will be victorious.'

We ought, then, to bear this point firmly in mind, that when he spares us for a time, we should not think that now we are on even terms; we should not ask for leave as if enough had been done. No, let us be prepared to withstand worse assaults than ever. We recall what was said to Peter: 'When you were young, you girded yourself as you wished with little to constrain you; but when you are old another will bind you, and you will be taken in bonds which you cannot undo until death' (cf. John 21:18). Why was that said to him? It was because he serves us as a warning that when we are young and weak in the faith God upholds us; but if, having upheld us for a time, he tests us more severely, we should have had much time to reflect, so that nothing should seem unusual to us and take us by surprise.

In this verse the devil is called 'the tempter' in order to put us on our guard. For this was not a craft which he practised only once: the gospel fastens this title on him so that we should know that this is his very nature. As long as we have to live in this world, since we cannot serve God without being soldiers who are required to fight, observe that our enemy, who is always watchful and who has his snares prepared, is called 'the tempter'—that is, he has the means to assail us with different temptations and to put many ideas and fancies into our heads, leading us to rebel against God, sometimes through lack of trust or through greed, sometimes through ambition. This we will shortly see.

Satan is therefore called our adversary: that is what the word 'Satan' means. And he is also called 'the tempter', to teach us that he is the one we must fight against. He comes, then, to our Lord Jesus Christ, and says, '*If you are the Son of God, tell these stones to change into bread.*' There are three kinds of temptation mentioned here. The first we have already read. The second is that our Lord Jesus Christ should worship the devil. It is true that the two Evangelists do not follow the same order, which is why I will not dwell too much on this point. He is thus tempted to worship Satan in order to obtain all the wealth in the world. Thirdly, he is asked to throw himself down from the temple in order to prove his worth, so that everyone should know that he is the Son of God. We will expound the last two temptations later.

As to the first, many of the ancients were badly mistaken when they said that Jesus Christ was tempted by gluttony or over-indulgence.[2] This was because they prized abstinence far too much. Of course, to be sober throughout our lives is a great virtue, and since we are especially inclined to over-indulge, we should cut back on our helpings. We should certainly value this as a virtue. It is not the same, however, with the abstinence practised by the hermits long ago. They did not dare drink water, except in measured amounts out of a walnut shell or something else; or else by weight, an ounce of water being a very large drink! Again, they were not supposed to sleep except standing against a wall, or they considered it unlawful to eat bread: they existed only on roots. So having abstained from the normal means by which we stay alive, they fancied they had been whisked off to heaven with the angels!

Paul, on the other hand, declares that nonsense like this is of little use; what is of use is godliness when it is truly rooted and engraved on our hearts (1 Tim. 4:8). For where is our perfection to be found? In the fear of God, in faith's reliance on him, in fervent prayer to him, in thanksgiving for the blessings he gives us, and in patience in adversity. That is where our perfection lies. But external practices (by which Paul means fasting, vigils and the like) are unimportant and a waste of time. Given, then, that the ancients had had due warning from the mouth of Paul, they ought to have been more cautious. What then? The devil had so blindfolded them that they thought it highly virtuous for men

[2] The reference is to the fourth-century commentator, Ambrose of Milan, who listed gluttony, vanity and ambition as the three temptations to which Christ was exposed (*Exposition of Luke's Gospel*, IV.3).

to kill themselves by excessive abstinence. They were completely useless, scarcely able to drag one foot after another or to move an arm in order to perform one good work. Such was their holiness!

Hence, since one mistake attracts another, they thought that the worst poison the devil could devise was to tempt us to gluttony. They believed that this led to the damnation of the human race, as if eating a pear, a cherry, a peach or apple—we do not know what fruit the devil offered Eve—was the greatest sin in the world! It is certain that the devil attacked Adam by tempting him to unbelief, rebelliousness and pride. This is clear from the words he spoke: 'It will not be as he said. You will be like God' (Gen. 3:4-5). He did not say: 'You will taste with the tip of your tongue a delicious fruit.' No, he said: 'You will be like God.' Thus Adam and Eve were assailed by pride. And by unbelief, for when Satan is told that death had been threatened, he says: 'Oh, that's not how it will be.' Lastly there is rebellion, which Scripture especially records since man deliberately dared to transgress God's command.

To say, then, that they were tempted to gluttony, as if the devil could not have dealt them a deadly wound to the throat, is a complete distortion. If the devil tempts us to gluttony, it is as if an enemy were to slash our arm or thigh with his sword: we would heal in time. But if he were to pierce our heart or throat, we would be dead. On the other hand, ambition and pride which raise us higher than is lawful, or unbelief which undermines God's word, or rebelliousness which openly opposes God and fights against him—these are deadly wounds which the devil inflicts on us. These poor fools, ancient though they are, were merely Satan's tools and servants. They showed no powers of judgment in saying what they did. In any case, we have faultless evidence which convicts them of error. Our Lord Jesus Christ was a better soldier than anyone else; he knew how to defend himself, and was much more alert than others in repelling the enemy's wiles.

From his method of defence, we may judge the kind of temptation to which Jesus Christ was subject. He was well armed with shield and sword. He knew which way to raise his shield according to the direction from which he saw Satan's darts coming. For Paul likens temptations to fiery darts which are hurled at us in order to wound us mortally (Eph. 6:16). What, then, does our Lord say? Does he say, 'Gluttony is forbidden'? Or that self-indulgence and gourmandizing are faults condemned by God? That would have been the truth, but he knew full well what Satan was scheming to do to him. He therefore replies: '*Man shall not live by bread alone, but by the word which comes from the mouth of God.*' In this way he clearly shows that it is God who feeds us, not bread, nor wine, nor any other provisions. He has no wish to diminish the power of God which Moses had proclaimed (Deut. 8:3).

By this means the devil attacked our Lord Jesus Christ, seeking to instil in him such mistrust as to make him look for unlawful means, as if God had failed him or as if there was not sufficient power to feed and sustain him. That, I say, was Satan's ruse. At first glance we might say that our Lord would not have sinned if he had miraculously changed stones into bread. He would thus have defied Satan, proving that he was his Master and that he should be worshipped. Jesus Christ, however, has the ultimate end in view. If he had chosen to be miraculously fed while not knowing the will of God his Father, unbelief would surely have got the better of him. Then too, he would have wronged God greatly by not being content with the grace by which we all are fed.

To understand this better, we must explain what Jesus Christ said by way of answer. Notice, first, that he does not reason at length or argue with Satan. He takes Scripture as his shield: '*It is written.*' This one word demolishes all else. We are therefore exhorted to arm ourselves with the word of God, so that we can withstand all the temptations which Satan brings before us, and can resist the attacks that he may mount against us. We must, I repeat, be equipped with Scripture: there are our true weapons. Accordingly, having spoken of the powers of the air which are against us and of the devils who are above us in order to oppress us, Paul adds, 'Be well equipped, my friends' (Eph. 6:10-11). The word he uses implies being armed from head to toe, as we say. He then goes on to list the helmet and the rest of the equipment, including greaves, which were used at that time (Eph. 6:14-17). Thus we have the helmet, the sword, the shield and all the other weapons. At the same time he speaks of faith, hope, the gospel and the word of God. Yet it all comes down to one thing: faith. From where does faith come? From the word of God. Likewise hope. And what is the gospel? It is the message by which we are born again. It is as if Paul were saying, 'My friends, be armed. How? It is not for you to forge your own weapons: God will give them to you. Seek them from his hand.' He calls God's word a sword and faith a shield; there is the helmet of the hope of salvation, together with the gospel, lest we be plunged into this earthly mire of depravity. 'The word of God,' says Paul, 'will arm you with everything you need from head to toe, so that no part of you will be exposed. Satan has no means of getting at you, as long as you are well protected to resist him.'

This is what Paul teaches us, and our Lord Jesus Christ shows how it is done in practice, for when he cites Scripture, he insists at the same time on faith. Faith implies hope, and hope produces endurance, enabling us to persevere to the end. It is in this respect that we must be conformed to him, not in respect of the miracles by which he sought to prove that he was God's true Son. We, on the other hand, are not. In sum, we see how our Lord fought against the devil. Let us, then, take Scripture in our hands so that we too may resist him.

Again, it is clear from this how much the devil has carried away those canting hypocrites who nowadays try to take holy Scripture from us and to rob the whole church of this priceless treasure. The papacy is based on ignorance and folly, for as soon as God's word is set forth, what idolatries and perversions are revealed! The pope has raised his horns against God and has blotted out the power and grace of our Lord Jesus Christ; he has corrupted and distorted everything, as we well know. If Scripture were buried, the pope would rule unchallenged. That is why the hypocrites who are in his pay are always harping on the theme: 'What then is Scripture? A nose of wax!'[3] That is the detestable blasphemy they spew forth, and not only in the presence of ordinary folk; their books are full of it. There is nothing certain in holy Scripture: such is the chief article of their faith. It can be twisted in any direction; it is both dark and deep. In saying this they simply reveal their depravity, as if admitting that if they came to Scripture they would be convicted of error.

They do indeed point out that the devil made use of Scripture. Heretics, too, have misused Scripture and have infected the world with their errors. No one doubts that. But if the devil misused Scripture, how did our Lord Jesus Christ resist him? By means of Scripture itself! If heretics have been able to twist the true and natural sense of the law, the prophets and the gospel, how did the holy teachers manage to rebuff them? Did they say, 'A holy council has settled this'? Much different weapons were needed! The word of God was sufficient for this purpose. It is the authentic test. We know the genuineness of God's word by the fact that although the devil tried his hardest, he could not demolish it: it remained intact. If there had been no conflict, we would not have had so clear an idea of the power of God's word to sustain us

[3] The 'nose of wax' image was employed by Roman Catholic apologists to demonstrate the need for a fixed centre of authority—the pope and his councils—which would infallibly interpret Scripture. Protestants argued instead for the essential perspicuity of Scripture, whose authority is confirmed and sealed by the Holy Spirit.

and to keep us always steadfast and immovable. So when fierce storms arise and when all seems as if it must collapse, while we nevertheless are kept on our feet and are victorious in our faith, it is then that we understand the majesty of God's word. Although it is assailed high and low, it can never be overcome.

The lesson which we must learn, then, is this: when we are stripped of the word of God, the devil will have us at his mercy. We will be out in the open, exposed. We will be like a man who finds that he has fallen into the hands of an enemy and has no means to resist. If he has acted in full knowledge, he deserves to perish. Thus we deserve to be forsaken by God when we do not deign to arm ourselves with his word, so that we may bravely fight against all of Satan's temptations.

Let us turn once more, however, to this word of Scripture: 'Man shall not live by bread alone' (Deut. 8:3). What we translate as 'word' may sometimes also have the meaning 'thing'. So following the natural sense we may take 'the word that comes from God's mouth' to mean 'all that God desires and blesses'. In the original passage Moses was reminding the people that they had been fed with manna, and he inferred from this that God was able to nourish us in the absence of bread, water or any earthly resource. Moses' meaning is therefore clear: although God gives bread and all other foods in order to sustain us, he has not surrendered to them his powers or his prerogatives. We are fed by a hidden grace which comes as it were from God's own mouth, from his merest breath. This is our true food. Bread itself cannot do it: it is devoid of strength and energy. How could it do it, since it is inert? How could it give us life? If we were not so blind and so thankless that we take from God what is his, and if we were not so sacrilegious that we rob God of his majesty, we would realize that it is neither bread nor meat nor provisions of any kind which can give us strength. What is it then that feeds us? The word of God.

In this passage Moses is not referring to the word which is preached to us, and which brings us spiritual life. No, he means the secret strength which God breathes into every creature. Moreover, when God gives us bread and other foods for nourishment, we must learn to look upward and always ascribe the title 'nourisher' to him to whom it is due. To call bread our nourisher would be blasphemy, open idolatry, for we would be transferring what God reserves for himself to a lifeless creature. We would, as I said, be making an idol of bread. Whenever, therefore, we have a meal, or have to eat and drink, let us learn to raise our eyes on high, and to make such use of these ordinary means that we remember that it is God who feeds us. True, he has provided bread as a staff to sustain us; but in doing so he has done nothing to detract from his glory or to diminish it, so that he might say, 'I do not now have what I had before.' It is as when he made the sun. Did that mean that he had ceased to be light? He appointed the visible body so that the sun's brightness might lead us higher up—lead us, that is, to the light inaccessible. This is what we are taught here.

To apply this verse properly, we must see that although everything should fail, God is sufficient to sustain us without any other means. It is to this that our Lord's example points. He says, 'I have no bread. Does God then have nothing with which to feed me?' Supposing there was no bread, would God cease to exist? Without bread or anything else to sustain us, God remains all powerful. And as without the sun he has the power to illumine the world—could he not illumine us in his own strength?—so too he can sustain us in the absence of food or any lesser means. Our Lord Jesus Christ has shown by his example how we should apply these words of Moses.

Our common experience proves that this is so. Although God may send us great fruitfulness, he does not cease to feed us miraculously. If we compare what the earth produces with what we eat, swallow and consume, we would surely be surprised. We would do well to leave such reckoning aside. God must feed us more by his power than by all that comes from the earth. Of course God's provision is rich enough for us to praise and bless him. Even so, the grace of which Moses speaks here far exceeds the natural order. Also, when there is barrenness and we are beset by famine, let us turn to our God and pray that he may graciously sustain us.

Now God rightly threatens those who transgress the law, saying that he will take away their staff of bread, and will make sure that though they eat their fill, bread will not suffice to feed them, since its strength has been removed (Lev. 26:26). He also tells them, 'I will make your sky like iron and your earth like brass' (Lev. 26:19; Deut. 28:23), meaning that he will see to it that the earth will have no substance to fortify them, for he has withdrawn his power. Even supposing, however, that we had enough to eat and drink, if God should curse us, we would certainly experience what God says through the prophet: 'They will bring wheat by weight to the mill, and will take away the flour by weight; it will be brought out of the oven undiminished, but it will have no strength in it. The stomach will remain empty, even though it is fit to burst. It will be full, but only of wind.'[4]

Let us therefore learn to trust in God, and when he is pleased to display his riches by blessing the earth, supplying both crops and vintage, this will teach us that in putting forth his hand he shows himself a Father to us. And when we ask him for our daily bread, let us recognize that he alone sustains us. If, on the other hand, we are threatened with barrenness, we should realize that he has withdrawn his blessing, but that nevertheless he is able to feed and sustain us without any other means. What Moses says concerning the manna shows us that in time of famine, however much people eat, they are never satisfied, yet sometimes our

[4] A free paraphrase of Lev. 26:19, 26.

Lord Jesus Christ can make a piece of bread suffice to make us feel that we have eaten more than our fill! How does he do it? We can argue the ins and outs as cleverly as we like. The fact remains that God makes food of manna, and that even if we were to eat wood, so to speak, he can use it to our advantage, as long as his arm is outstretched in blessing. That, in short, is what we may gather from this passage.

So if we take to heart what our Lord Jesus Christ teaches us here, it is clear that in times of abundance, or in times of barrenness and famine, we will always be lifted up to our God, ascribing to him the honour he deserves. We will know him as the one who, in his sheer grace, feeds us by giving us bread to eat. We will also know that he is the one who provides for us and who remedies whatever it is we lack. Thus, with Paul, we will learn how to suffer hunger and thirst, and to have plenty (Phil. 4:12). This is the way faith always triumphs in us: our eyes will not be heavy with fat, but will behold the grace of the invisible God. In time of need we will always pray to him, and will wait for all that he holds ready in his hand to give us, providing we seek it only in him.

Now let us cast ourselves down before the majesty of him whom we have much offended, that we may obtain pardon, asking him so to remake us that we may forsake all our accursed desires. May we above all be as those who depend wholly on him, and who are grounded solely in his goodness and mercy, to the end that we may look to him for all good things—though already they are ours—and may give him thanks for them.

8

THE PINNACLE OF THE TEMPLE

Then the devil took him to the holy city, and set him on the pinnacle of the temple, [6]*and said to him, 'If you are the Son of God, cast yourself down, for it is written, "He will give his angels charge of you", and "On their hands they will bear you up, lest you strike your foot against a stone."'* [7]*Jesus said to him, 'Again it is written, "You shall not tempt the Lord your God"'* (Matt. 4:5-7).

And he took him to Jerusalem and set him on the summit of the temple, and said to him, 'If you are the Son of God, cast yourself down from here, [10]*for it is written, "He will give his angels charge of you, to guard you",* [11]*and "On their hands they will bear you up, lest you strike your foot against a stone."'* [12]*And Jesus answered him, saying, 'It is said, "You shall not tempt the Lord your God"'* (Luke 4:9-12).

LAST Sunday we noted the kind of temptation to which Jesus Christ was subject at the hands of Satan, and how he was victorious. The devil's purpose was to make him seek illicit ways, as if God had failed him. That was the attack which our Lord had to overcome. The devil tried to instil in him mistrust, because he lacked all earthly means. At such a time we need to rely on God, even though, after looking high and low, we find there is no way out of our afflictions.

When we are dismayed and in despair, we must make up our minds that God is well able to provide for all that we lack, even if, to our way of thinking, there is no way we can win. That is why our Lord says that man does not live by bread as such, but that God endows it with hidden power. Bread in itself is nothing: life cannot be said to reside in it. So supposing there were not a grain of wheat in the world, God is sufficient to feed and sustain us and to make our faith victorious to the end. As we read in Psalm 33: 'The eye of the Lord is on those who fear him and who hope in his mercy, that he may feed their souls in time of famine' (Psa. 33:18-19). We are thus taught to acknowledge God as the Father who nourishes us, not only when he puts bread in our hands and gives us all that we need by way of food, but also when we are in want and when famine threatens us with death. At such a time let us not fail to call upon him who is careful to sustain us and to watch over our lives. As for the means he employs, let us not call into question his power. Let us recognize instead that, whenever God wills, he makes use of his creatures, working in them freely as he pleases. We must not limit him to external means alone.

Matthew and Luke now record a second conflict: *The devil took Jesus to the summit of the temple, and told him to cast himself down*, using as his excuse Psalm 91: '*God has given his angels charge of you, to bear you up in their hands*' (Psa. 91:11-12). They also declare that Jesus Christ overcame this temptation by quoting Scripture to the contrary: '*Do not tempt God.*'

The two Evangelists do not observe the same order. Matthew relates what we have just read, while Luke places this temptation third. This is not at all unreasonable, for as we know they did not always adopt the same style; it was enough if they gave a summary account of what was useful for our salvation. It is therefore immaterial whether, on his second attempt, the devil urged our Lord Jesus Christ to cast himself down, or whether this was the last such struggle. The essential thing is that we should understand the devil's intention.

We cannot really profit from this story if we do not see why the devil quoted this Scripture, and if we fail to note the contrast between Satan's wiles and the traps he set, and the wisdom given to our Lord Jesus Christ which allowed him to resist and to close the door to him. As we said before, there is no question that the devil meant to tempt God's Son to unbelief, so that he should cease to depend upon God's will. The devil further wished to provoke him to pride and arrogance. So he attacks him by getting him to venture more than is allowed him—to act without his Father's permission. The devil undoubtedly sought by craft to lead him into error and to make him stray from the right path. He strove with might and main to accomplish this, for he knew that if he overcame the Head, he could easily inflict a mortal wound on those who were his members. The devil therefore tested our Lord Jesus Christ by employing all the wiles and terrifying attacks which he has at his command.

Since we also must prepare ourselves for combat, we should know what it is we chiefly have to guard against in order to resist the devil. For those who go to war must be aware of the enemy's methods, his traps, his weapons and his tactics. We thus have to consider the weapons which Satan uses and his designs, as Paul reminds us (2 Cor. 2:11). The point, then, which we should note, is this: just as the devil first tempted our Lord to unbelief, and later tried to provoke him to ambition, recklessness and daring, we too must be on our guard, for we will not be spared Satan's attacks from both right and left. When Paul speaks of having been tried by affliction of many kinds, he says he had to be well armed on every hand (Eph. 6:10-11). The same will happen to us. Sometimes we will be deprived of everything we need; it will be as if our hands were tied or our arms broken, so that it will seem that God has forsaken us and that we call upon him in vain. We will accordingly be cast down. The devil will attempt to plunge us into the deepest mire and will drive us to such despair that it will seem a waste of time to turn to God for help.

On the other hand, when he finds that he has the chance to fill us with excessive pride, he puffs us up with wind and allows us to promote ourselves more than God permits. Let us beware, then, of either kind of assault. And if God at times should bring us to such extremes that we do not know what will become of us, we must lay hold of his help by faith, and rest in that assurance. If, however, we have reason to swell with pride, we should know that the devil has carried us off with over-confidence, so that we take more liberties than we should. Let us beware lest he takes us beyond the bounds so that we flutter about in the air, or lest he sweeps us away so that we happily indulge our whims and fancies. This is the first lesson, then, that we must learn, when we are told that the devil sought to persuade Jesus Christ to throw himself down from the temple.

Now to ask whether our Lord was taken to Jerusalem in a vision or in actual fact is a question more intriguing than useful. It is probable that it was a vision only, since Luke tells us that it happened 'in a moment of time' (Luke 4:5). He could not have been actually carried from the wilderness to the summit of the temple, and the objection according to which he could not have been subject to an illusion can be easily answered. He submitted voluntarily, and it was not his soul that was deceived, only his bodily senses. It is not absurd to think that the Son of God so humbled himself that he allowed Satan an opening in order to offer combat. However, since there is no point in stirring up a heated argument or dispute, we would do better to put this aside, to look at the substance and to consider why these things are told to us.

I said earlier that the devil sought to get our Lord Jesus Christ to act rashly. I call 'rashness' anything a man does when heedless of God's order or command, or when heedless of his own ability, so that he has not the wit or judgment to say, 'This thing is worthwhile; that thing ought to be done.' Instead he acts capriciously, on impulse. That is the kind of daring which the devil tried to instil into Jesus Christ.

We turn now to the pretext which Satan uses. Once again he cites Scripture—verses from Psalm 91, where it is said that those who come under God's care will dwell in safety. The Psalmist goes on to say that God has commanded his angels to keep his people from stumbling, so that they may continue in all their ways (Psa. 91:11-12). If this is true for all believers, how much more true is it for our Lord Jesus Christ! It is through him that the angels keep watch over the faithful, for he is their Head. That is how the angels commune with us and act as our protectors. They would be our enemies if we were not united to them by a common bond, our Lord Jesus Christ, who is supreme over his whole church. In this way the angels are like brothers and servants to us, as we read in the letter to the Hebrews (Heb. 1:14).

There is thus a semblance of truth in what Satan says to Jesus Christ, that God has commanded his angels to bear him up in their hands. We gather from this that the angels take good care of us, since God has entrusted us to their protection. When we keep to our path, they will defend us by the power which God has given them for that very purpose. At first glance, then, Satan has not falsified Scripture. Nevertheless he has been doubly cunning here. First, he turns what is meant to comfort the faithful into an excuse for recklessness and over-confidence. Second, he omits words which are not incidental to the passage: 'God will guard the faithful in all their ways.' That is the sentence he omits: 'in all their ways'. He intends to lead Jesus Christ astray, while having him believe that he will be protected by the angels.

It is as if a house had been got ready for someone; nothing had been omitted. 'Look,' the man says, 'up there is my room, well furnished, and there I will sup.' But he tries to get to his room through the window, and in leaping into the air he hits his head against a wall! Are there not stairs that go up? In the same way Satan has falsified Scripture. He wants to make Jesus Christ over-confident so that he will attempt more than is allowed him. That is the clear, natural meaning of this text. When we walk in our ways, the angels will always keep careful watch over us.

What does it mean to 'walk in our ways'? We are subject, it is true, to a countless number of afflictions. Every element threatens us; we are surrounded by endless dangers and exposed to very many perils. We do not recognize a hundredth part of them. Still, were it not for the angels, our plight would be the most miserable of all, and we would be forever stricken with fear and terror. That is how we would be. Now it is said that although there are many hindrances in this world, and although we may go backward rather than forward, bereft of purpose and entangled in many cares, God will provide. How can that be? Because, as Psalm 34 says, the angels are encamped around us; we are always protected by them; power is given to them to defend us (Psa. 34:7). The angels have been appointed to bear us up in their hands and to keep us from stumbling.

This truth, therefore, gives us full assurance, first, that having committed ourselves to God and to his guidance, we can defy all that Satan can conceivably do against us. In the second place, when the devil endeavours to stir up wrath against us, let us make sure we go on regardless, for God will help us overcome everything. Of course, if I strive to do my duty, some will hate me and others despise me; I will make many enemies; nets will be laid to trap me. Even so, as long as God has promised to lead me in all his ways and not to forsake me, I will continue on. That is how this message can be profitable and instructive for us, and how, amid all our sorrows, we are strengthened and gladdened by the knowledge that, if by finding favour among men we might think ourselves doomed, God has given his angels power to defend us.

The devil thus interpreted this passage the wrong way round. What is it he says? '*Cast yourself down!*' Those are not the ways of God. He could indeed bear us up in the air, as the eagle is said to bear its little ones up (cf. Isa. 40:31). Consider, however, whether God wants us to fly without wings, and to put his power to the test by throwing ourselves from a very high roof. That is not walking in his ways. When we struggle to walk through narrow gaps, woods, thorns and brambles, and when there are mountains to be crossed, then he will do as he says elsewhere in the Psalms: he will give us the feet of hinds and deer (Psa. 18:33). He will lead us at all times and in all places, yet we must be mindful of our ways. Let us walk, as is said, when the path is good, but let us also walk when there is mud and swamp, when there are bushes, mountains and stones. Let us walk there too: God will give us grace to overcome everything. Let us take our stand, then, upon God's word. Whoever neglects God's will acts recklessly. You might think, 'God is on my side.' Is he? No, you falsify his word. He has promised to lead you when you walk in your ways, but when you act heedlessly, when you do not keep to the path or track but are merely rash, presumptuous and bold, is God obliged to serve you?

We know that children's nurses hold them from behind when, small and weak, they begin to walk. But could they reach up high if the children wanted help to fly through the air? God wants to be a nurse to us by being our protector, and by using his heavenly host to keep watch over us and to direct our feet. He does this, however, to remedy our weaknesses and failings, not to inflate our sense of pride or to make us raise our horns, nor to enable us to take hellish liberties or to drive us to extremes of folly.

This, therefore, is what this passage teaches. First, whenever we read in Scripture that God will not fail us, that he will be our fortress, our rock, our rampart and security, that his arm will be outstretched to aid us, that in the midst of death he will greatly strengthen us, despite our frailty—when we have such an array of promises, we should know that their chief purpose is to make us fear God, as we saw earlier in Psalm 33 (Psa. 33:18). Then too, we should hope in his mercy, and not act according to what comes into our head, thinking that we can bind God to our wishes. Let us beware of such caprice and recklessness, knowing that this was how God's Son was attacked and that Satan today has similar schemes afoot. Let us be on our guard, giving no thought to either arrogance or presumption. May we say with David, 'I have not walked in pride beyond my powers or understanding.' And may we also be, as David goes on to say, 'like children weaned of their mother' (Psa.131:1-2).

The devil's wickedness is thus shown by his attempt to twist Scripture, to make it say the opposite of what is given to us. Satan tried to change the spiritual bread that feeds our souls into poison. However, he did not succeed with our Lord Jesus Christ, nor will he succeed with us. Only let us fight according to the example of our Head, and let us walk in our ways. Whatever promises we have from God in Scripture, we should always be careful to keep within our bounds and not bolt as horses do, following the whims and fancies in our head. Let us not lose sight of all that God commands.

It is true that we cannot be too bold when it comes to following the path which God has appointed for us, and to which he bids us keep. We should not be afraid to dare too much! However, even the tiniest boldness is excessive—more indeed like intoxication—when men fail to consider their abilities, their calling, and the will of God as it has been taught to them.

Accordingly, our Lord Jesus Christ says to Satan, 'You shall not tempt the Lord your God.'

Here we see again what was explained to us last Sunday. Although the devil may falsify Scripture, he cannot snatch it from us so that it ceases to be of use to us. Jesus Christ does not abandon the struggle to which the devil challenges him, for he knows him to be the father of all sacrilege. Now the greatest sacrilege is to misuse God's name. Our Lord knew this, but he felt no dread, even as today there are many who disturb the church by distorting the meaning of Scripture, by manipulating it and by changing its truth into a lie. Paul says that there must be heresies (that is, sects), so that the upright in heart might be tested (1 Cor. 11:19). When we see Satan resorting to such things, let us be resolute, as was Jesus Christ who made Scripture his shield and who armed himself with every weapon from head to toe, as we saw in Ephesians (Eph. 6:13-17). So when we are equipped with the whole of Scripture and are faced with a thousand traps set by Satan, it will be an impregnable fortress for us. May the example of God's Son therefore be our bulwark. He is given to us as a model and mirror, but also as our teacher. What he teaches us, as we see, is that although the devil lays false claim to Scripture, we should not be moved on that account, but should courageously resist him. How do we do that? By Scripture itself: 'It is written.' That is the way to rebuff Satan's temptations.

Our Lord cites the words, 'You shall not tempt your God' (Deut. 6:16). Moses, when he said this, simply meant that we must not think that we can bind God to our whims and wishes. Let it be enough that we accept what he says. We can tempt God in many ways, but here the word 'tempt' has the sense of trying to bend God to our wills, to make him subordinate so that he conforms to what we want, instead of our conforming to his word. That is the meaning of temptation here.

It is important to bear in mind the failing which Moses was trying to correct, given that the Israelites were always demanding fresh miracles. 'Why does not God do this?' 'Why does God not work this way or that?' Such was the impudence of this people. It was a far too common fault, since they tried to make God jump through the hoops, so to speak, and to get him to change, as if they were laying down the law to him. Hence Moses told them: 'It is not for you to test and probe him to see what he wants, or whether he will attempt one thing or another. Be content with his will, for you must yield to his command and must not go beyond it.' We see clearly, then, how useful this verse is, and what it means. We see also how our Lord put it into practice, as he was bound to do.

Now it is not enough to understand all that we read in Scripture or that is preached to us. There are many of course who are content to say, 'Oh, that's that verse explained. That's how it's to be interpreted.' No, the main thing is that, having got the meaning, we lay hold of it for our instruction and practise it as often as we need to. It is like a man who has locked away his treasure, but who in time of need does not have the wit to take his key and open his chest, or to dip into it whenever he is in want. So with the chest beside him, he lets himself starve to death. What, then, do we make of that?

It is the same with us. Supposing we have understood the whole of Scripture, what good will it be to us if we merely read it but cannot apply it for our use or instruction? Or if we do not use the key to this treasure whenever necessary? From our Lord's example, we gather that the only way that we can be kept in check, so that we are not puffed up by recklessness or pride, is to remember the lesson: 'You shall not tempt the Lord your God.' That is one point.

Overall, however, as I have said, this verse warns and urges us not to try to change God according to our own ideas. Let us allow him to work according to his own will and pleasure. For although he invites us to make our way directly to him and promises to do the will of those who fear him, this does not mean that he will bow to the will of each and every one, and that we should think that we have the upper hand, as if he were not supreme over us. No, it is assumed that we must pray that his will be done, and that our requests, as is said in one of John's letters, should be restrained. We should ask for nothing which is contrary to his will or which we believe is displeasing to him (1 John 5:14). If, therefore, we want God to do a miracle, to descend visibly from heaven, to change mountains into valleys, wells into springs and trees into vines; if we want to rush pell-mell at things, as we say, we would be tempting God. Why? Because we would be trying to test his power, to see what he could do. These things he can do, but if he chooses not to do them, are we then to despise him, instead of allowing him to rule us as he should, and instead of showing him such reverence that we neither do nor wish anything except what pleases him? So when Moses says that we must not tempt God, this is what we have to understand. It ought to be enough that God has said, in each and every way, 'I will not fail you.'

Much patience is needed if this is to happen—patience of two kinds. First, we may feel that God has drawn away, and that he shows no sign that he is willing to aid us. Even so we are to remain calm until he proves that the opposite is true. Patience of a second kind is needed when God does not deal with us as we would like; yet still we do not cease to glorify him. He does not always make it easy or hard for us, since knowing what is good and necessary for us he treats us as he wills. We thus need patience. Whenever we fail to be patient in either way, we will find it impossible not to tempt God. As we all know, when we are troubled and perplexed and when God does not promptly produce a remedy, we seethe with impatience and are even driven to defy him, demanding that he act immediately. 'How long is this to last? Why must I suffer such distress?' To hear us speak, you might think that God had done us wrong. Nevertheless, it is certain that all that he does is righteous and proper, just as it should be. For our part, we generally do not know what to ask for, as is said of the sons of Zebedee (Matt. 20:22).

Men sometimes, it is true, seem to yield in all humility to God, when things turn out exactly as they like, and when he showers them with his generous bounty, as if in miraculous fashion. Later, however, being fickle, they change their minds and ask for something new. If he does not comply, they lose control and lay down the law to God as if he were not sovereign over them. This is the sort of impetuousness we display, so that we inevitably end up tempting God. We would like to pen him in, as if we were to imprison someone and say to him, 'Don't move from there!' If an officer of the law is hauling someone off to prison, but stops when the other says, 'Let me go home', he will reply, 'No, you've got to go to prison. Whatever you want, do it now!' God therefore complains that he has been penned in by his people. As the Psalmist aptly says, he is kept as if bound by their presumption: 'Did not God cause water to come forth? Can he not also prepare a table for us laden with meat?' (Psa. 78:19-20). They tried to confine him as in a circle, to shut him up as if in prison. This is too vile a blasphemy to utter! Not even the wicked when speaking candidly would say that God should be made a prisoner. And where would it end? Here is evidence of woeful arrogance, yet this is what we do. It is far too common a failing, for when we are so unstable that we cannot wait till the next day, when we want God to do exactly as we please, we surely hem him in and try to make him submit to us. We make a prison for him, as if it were capable of shutting him in. We should learn therefore to keep calm, even though God might leave us to languish. Let us not tempt him in this way.

We need also to be patient in another way, by wanting to arrange things as though we were their master. There are people so foolish that they want the sun when it is shining to be dark, to move away when it is coming closer, or to come closer when it is moving away. They would like to change mountains into valleys and lakes into rivers. There are arrogant people like that. Be sure that if we try to change God's appointed order so as to suit ourselves, we are going against him. Let us be patient, then, accepting all that he has told us is agreeable to him and regarding it as good. He has revealed what is useful for us to know; his will alone is the measure of all wisdom and righteousness. So to avoid tempting God, we must be patient: we must not go beyond our bounds, but must allow God to be master of all and to have dominion over us.

How profitable this passage is should thus be clear. Not only does it have something to teach us when we are calm and tranquil, it also helps us in our battles to resist both on the right hand and the left. And when we are attacked from all sides, it helps us turn our shield against the blows, as our Lord Jesus Christ has taught us.

If we walk in all humility, we cannot doubt that the devil will depart, vanquished. This will not happen at the very first, much as we would wish. We see this in our Lord Jesus Christ. Was he victorious? Then the devil redoubled his efforts, persevering in his proud design to spite God by perverting Scripture and by turning black into white. When the same happens to us, let us resist by readying ourselves for a second battle. Then, having been helped once or twice, let us expect this same God who has aided us, not to fail us.

Now let us cast ourselves down before the majesty of our good God, acknowledging our faults and asking that, by his grace, we may find them more and more displeasing. Corrupt as we are by nature, may we nevertheless seek only to be led and governed by his Holy Spirit, walking in his holy commandments and living our lives to his honour and to our neighbours' edification. And though we must pass through many hardships, let us not lose heart but follow our calling, knowing that he will keep us in all our ways.

9

THE KINGDOMS OF THE WORLD

Again the devil took him to a very high mountain, and showed him all the kingdoms of the world and their glory; [9]*and he said to him, 'I will give you all these if you will fall down and worship me.'* [10]*Then Jesus said to him, 'Go, Satan, for it is written, "You shall worship the Lord your God, and him alone shall you serve."'* [11]*Then the devil left him, and behold, angels came and ministered to him* (Matt. 4:8-11).

And he was in the wilderness forty days, tempted by Satan; and he was with the wild beasts; and the angels ministered to him (Mark 1:13).

And the devil took him away into a high mountain and showed him in a moment of time all the kingdoms of the world. [6]*And the devil said to him, 'I will give you all the might of these kingdoms and their glory, for it has been granted to me, and I give it to whomever I will.* [7]*Therefore if you will fall down before me, all this will be yours.'* [8]*And Jesus answered him, saying, 'Get behind me, Satan, for it is written, "You shall worship the Lord your God, and him alone shall you serve."'* … [13]*And when every temptation was finished, the devil left him for a time* (Luke 4:5-8, 13).

WE heard in the Psalm which was sung a little while ago that the inheritance of the world is for the faithful, since they are God's children, and since it is from him that they must seek every blessing.[1] God is therefore glorified when we do him homage, not only with our lives but with all the good things which we enjoy, knowing that they come not from us but from no other source than his sheer generosity.

Now the devil tries to snatch for himself God's honour and dominion. He would have believers think that they must receive from him all that God gives, and that it is to him that praise is due. Daily experience shows this to be true, as we know by the way he tempts us to turn away from God and to come instead to him. However, our Lord Jesus Christ fought hard to help us see that there is nothing strange in following his example, and that we can be sure of victory, since it was for our sake—in our very persons, so to speak—that he was attacked, but won the day.

Here we find the devil trying to get our Lord to worship him, and promising him all the world's kingdoms, honours and dignities—everything that men desire by way of ambition or greed. His objective, as I have just mentioned, was to rob God of his majesty and to take his place. That was his aim. I said previously that unless we carefully consider how our Lord was tempted, the story will leave us cold. It will be of little profit to us. When, however, we look closely at what the devil strove to do, we will recognize his deceits and illusions; and when we recognize them we must be armed and on our guard against them. We must also be armed with power from on high, so that we do not fail.

From our Lord's reply we understand the nature of the temptation. 'You shall worship the Lord your God,' he says. His

[1] A marginal note indicates that it was Psa. 33 which was sung. By 1560 some eighty-three Psalms had appeared in metrical form with musical notation. The Psalms were sung in a set order over a twenty-eight week cycle, and preceded the sermon. Psalm 33 belongs to the twelfth week of the cycle, the first six stanzas being sung in the morning service, and the remaining five in the afternoon.

answer shows that the devil sought pre-eminence, hoping to attract the homage which is due to God alone. Consider what he says: '*All the kingdoms of this world are given to me; if you will worship me, I will give them to you.*' Here the devil represents himself as God's deputy, holding all things in his hands as if he had taken them from God, as if they were his prey, booty which does not belong to him. It is as if he had taken over a country by force, by the sword and by right of war. So Satan spews forth a blasphemy against God, quite apart from the hateful sacrilege of rising up against the one who made him. He is well aware that God created him, yet he pushes in and says that everything is his, not God's. From this we see the fury that possesses him. Not that he believes the words he says, for we know that he is the father of lies (John 8:44). It should not surprise us, then, if he lays false claim to what does not belong to him. That is one point.

The devil wants our Lord to worship him, by offering him the wealth of the world to be received from him. Moreover, there are two temptations here. First, he urges Jesus Christ to crave the world's lordly powers, greater indeed than those appointed for him by God his Father. For, as we know, he said that he had come to serve, not to be served (Mark 10:45). It was necessary, too, that humanly speaking he should be of lowly rank. 'Who made me a judge over you?' he asks (Luke 12:14). We know also that he had to flee and to hide in a deserted place when men sought to crown him king (John 6:15), since that would have obscured his office as Redeemer and would certainly have destroyed his spiritual rule. Such were the struggles he had to endure, scorning wealth and all the pleasures of this world, despising whatever delights men and whatever inflames their greed.

There was a second trial which was even worse. The devil tempts our Lord not only to greed but at the same time to sacrilege, the forsaking of God. Now although this might amaze us, it happens all too often. Paul rightly calls greed 'idolatry' (Col. 3:5). Every day, indeed, we see that those who covet wealth pay homage to the devil. They will not say so openly, but the facts prove that this is their intention. They are so carried away that God means nothing to them; Satan is everything. When someone practises deceit and theft, or extorts money from his neighbours, he cannot grow rich by these means without believing that the devil is in complete control. For if we were really convinced that it is for God to supply all our needs, to sustain and feed us both in poverty and in wealth, we would certainly expect nothing good from this world, but only from God's simple blessing and generosity. Do not those who indulge in robbery, deceit, trickery, pilfering and all such acts, frankly despise God and try hard to deny his blessing? They worship Satan; nothing could be clearer. Thus Paul declares that greed involves idolatry, and he tells us why in a verse in Timothy. 'Those,' he says, 'who desire to be rich fall into many tribulations, and in the end must suffer distress in a kind of perpetual hell' (1 Tim. 6:9). Why? Because they fall into Satan's nets; the devil takes possession of them and keeps them as his prey. So having robbed and pilfered on every hand, they must stumble into all kinds of misfortune. Satan is sure to capture and enslave them.

We can now appreciate how helpful Matthew and Luke's account is to us. The devil, as we said, employed every means against our Lord Jesus Christ. So when we want to be equipped to resist him, let us think of how our Lord was attacked and how he withstood, for we often struggle when we find ourselves desiring more than is allowed us.

As Solomon says, God made both rich and poor (Prov. 22:2), meaning that had God so wished, everyone would have enough goods, money and all that the world considers desirable; there would be the same measure for all. God, however, knows why he has created wealth and poverty, and so it will be to the end of the world. God shows the rich special kindness, however, in order to bind them more tightly to himself. This is how he seeks to test their love, to see whether they will be good and faithful stewards of the resources he has entrusted to them, when their neighbours are in need of help. He also wishes to test their self-restraint. As Paul aptly says, those who are rich in the world's eyes should not be puffed up with pride or boast on that account (1 Tim. 6:17). God reveals whether a man is walking in humility when he gives him a sufficiency, a measure of wealth in this world.

As for the poor, God knows what is good and necessary for them. He supplies medicine which will preserve them, because if they were more affluent they would often forget themselves. At the same time he is testing their endurance. On the other hand he seeks to deprive the rich of every excuse, so that their wealth might serve as a rope to throttle them. It is like a great pile of wood which will fuel the fire of God's vengeance against them. Again, as to the poor, many of them scorn God and give themselves to much ungodliness. When oppressed by want they grumble, become annoyed and blaspheme, displaying the venom which before was kept hidden. Rich and poor exist, because God has willed it so.

Now a person may be rich whose heart is not set on riches. Thus the Psalm exhorts us: 'If you have great wealth, make sure you do not set your heart upon it' (Psa. 62:10). In any case, those who covet wealth most certainly forsake God, because there is no restraining their covetousness: their appetite is bottomless, insatiable. In the first place, whoever aims to be rich defies God for no good reason; he is cruel, too, toward his neighbours. His craving knows no end; nothing will satisfy him. When the devil therefore succeeds in planting the root of greed in our hearts, he owns us and deprives us of our freedom, for God abandons us, just as we have abandoned him. Accordingly, to serve God truly and to withstand Satan, let us each be content with our own portion. The rich should know that they have a heavier responsibility and must account to God for the wealth he has placed in their hands. The poor should understand that God deals with them according to what he knows will benefit them most. Let all of us, then, keep to our rank and condition.[2]

If someone has the means to increase his wealth, let it not cause harm to another or kindle the flame of greed. The rich should not only be content with what they have: let them be poor in heart. That is, let them be ready from one day to the next to abandon everything that God has given them, and let them not be distressed on that account. If God wants to augment them, they should accept the blessing which is given; if he wants to diminish them, they should know that it is for their own good. That is one point. A second point is that if greed is already one of Satan's lures which are meant to catch us in his nets and to lead us away from God, not only does it, as I said, make us covet this world's goods and remove any reluctance on our part to overturn God's order; it will also turn us into wild animals intent on theft, abuse, violence, deceit, evil and other offences. To do all this is to pay homage to Satan.

Bear these two points, then, carefully in mind. As long as we live in this world we cannot avoid being attracted by some excessive craving; and when the devil has completely thrown us off balance, we will do homage to him and will turn our backs on God. That is why, if temptation does not defeat us, we must battle on.

Our Lord Jesus Christ was not himself subject to the same desires as we are. He naturally wanted normal things. He

[2] Calvin's comments should be seen in the context of a society which offered relatively few opportunities for upward mobility. In any case the preacher's concern is not with the possibilities of individual betterment, which he does not discount, but with the responsible use, here and now, of God's bounty, and with the exercise of trust in God's fatherly provision. Where need exists, in the name of Christian love Calvin urges a mutual sharing of God's gifts which, while not eliminating economic inequality, is meant to attenuate its harshness.

accepted the gifts which were offered to him; he valued the world's resources and its opportunities for rest; he shunned grief and poverty, hunger and thirst; he felt joy, sadness, love, hate and similar feelings which are part of human nature. Yet he always remained entirely innocent. He was not tainted by the turmoil typical of our desires, for while many vain things transfix our gaze, they also penetrate our hearts. Why? It is the venom of original sin at work. When we see a lovely piece of country and fine possessions, we are moved by joy and delight. We not only appreciate them but some inner impulse goads us to say, 'If only I had as much!'

While it is impossible for us not to be touched by covetousness, since we are corrupt and since our nature is defiled by original sin, our Lord Jesus Christ possessed such holiness that the devil could not induce him to do anything evil. As for ourselves, however bravely we fight and do our utmost to resist, there will always be some sting of sin in us, and God will uncover the evil which is hidden within. He will show that our wants are like a continually burning furnace, or like a smouldering fire which now and then bursts into life, according to what is set before us. We must, then, be all the readier to repel the blows which Satan aims at us, for however strong we are, our weakness is sure to surface. In these circumstances we easily forgive ourselves; we are so careless that the devil would defeat us a hundred times over if we had not taken up the shield with which our Lord withstood Satan's temptations, and if we had not been good soldiers who followed his example.

For this is how he answered Satan: '*You shall worship the Lord your God, and shall serve only him.*' As we said before, this reply shows that the devil sought to wipe out the majesty of God and to transfer it to himself. Not that he thought that this was possible, but such was his rage that he could not help revealing his true self. He is, as I have said, the father of lies and deceit

(John 8:44). Our Lord therefore quotes Scripture to him, demonstrating that we too must make right and proper use of Scripture. It is not given to us so that we might vaguely attend to this or that, but so that we might use it with discernment, as we should. Accordingly Paul tells us that those who are teachers in the church must be wise, carving and cutting up the word of God (2 Tim. 2:15).[3] It is not enough that they should faithfully expound it: they must lay hold of what they know is profitable, so that the people may receive its fruit.

We are thus to worship God and to serve only him. The word 'worship' signifies that we must duly bow down before God and pay all homage to him. Not that we may not lawfully bow down to men, but we must distinguish between the earthly or civil honours which we render to men, and the spiritual honour or reverence which we owe solely to God. When speaking of God's worship, Scripture assumes that God is without peer. In worshipping him we render to him the spiritual service which he asks of us, and we offer him the homage of our bodies and souls. When Scripture speaks, as it often does, of worshipping men, it means that we pay them respect, as courtesy requires. But this respect does not detract from the homage which we owe to God and to his spiritual service. Our homage is termed 'worship', and is evidence that we put our whole trust in God alone, and that we want him to rule our bodies and souls and to have authority over us.

Notice how foolish the papists are in this respect. They speak of twofold worship. One they call 'reverence,' and the other 'service'. They do not make the distinction which I have made. If they distinguished between the honour which is a mark of social respect or courtesy, and the spiritual honour owed only to God

[3] Paul urges Timothy to 'rightly divide the word of truth' (2 Tim. 2:15, KJV). The basic sense of the verb is 'to cut straight,' hence Calvin's reference to carving and cutting. In his sermon on this verse he likens the action to that of a householder who slices or carves a loaf of bread, so that his young children may eat it more easily (*CO* 54:150-51).

and which is in fact religion, the affair would soon be settled. They say, however, that the honour of reverence, which they call *latria*, belongs to God, and the honour of service to the saints. In short, they ascribe the honour of spiritual service to creatures, while God has something separate, which they call 'the honour of reverence'. In this way they reserve their chief worship for the saints—indeed for their images, their bones, their shirts and their shoes. This they call *dulia*, that is, honour of service.[4]

Now when Paul speaks of the Galatians' former ignorance, he says that they served idols (Gal. 4:9). He does not only say that they worshipped them and gave them the reverence which the papists call *latria*. No, he says they served them. So this distinction which they draw has nothing in common with Paul: it is as if they meant to contradict the Holy Spirit. Yet they have gone even further. Believing that the Virgin Mary, the true cross and the blood shed by Jesus Christ should not be ranked with ordinary images, paintings, shoes and all the other nonsense they worship, they have thought up a different, superior sort of service which they call *hyperdulia*, to show that the Virgin Mary and the cross deserve a higher place. We see, therefore, what madness has taken hold of these poor blind souls, who exalt creatures instead of God so that they not only worship the saints themselves, but their shoes, breeches and a dreadful hotchpotch of other baggage. This shows us how deep was the pit from which God rescued us, the pit of misery where once we lived. With feelings, then, of dismay and shame, we learn from this verse an important lesson for the future. Its meaning is clear: we must worship only God.

There is no question but that God reserves for himself alone the reverence which is the mark of piety and religion, reverence which is called 'spiritual service'. For the word whose meaning

[4] On the distinction between honour paid to God (*latria*) and honour paid to the saints or their images (*dulia*), see *Inst.* I.11.11 and I.12.2-3.

we said is quite different—the word 'courtesy'—proves that we in no way detract from God's service when we honour someone. To claim that we are attributing some godlike quality to him should never cross our mind. If, however, I honour someone out of devotion, I surely rob God of a portion of his honour. For example, although Cornelius the centurion was a God-fearing man, he knelt before Peter (Acts 10:25). He knew that Peter was a man, not God, yet he treated him with foolish, inordinate devotion. Peter would not have rebuked him so sharply if he had not realized how bad a mistake this was.

Consequently, so far as spiritual service and devotion are concerned, we cannot elevate men in the smallest degree without demeaning God, and without depriving him of his honour by an odious act of sacrilege. Such is the plain meaning of this text: we are to pay God spiritual homage with our bodies, souls and goods, and if necessary we must demonstrate our homage by external rites, as proof that God can have no peer. For these are the words which Moses adds: 'You shall serve only him' (Deut. 6:13). In saying this he rules out everything that men might propose out of their own heads. That is why we read in Psalm 73: 'Shall I look high and low for any other God?' (cf. Psa. 73:25). Here David is describing a common, everyday fault which is deeply rooted in our souls. We protest well enough that God is sovereign, but not a word is said about safeguarding his honour. The heathen said exactly the same. They never thought that all their gods were supreme: they believed in one absolute ruler. They went on, however, to imagine that God was in a place all by himself, and that there were smaller gods, each with his particular responsibility. In a word, there is nothing to choose between the heathen with their multiplicity of gods, and the papists with their angels and departed saints.

However, while people have always been convinced that there was a God who ruled all things and who made the world, they did not fail to endow him with many partners, thus making many gods. Every man made his own god, and every town had its protecting deity. This was so even in Judaea at the time of the prophets, as they tell us, and the same is apparent today among the papists. All have their patron saints, and all go off looking for places to make their devotions. One person will swear by St Barbara, another by St Catherine. If, then, we are to end all such superstitions, and if we are to be truly cleansed of them, let us take to heart the lesson taught to us here: God alone desires to be served and worshipped. He disowns any service in which he is made to share, and of which a portion, however small, is assigned to someone else.

If we would worship God, we must render to him all that is his. We must thus acknowledge that all dominion, glory, praise, wisdom, righteousness and power belong to him, as Paul says to Timothy (cf. 1 Tim. 1:17). That, I repeat, is the true worship which we owe God. And let us also demonstrate this outwardly when circumstances require. As to the question of bowing down, we see that those who pretend to venerate idols and statuettes, though their heart may not be in it, are committing sacrilege. For it is not said, 'You shall worship in your heart', but simply 'You shall worship.' Since God has strictly forbidden any ceremony which harms his majesty, we know that all that pretence which many use as an excuse is merely a delusion of Satan. Because of their stubbornness and impudence they ought to be doubly punished, since they openly mock God.[5] Seeing, then, that it is God alone whom we must honour, and that no creature can be allowed to rank with him, let us do as Jesus Christ did, and

[5] The preacher alludes here to the conduct of those who, living under the jurisdiction of Roman Catholic authorities, conformed outwardly to the rites of the papal church while holding inwardly to the truths of the gospel. Lip-service, they argued, did not constitute infidelity. Calvin commonly terms such people 'Nicodemites' (cf. John 3:1-2), since they choose concealment to the open confession of their faith. For more on this matter see John Calvin, *Faith Unfeigned* (Edinburgh: Banner of Truth Trust, 2010).

confess that our only good comes from God, that we seek it only in him, and that we render to him what we know to be his.

It is of course true that men may serve as God's agents and ministers to impart his good gifts to us, but this in no way diminishes his power. If someone were to do good to me, I would not then say that God meant nothing more to me, nor would I put that person in God's place. If I did that, how ungrateful would I be! The fact is that God allowed that person to be his hand. And if I made an idol of the hand that did good to me, but ignored the person himself, I would give great offence. If someone gave me money for food and drink, but if I only honoured the hand that gave it as if it were separate from the body, and if indeed I forgot about the body, how ridiculous would that be? Among men such a thing would never happen. Yet this is what we do. God bestows his gifts on us through the agency of men. They are only his hands. But when we fix our attention on them, we demean God and think no more of him. Let us learn, then, so to honour him that we acknowledge that he is the source of all good things, and that they flow to us from him.

That is why Paul says that immortality belongs to God (1 Tim. 1:17; 6:16). Although our souls are immortal, they have no life; nor do the angels, unless God imparts immortality to them. If he alone is immortal, we must conclude that all immortality comes from him, just as, if he alone is wise, we must seek all wisdom in him. Because it is for him to feed and sustain us, because all goodness and abundance are in him, we must ask him for our daily bread. There is nothing that God reserves more strictly for himself than the claim that all good things come from him, and that all praise for them must go to him. So whenever we feel the urge to obscure God's glory, let us reject the temptation with the words which have been written: 'You shall worship and serve only God.' Thus when the devil lures us and spreads his nets to beguile and trick us, if we try to enrich ourselves by wicked dealing and crooked means which God condemns in his word, we must say to ourselves: 'What's this? We are setting idols up in place of God!' And what will the result be? Shame upon our heads! Every time we acquire goods by unlawful means we are worshipping Satan and robbing God of his majesty. Again I quote Paul: 'Covetousness is idolatry' (Col. 3:5).

Whenever we need to know how to behave in this world, we should look to God. We should give no thought to becoming rich by cheating, clever dealing, deception or theft; in doing these we wrong God, whatever means we use. We must keep coming back to the thought that God alone is to be worshipped, and that he is not content for us to bend the knee before him, to raise our hat as a token of respect or otherwise to look our best. We must be earnest in our worship of him. We must, that is, make sure not only that the title 'God' is reserved for him alone, not only that we acknowledge one God whom we must serve, but that we ascribe to him all his qualities, centre our whole life on him and seek only to glorify his holy name. Once we resolve to worship only God, and once we know how he wishes us to serve him, we cannot doubt that we may bravely rebuff Satan and that we have the resources to resist him, as our Lord's example shows. Have we fought, then, as we should? Satan must be driven off. Not that he will not return later, but for us the outcome can only be successful, provided we arm ourselves with the shield given to us by the Son of God.

That said, Mark relates that *Jesus Christ was among the wild beasts*. Yes, and Matthew adds that *the angels came and ministered to him*. Luke for his part tells us that *the devil, having ended all these temptations, departed for a time*. We should attend to all these points, for they contain sound instruction for us.

The fact that he was among the wild beasts conveys the idea that he was without any human support. If we are tempted, or if we are distressed or perplexed in any way, it means much to us to have a friend in whom we can confide; though our appearance may be sad, we find this encouraging. However, if someone has been banished from society and meets only wild animals in the wilderness, his struggles will be so much more severe. That was how our Lord Jesus Christ was placed. So when we are bereft of all human help, and when men have neither the strength nor the ability nor the zeal to aid us, we should remember that our Lord himself passed this way. It is only right that we should follow him, since he has gone before and has pointed out the path. That is one thing.

When Luke records that the devil, having ended all his temptations, withdrew for a time, what we must notice is that our Lord Jesus Christ was tested to the very last. That is what the words 'all temptations' mean. It is as if our Lord was said to have passed through a sieve, to have been probed almost to the depths, to have been assailed on every side. It is as if the devil, having had one blow parried, tried to land another one. The devil therefore has so many wiles, so many evil tricks, so many fiery darts to pierce us fatally, that he will use them as much as he can, as he did with our Lord Jesus Christ. What did he gain? Nothing! He was obliged to withdraw.

What we learn from this verse is that if our Lord allows us to be tempted in different ways, we need not fail, come what may. Let us practise what we are taught in the Psalm: 'We have passed through fire and water, yet we are not consumed' (cf. Psa. 124:3-5). When believers apply this Psalm to the church itself, they sing not of one temptation only, but of a succession through which they pass.[6] Let us allow God, then, to test us as long as he chooses. It is not for us to lay down the law to him: we must accept the portion that he sends us.

[6] Psalm 124 was one of the metrical Psalms sung in the Genevan church. Calvin had preached on the text in November 1545; his sermon was one of the first to be recorded and published (*CO* 32:467-80).

Notice also that Satan is said to have left him 'for a time', showing that Jesus Christ had opportunity for rest, since we need God to sustain us. If we were warring constantly and endlessly, having not a minute in which to draw breath, what would become of us? Our Lord Jesus Christ would have overcome all of that with his boundless power, it is true. Nevertheless God meant to show as in a mirror that he can temper Satan's trials, and will not allow us to be attacked beyond our strength. This we experience when, like men bewildered and confused, we find that Jesus Christ brings us relief, and eases our temptations so that we are not wholly overwhelmed by them. Admittedly we must engage in conflict, and God will allow us to be attacked. But the alarm is not always sounded, and the trumpet is not always heard. Our enemies do not always brandish their swords in order to assail us. Our frailty, as I said before, could not cope with it.

When, however, we have endured misery for a while, our Lord takes pity on us; or if we suffer some other affliction, he will sometimes grant us a happy escape. This is how every day God gets Satan to withdraw. It is, however, only for a time, and we should not make the mistake of thinking that, having fought for a while, we are sure we may take leave and find rest. As long as we live in this world, let us not imagine that we will enjoy a peace which lasts for ever: Satan is our adversary, and he never sleeps. There will be periods of truce when God is pleased to support us, but we must always return to the fight. War does not cease, and we must always be prepared for it. Especially, then, when God has given us time to relax and does not continually press us hard, we should say to ourselves: 'How well have I laid up a supply of arms in order to resist Satan? I know that I am not yet well enough equipped with the word of God. From now on I must prepare myself and get a good supply together, in order to repel the enemy when he comes to attack me.'

Remember also that, as to the angels, although we have enemies, they keep close watch over us, for God is not only on our side but he has angels who will uphold us. He has charged them with the task of defending us and has appointed them to serve us, not only for a while but for ever, even though we do not see it. Most certainly the angels served our Lord Jesus Christ when Satan was attacking him; yet insofar as he was a man this was hidden from him. It was necessary for him to be deprived of any kind of aid, so that he should later experience the angels' help. In the same way, God will sometimes make us conscious of his grace, through the agency of angels whom he has chosen to serve us. See, then, how fortunate we are, despite our failings, to be able to fight in his power, until we reach at last our heavenly rest.

Now let us cast ourselves down before the majesty of our good God, acknowledging our faults and begging him so to make us feel them that we may come to hate them. May he help us fight with Satan and repel all that he would do against us. And may we overcome all our evil appetites, and so yield to his holy will that nothing may prevent us from honouring him as he deserves.

10

THE GOSPEL OF GOD

Now when Jesus heard that John was in prison, he withdrew to Galilee ... [17]*From that time on he began to preach, saying, 'Repent, for the kingdom of heaven is near'* (Matt. 4:12, 17).

Now after John had been put in prison, Jesus came into Galilee, preaching the gospel of God, [15]*and saying, 'The time is fulfilled, and the kingdom of God is near. Repent, and believe the gospel'* (Mark 1:14-15).

But Herod the tetrarch, who had been reproved by him because of Herodias, his brother Philip's wife, and for all the evil things that he had done, [20]*added this to the others, that he put John in prison* (Luke 3:19-20).

And Jesus returned in the power of the Spirit to Galilee, and a report concerning him went out through the surrounding country. [15]*And he taught in their synagogues, and was honoured by all* (Luke 4:14-15).

WE have seen how John the Baptist fulfilled his duty by preparing the way for our Lord Jesus Christ, so that he might be welcomed without reserve as the looked-for Redeemer. John had been appointed to this task, as we noted earlier, and as we will see more fully later on. His calling, however, was not clear-cut, which is why he is said not to have been a prophet, but to have acted as a herald. He was to make a way for the Son of God, to whom all should submit and to whom all authority was due. Thus God's Son receives firm endorsement from him who surpassed all the prophets in rank.

We now learn that our Lord Jesus Christ began to do the work entrusted to him by God his Father. For not only did he have to suffer for the world's salvation, he also had to bring to men the fullness of all truth and wisdom, as it is written: 'In him are found all the treasures of wisdom and understanding' (Col. 2:3). He was also the Father's ambassador, who perfectly revealed what the fathers of old understood only in part. He said, as we will later see: 'Blessed are the ears which hear this teaching, for the prophets and kings of old desired to hear it, but did not enjoy this priceless blessing' (Matt. 13:16-17). Likewise the apostle declares that formerly God spoke by the prophets in many ways, but that in these last days he has spoken by the mouth of his Son, to bring finality to all of prophecy (Heb. 1:1-2). This truth was instilled even into the Samaritan woman and all her nation, who nevertheless were not instructed in the law. The fact is that, since time immemorial, God wished this to be engraved on the hearts of men, and that it should be spoken of by all. 'When Messiah comes,' she said, 'he will show us all things' (John 4:25).

It is time for us to hear the essential teaching of our Lord, as revealed by all three Evangelists: *Jesus began to preach in Galilee, at the time that John the Baptist was put into prison.* As we said a little while ago, John did not need much time to perform his appointed task. It was enough that he should fulfil Isaiah's testimony by being the voice crying in the wilderness: 'Prepare the way of the Lord. Let rough places become plain, let mountains be made low and let valleys be exalted. Let nothing hinder him to whom all praise is due from being seen and known, and let each give obedience to him' (cf. Isa. 40:3-5). To do this did not require a great deal of time, which was why God allowed Herod to put him in prison. Luke mentions the reason. It was because Herod could not bear to be rebuked both for his evil deeds and for the incest which he committed with Herodias, whom he had taken from his brother. Also, God's law made it illegal to take her as his wife. And in the third place he had repudiated his legitimate wife, who was the daughter of the king of Arabia. (This was not Herod the Great, who, seeking to kill the one born to be king in Judaea, caused the young children to be murdered. It was one of his successors, who bore the title not of 'king' but of 'tetrarch'. According to the pleasure of the Roman Emperor, the country was divided, like some prey, now into four parts, now into three, now into two. And according to his favour, the title 'king' was granted to one man, and the title 'tetrarch' to another.)

What we must notice here, then, is the steadfastness of John the Baptist, who did not spare the ruler of the land but sharply rebuked him for his incest, his unlawful divorce and his other crimes and offences. From various histories we learn that Herod was an arrogant and cruel man, licentious and given to all sorts of passions—a man who, in the eyes of all, was devoid of integrity and decency. John, knowing that this man, who should have been an example and mirror for everyone else, was thoroughly evil, could not abide him. We see very clearly that he was armed by the Spirit of God, for by nature men are fearful, which is why they strike sail when it is a question of calling the great to account. For the great can bite and scratch: annoying them is as good as digging one's grave! God must therefore work in those whom he sends, giving them valour so that they do not flinch or show undue favour. John the Baptist was such a man.

Here, therefore, is evidence that he was led and controlled by God's Spirit, for the very boldest of men may in the end prove to be fainthearted. When only a clash is involved, they will immediately foam and fume—when, that is, they are safe from blows; but once battle is joined they are petrified, changed beyond recognition! So when we hold fast and refuse to strike sail, even though in the course of our duty we may provoke the wicked and may put ourselves in danger because of their audacity—when we persevere regardless, it is a sign that we are led by the Spirit of God. This, then, should give us even greater certainty concerning John's message and the witness he bore to our Lord Jesus Christ, whom we may indeed accept as our Redeemer.

We see, however, in the example of Herod, how difficult it is to accept rebuke calmly and in all humility. This is the true test by which we show whether or not God's fear is rooted in our hearts. If we simply present our teaching, it will pass unhindered and most of us will not object. If a few warnings are added, provided no one is nettled we continue to be relaxed. But when some sore spot is scratched and each of us is seriously tested, then we begin to protest: poison and bitterness come dribbling out. In short, the worst hypocrites in the world would gladly give God obedience except that reproof shows them as they really are. It is just as I said: by nature we love and indulge ourselves; we like to be petted and to be spoken to in honeyed words; we like our faults to be concealed and turned indeed into virtues! That, in our own way, is what we all want. Consequently, when Jesus Christ makes our faults known to us and brings, as it were, a case against us; when he acts as judge toward us and summons us to appear before him, it is then that the wicked and despisers of God rise in rebellion. We should therefore learn all the more to submit willingly to all the warnings we receive. And although it is upsetting when our wickedness is disclosed, and when we are scratched where we do not itch, let us consent to God's judgment and accept reproof from his lips. This is the most important thing if we would show true obedience of faith.

Luke says something else which we do well to note: *To all the evil which he had committed, Herod added this, that he put John in prison*. What Luke means is that it is the very height of godlessness when men rage against the prophets, and when like wild beasts they defy rebukes, striking out with tooth and claw. This is a sure sign that they are hopeless and past correction. So when we fail, if God is gracious and gives us warning, may it move us to repentance, and may we not only hang our heads but bend our necks and allow him to humble us. And if we find this hard, remember that however bitter the medicine may be, the sick do not refuse it. Why? Because their life depends on it. We need medicine because we are all sick in our souls. Our Lord has thus appointed reproof as a means of making us feel our misery and of making us groan, to the point that we are anguished and ashamed in the presence of his judgment. Given, then, that this is the real remedy which will cure our spiritual ills, let us receive it with meekness, and since we have offended God in many ways, let us not scale the heights of godlessness by rejecting his word, and by rising up in fury against his servants whom he has appointed for our salvation. Let us beware, I say, of such heights of wickedness of which Herod is accused here. In him we are meant to see the mark of the reprobate, of all who are wholly forsaken by God. In setting themselves against the prophets, they give no sign that they can be brought back or be converted.

We come now to the main verse, where it is said that *Jesus came into Galilee and there he preached*. Following his baptism and Satan's temptations, about which we heard, God made him a teacher, the task for which he had been sent. He might well have begun in Jerusalem, but God chose to act as he did for two reasons. First, as we know, there are Paul's words, that all haughtiness must be brought low (2 Cor. 10:5). God sought to work by feeble means, by what was despised, when he revealed the treasures of his grace (1 Cor. 1:27). True, he exalted his gospel when necessity required, as we saw and as we will see again in respect of the miracles which revealed the glory of God's only-begotten Son. Nevertheless, humanly speaking, our Lord Jesus Christ was required to begin in a weak way. In the second place, God condemned Jerusalem by preferring Galilee, which was a backward place. Jerusalem was greatly esteemed: its inhabitants thought that since God had his seat and temple there, they were the worthiest people on earth. Yet our Lord turns them down. Not that he completely rejected them, but it was necessary to humble them, so that they should no longer presume on their own worthiness. In this way God's glory was more brilliantly displayed, for the world's salvation was seen to come solely from his free goodness.

Consider, now, how this message is described. A fuller explanation will be given in due course, but the Evangelists here have sought to supply an outline which fully accords with what they said concerning John the Baptist. Jesus Christ speaks these words: '*The kingdom of God is near: repent, therefore, turn to God, and believe the gospel.*' Matthew for his part says that *he preached the gospel of the kingdom*. We earlier explained the word 'gospel', saying that it meant good or joyful news. For although men find joy in their vain pursuits, their joy is cursed by God if it is not referred to him. So let us learn to rejoice when God is well disposed toward us, when he counts us as his children, when he rules and governs us, when his name is blessed, when we honour and worship him and devote ourselves to his service. In these things, I say, we must above all rejoice. But when some rejoice in their pleasures and delights, and others in the attainment of honours which quite carry them away, and when others still find joy in goods and riches—alas, it is mere stupidity, for men do not know the purpose for which they were created.

Whenever, then, it is a question of rejoicing, let us learn to lift our heads high above the world and to make sure we glorify

God, giving to him the honour which is his due. Again, let us look to him that he may receive us in his mercy and acknowledge us as his children, since he does not impute our sins to us. Accordingly, the message proclaimed to us by Jesus Christ is called 'gospel', showing that we have cause to rejoice because through him we are reconciled to God his Father. May he moreover rule us in peace, that we may no longer be in wretched thrall to the devil, the father of all iniquity, who would drag us after him, this way and that.

When our Lord was born, we learn that already the angel said, 'I bring you news of great joy' (Luke 2:10). Only the shepherds, however, were able to hear it. There was joy again when Jesus Christ revealed that he had come to establish his Father's kingdom, and to rescue poor sinners from captivity to the devil and from bondage to sin and death. Mark records that our Lord preached the gospel of the kingdom, the good news that God's kingdom is established in our midst. Imagine we were asked, 'What would it be like if God were not in control?' We would all be in a dreadful plight. It would be unnatural if God, who directs and upholds all things by his power, and who has made everything in order to rule and govern it, were denied his sovereign sway, and if men were so devil-possessed that they refused to submit to him. We would all think that such a thing was monstrous. Nevertheless, however good a face we put on it, and whatever profession we make with our lips, we are clearly estranged from God. Until Jesus Christ comes to put things right, we rebuff God as much as we can and drive him far away. God therefore disowns us and regards us as his deadly foes; we have no part in him until Jesus Christ becomes our Head, shows us how we must be ruled and reveals God's will to us. Then, being taught the truth of the gospel, we accept it by faith. Until that time we are so far removed from God that he forsakes us and leaves us to ourselves, as if we were creatures under his curse.

The gospel message should therefore be all the more precious and pleasing to us, since it brings us such great good. For our part we have every reason to dislike ourselves and to feel ashamed, as long as we have not been taught in the school of God's Son; as long, that is, as we have not tasted the gospel but have lived as we thought best, rather like the papists who take as their sole foundation the opinion of their fathers and forebears. As long as we remain ignorant, God counts us as his enemies. And since he is not our king and does not enjoy the sovereignty he should have over us, we have every cause, as I said before, to be utterly ashamed.

We are told, then, that because the kingdom of God is near we must be converted and believe the gospel. We have already explained, though rather briefly, what is meant by 'the kingdom of God'.[1] It means that God has chosen to reveal himself to men from whom he was formerly estranged, and who were more or less cut off from him. We have all been banished from the heavenly life by Adam's sin and fall. God therefore sends his only Son and, as it were, with outstretched arms asks us to turn back to him, for he is willing to receive us. Although we have strayed and are lost because of our demerits, he still wills to show us mercy. Because the kingdom of God is near, our Lord Jesus Christ urges men to repentance and faith.

Notice first of all that nothing should move or inflame us to yield to God more than his offer of infinite grace and goodness. When Paul, for example, seeks to pierce men's stony hearts and to soften their hardness and obduracy, he appeals to 'the bowels of God's mercy' (Phil. 2:1). In speaking thus, he is really saying: 'Will you now continue in your madness? Must you be worse than the devils? And when God comes to you, displaying his mercy and opening his heart to welcome you as his own children—when he gives to you his own Son, will you be so

[1] See above, pp. 2-6.

unfeeling as not to be softened or inflamed by love for his grace? Will you not allow him to lead you, and will you not delight in the goodness he shows you?' It is in just this way that Jesus Christ urges men to repentance and faith. But on what does he base his appeal? On the fact that God wishes to draw near to those from whom he was once estranged. God, therefore, in receiving us in mercy, sets his goodness before us without waiting for us to seek him out; he forestalls us with such exceptional grace that we cannot grasp even a hundredth part of it. Since he is so kindly disposed toward us, we should be rightly and deeply touched, to the very core of thought and feeling.

Now although our Lord is no longer living in this world, his message goes forth and is preached in his name. Remember what he said on one occasion: 'He who hears you, hears me. He who receives you, receives me' (Matt. 10:40; Luke 10:16; John 13:20). So while we do not visibly see the Son of God, and while it is a mere man, like us, who goes up into the pulpit, it is in his power and on his authority that we daily hear that God's kingdom is near. Whenever God blesses us by making known his will, it is as if he had set up his royal throne among us, sitting in state with his sceptre in his hand and his crown on his head, and bidding all of us submit to him. In a number of passages, indeed, as we will see, the gospel is called 'the kingdom of God' (Matt. 13:11, 19, 24, 31, 33). Why? Because we are alienated from him and are cut off like rotten limbs, until he is pleased to be reconciled to us and to accept us as his children. When we seek his grace through our Lord Jesus Christ, he testifies that he is well disposed toward us.

The kingdom of God has drawn near. Not once only, but each and every day God wills to rule and govern us. Nor was it in Judaea only that he sought to be known and worshipped. He extended his grace much further, as we read in Psalm 110: 'The sceptre of Christ will go forth from Zion' (Psa. 110:2). Scripture does not say that his sceptre will be in Zion, where the sceptre of David and Solomon lay. Scripture says that it will come forth from Zion, meaning that among distant nations and in every direction on earth we shall know the great King whom God has established, and will give free and willing obedience to him if we want him to rule over us for our salvation. Otherwise we will be forced, despite ourselves, to bend our necks and bow our knees—or else we will see them broken!—just as the devils in hell are made to do homage to our Lord Jesus Christ. This is how it will be for all the faithless and rebellious.

As to God's kingdom, however, it is assumed that we calmly allow God to exercise his rule over us. As it is written in the psalm, 'The Lord is coming: let the earth rejoice' (Psa. 97:1). For these two things are unbreakably bound together, that God should reign, and that we should come to him, truly humbled and content for him to have sovereignty over us. God's kingdom cannot be severed from the joy we feel in knowing that we have cause to exult over Satan, the world and all our enemies. Think also of this, that if we are so evil and depraved that we cannot rejoice when God takes up his right to reign, we will end up gnashing our teeth, and with the devils in their disobedience we will be utterly undone when we see joy among the angels in heaven, among the holy patriarchs, prophets and apostles, and among all who have followed the message of the gospel.

Consider, now, how and in what way we should accept God's kingdom, lest we protest that we are ignorant, incapable of ascending to secrets so high that we cannot grasp them. Only two expressions suffice to show Christians what should be the sum total of their wisdom and knowledge: 'Repent' and 'believe the gospel'. Who now will dare to protest: 'Look, I know pitifully little. I'm certainly no scholar!' Well, what of it? Then think only of these two words, 'repent' and 'believe'. There might be an excuse if it was all in one enormous book, as when we study different branches of human knowledge and have to read book after book, for one book does not make sense without another. Also, a great deal of time needs to be spent, and sometimes we make little headway. Here, however, only two words have to be remembered. And if we do not learn them, what will become of us?

Without question, God meant to deprive us of every excuse, and to teach us that nothing stops us from making progress in his school for our salvation, except our thanklessness, sloth and wickedness. We choose to be mindless, seeing that the whole gospel can be summed up in these two words, 'repent' and 'believe'.

Now it is true that earlier we explained what repentance was, and similarly faith, so there is little need to dwell on them again.[2] Nevertheless, it is necessary to refresh our memory of what was said before. In the first place, then, we must turn to God; we must be converted. But what does conversion involve? It is not simply a question of changing tongue, hands or feet. We must start higher up: we must be wholly remade in all our thoughts and desires. Our life must then reveal that we are inwardly changed, as was earlier expressed by the metaphor of the tree and the fruit which comes from it. Just as the root of a tree is hidden in the earth, so repentance cannot be seen. It lies in the mind and heart; it leads us to deny self, and to give up arrogantly wanting our own reason and judgment to guide us. We are to be teachable and easily managed, so that our Lord Jesus Christ is able to direct us as he wills. Repentance also involves a change of disposition so that our nature no longer controls us, and so that all the filth that it contains is cleansed. Our Lord must so renew us by his Holy Spirit that we gladly conform to his will. There you have the root.

After this the fruits appear, that is, all our works, for the life of the Christian man must bear witness to the fact of his

[2] The reference is to the fortieth sermon of the *Gospel Harmony*, preached on Matt. 3:1-3 some two months earlier.

repentance. Repentance or conversion, therefore, means that the sinner should be upset and disgusted with himself, should find nothing to like about himself. This is why conversion is called repentance, for we can never give God our obedience until we are unhappy with ourselves and loathe being the way we are. The word 'conversion' implies that we have gone astray, have turned our backs on God and sought the things we madly crave; but then God turns us around and makes us obedient to him, so that we listen when he speaks and follow the path he traces for us.

We can now see why these words are used and what they really mean: we must be changed in order to be remade in obedience to God. As long as God keeps a loose rein on our necks and does not recall us to himself, we are lost. Such a change means that we were previously lost; in all our thoughts, wants and feelings we were dead. Let us acknowledge, then, that our entire life is hateful and cursed until God makes us new.

So much, then, for free will! So much for all those fine virtues these madmen boast about, since they fancy that within them there is some good seed, some prior disposition to goodness! On the contrary, when it is said that we must be changed and refashioned, it is a sign that from birth onward we are thoroughly defiled, that we are nothing but sin and fit, therefore, only for death. It is only right that our lives should change, and our thoughts and feelings too, since our Lord Jesus Christ calls us so lovingly to himself. For how would it be if his goodness gave us even greater licence to do wrong? That would be like setting up Satan's kingdom! God, as we said, desires to rule in our midst. The message of our salvation should lead us to repentance and conversion.

It is further said that we must believe the gospel, for if we did not have God's promises, conversion would surely be impossible for us. It would be like telling a mountain to fly away! Of course, we owe God our obedience, and we are convinced of this ourselves, for we are not like blocks of wood, devoid of feeling, as if we might somehow make this our excuse. Even so, evil is so entrenched in us that we cannot think one good thought which might make us want to take the proper path, or to dedicate ourselves to God's service. Here, of necessity, all human powers must end. What then is to be done?

If the gospel is not to be preached in vain, we must add faith. Now what does faith mean? It means knowing that God is willing to bury all our transgressions, and that he chooses not to reckon with us as our judge but will accept us as righteous, because our stains have been washed by the blood of his Son. Moreover, what we cannot do for ourselves, he will do by the grace of his Holy Spirit. Since we are incapable of changing ourselves, he himself will change us, writing his law in our inward parts and inscribing it on our hearts. In short, he will cause us to dedicate ourselves to him, even though by nature we are inclined to every kind of evil—indeed we are steeped in it!

We see now why belief in the gospel has been added in the second place. Repentance would be preached to us in vain, fruitlessly, if God had not added the promise that he will help us by his Holy Spirit. For we are completely frail and so prone to evil that he must supply all that we lack, and must cleanse us so that we can show that we are changed and no longer the same as we once were. When we know this to be so, we can be sure that there is nothing idle about the expression, 'believe the gospel'. It is the same as saying that God receives us in his mercy, and that although we deserve to be swallowed up by his wrath, he desires to treat us with compassion. When, therefore, we are told this, should we not be moved to accept his promise and to rely on it? For here God shows himself to us in such a way that his grace is openly displayed, in that he forgives our offences, renews us by the grace of his Holy Spirit and does not allow sin to always rule within us. He gives us strength to master it and so to fight against it that we can triumph over it. When we take all this in, we have the sum total of the gospel, which is something we need to learn every day of our lives.

If we fail to remember these two words, we cannot use ignorance as an excuse, since God has sought to teach us in so simple and direct a way. Yet let us not be stupid as many people are who say, 'There are only two words we need to know.' We are familiar with these rascals who remember that the essence of the Christian faith lies in two words, but they mistake one set of words for the other. They say that all we need to know is to love God and our neighbour. They know no more about God's word than the Turks do—much less, in fact! For the Turks have some understanding of God's goodness and mercy, whereas these devils have none at all. They have become senseless, and God has taken vengeance on them, giving them the spirit of madness so that they are quite beyond hope.[3]

Although these words sum up the gospel, we should not be annoyed if we hear them tomorrow, later on or even throughout our lives. They will always do us good, provided our ingratitude does not get in the way. Let us continue, then, to be good pupils of our God, and let us not tire of his teaching. May we keep following the path he shows us. Experience will tell us how much progress we have made, as God reveals himself more and more intimately to us. In short, those who profit most in God's school are those who need to grow still stronger in their faith, knowing that so far they have learned only in part. That is the lesson for us here.

Luke remarks that *Jesus Christ was glorified by all.* This serves to condemn the Jews all the more. They knew that the news concerning God's Son was the truth they should have obeyed, but in a spirit of rejection they resisted the Holy Spirit, to their

[3] The 'rascals' whom Calvin denounces here are critics, many doubtless local, who disliked the preacher's hortatory style and his insistence on expounding the whole counsel of God. A gospel of simple love would have been more to their taste.

utter shame. For our part, let us learn to glorify our Lord Jesus Christ and to give him, as long as we live, all due honour. We should not be like those with ticklish ears who, having heard two words of the gospel, think they are great scholars, but who weary of it or else grow cold. This is particularly true when we happen to lance their boils to let the pus escape—that is, when we speak forcefully; it is then they spit their venom out and, like rabid dogs, spew forth their blasphemies against God. We must not be like them. Instead, let us give God's Son our obedience, in order to make him our teacher and instructor. Let us embrace his truth as long as we live, so that the more progress we make, the easier it will be for us to learn.

Now let us cast ourselves down before the majesty of our good God, acknowledging our faults and begging him so to make us feel them that we may be brought to true repentance. May he so work in us that we become our own judges and condemn ourselves. And being received by him in mercy, may we be lifted up, and may our whole lives testify that we seek only to dedicate ourselves to him, rendering to him the service that we owe.

11

GOOD NEWS TO THE POOR

And he came to Nazareth, where he had been brought up; and on the Sabbath day he entered the synagogue according to his custom; and he stood up to read. [17]*There was given to him the book of the prophet Isaiah. He unrolled the book and found the place where it was written,* [18]*'The Spirit of the Lord is upon me, because he has anointed me to preach good news to the poor, to heal the broken-hearted, to proclaim deliverance to the captives and the recovering of sight to the blind, to set free those that are oppressed,* [19]*and to preach the acceptable year of the Lord'* (Luke 4:16-19).

WE have seen already that it was necessary for our Lord Jesus Christ to begin to preach the gospel, in order to fulfil the task which God his Father had given him. He had been sent not only to offer himself as a sacrifice, and thus to reconcile the world to God by wiping away sin; he had also been appointed to teach. What we must remember about the passage we have read is this: our Lord appeared as a witness who would proclaim the grace that, through him, would be given to the world. Thus Scripture says that he entered the synagogue as was his custom, and was given the book of Isaiah to read. What he read was part of chapter 61 of Isaiah (Isa. 61:1-2).

Before we come to our main point, however, we should notice that, although the church in Judaea was then in a ruinous state, there still remained traces of what God had established. The day of rest had not been appointed merely to make men idle, but to help them gather in the temple to pray to God, to offer sacrifices and to be taught holy Scripture, since sacrifice without teaching would have been pointless. That was God's purpose in wishing that one day a week should be for rest. It is true that it also contained a symbolic meaning, by which the Jews were urged to rest from their own labours, that is, to deny themselves, and to allow God to govern them. That was the purpose of rest. It was, however, also a matter of organization, since the people could not assemble every day, desirable as that might be. There was thus one day fixed, not only for offering sacrifice to God but for expounding the law and the prophets.

The custom, as we see, had been retained, even in those times when all was corrupt. God had not yet allowed religion to be abolished in this nation which he had chosen; he wished that some mark of it should remain until the coming of our Lord Jesus Christ. And although the majority had become degenerate, there were still a few who persevered in their worship of God and in the faith which was grounded in his promises. It is clear, then, that no church of God can be said to exist unless his word is proclaimed, for that is its soul. If someone therefore pointed to a statue or to a lifeless corpse and tried to make out that it was a real man, that would be rank stupidity. Nevertheless we know that the papists boast out loud that they are the church of God, even though God's word is banished from it. For although these hypocrites pretend to preach, it is nothing but lies. It is forbidden to read the law, the prophets and the gospel in the common tongue. They drone on well enough, but without anyone being taught or edified. Since this is so, it will be easy for us to judge whether the church is to be found among them.

Under Annas and Caiaphas, who were God's deadly foes, there was more order and consistency in Judaea and the synagogues than exist today in all of popery. For here we are told not only about Jerusalem which was the capital city, and where the high priest acted as God's prophet charged with expounding the law, but also about a simple village in Galilee, called Nazareth.

Seeing, therefore, that the blessing still remained that God's word had not been buried but was read and expounded before all the people, the very least that we can do when we assemble in God's name is to hear his word, which should sound forth among us. Otherwise all our protestations are empty, and our Lord Jesus Christ will not sanction what we do, but will condemn it as a sham.

We gather, then, from this passage, that everything in popery is in disarray, and that nothing in it comes close to being what Scripture says the church was under the Old Testament, or after the coming of our Lord, or in the time of the apostles and their faithful followers. As for us, we have cause to boast, but we must understand that to retain possession of so great and priceless a blessing, we must be careful to have ears which are attentive and receptive to the teaching of God's word.

Luke declares that *Jesus Christ stood up to read*. He did so not only in order to be heard, but to demonstrate a greater reverence for God's word. This was the custom, as Paul reveals in the fourteenth chapter of First Corinthians, where he says that the man who speaks should stand up, but that, having spoken, if a better and surer revelation has been given to another, he should sit down and remain silent, while the other to whom God has shown more grace should stand up (1 Cor. 14:29-30). Here, then, we see our Lord Jesus Christ who stands and reads a passage from the prophet. True, this formality was not strictly required, but since we are ignorant and slow of wit, we need to be aroused by signs and gestures to lift up our hearts whenever we are presented with the message of salvation. We should also accept it in all humility, knowing that if we are to offer God praise which is pleasing to him, and to show our deference to his majesty and glory, we must do so by agreeing with his word. That is what this formality implies.

Now we will never be capable of being taught by God, or of being good scholars, equipped to profit in his school, if we do not raise our minds on high. As long as we linger in this world God's word will never reach us, and we will never lay hold of it. Yet not only must our minds be lifted high if we are to receive God's word, we must also submit to him, and must prove that we are not being false when we call him our God, and when we boast that we are his people. Consequently, whenever we come to church, we must have these two things in view: first, we must cast aside all earthly worries and concerns, all empty desires and other such things which stop us drawing near to God; second, we must feel such deep reverence for what we know comes from God that we receive and accept it without dissent, and that we allow him to place his yoke upon our necks, being ready and willing to bend beneath its weight. The main point to note here is that Jesus Christ has made it clear that he is the church's supreme teacher; on him the law and prophets all depended, and he is the goal to which all things tend. To learn this is work enough for one day. If we know why our Lord Jesus Christ was given to us and what task the Father gave him to perform, we should calmly bow to his will and receive instruction from him. That is one point.

There is another. Our Lord here ascribes authority to himself: we must hear him. In addition, he reveals the work which has been entrusted to him, and thus the sum and substance of the gospel. He has been sent, he says, *to proclaim salvation to those who are lost and condemned, to bring to life those who are in death, to give light to the blind, to free the captives and to heal the sick.*

In short, he shows us that his teaching bears witness to God's fatherly goodness, in that he has pity on those who are wretched and in dire distress. He desires to be merciful to them and to gladden them in their sadness. That is the tenor of this passage.

As the supreme teacher of the church, Jesus Christ has full control, for heaven rang with a voice commanding all of us to listen to him: 'This is my beloved son; hear him' (Matt. 17:5; Mark 9:7). With these words, our Lord is placed, as it were, in a pulpit, in order to teach us that it is for him alone to be God's messenger and to testify to his will. Admittedly, he is not now living on earth and doing the work of a teacher, but it is in his name and by his power that this work is done.

When it is said that *this Scripture has been fulfilled in your hearing*, it is not that this saying does not also apply in part to all the prophets who went before. When the prophet Isaiah says, 'The Spirit of the Lord is upon me, and has anointed me to be a messenger of God's grace' (Isa. 61:1), without doubt he would also say the same of those who came after him—especially Haggai, Zechariah and Malachi—who lived after the return of the people from exile, when God set up his church once more, bringing about a restoration and leading to that perfect grace made manifest in the person of Jesus Christ. The prophets thus possessed God's Spirit and were sent as witnesses to proclaim his grace; yet they spoke by the Spirit of our Lord Jesus Christ, as Peter says (1 Pet. 1:11). Being directed by him, they brought nothing of their own. Since the time of the prophets, however, our Lord gave firm proof that he is our appointed teacher to testify to the grace of God his Father. Although he is not visibly present, he maintains his authority, so that we must all be scholars under him. Whoever speaks cannot fail to have Jesus Christ as his teacher.

Accordingly, Paul declares that when Jesus Christ came, he preached peace to those who were near, and peace to those who were far off (Eph. 2:17). Certainly our Lord did not preach the gospel to the Gentiles. If Paul says something different, it is because there is nothing in our preaching today which is ours; it is because Jesus Christ retains his right to teach. The fact that he uses us and our efforts does not detract from his worth or pre-eminence. Hence it is right to say that this prophecy was fulfilled in his very person. While the prophets indeed received God's Spirit, it was only in part, each according to his share. Jesus Christ, however, received grace in all abundance and in such perfection that we must draw on him. He is the only source who can fully satisfy. There was never a drop of the Holy Spirit in any mortal being except in and through our Lord Jesus Christ. He, I repeat, is the source from whom all blessing flowed, and continues still to flow.

We will understand this more readily, however, if we look more closely at the prophet's words: 'The Spirit of the Lord is upon me, for he has anointed me.' There is no question that what is meant here is the special unction which belongs to those to whom God entrusts public responsibilities. Now all believers without exception receive the Spirit of God, for neither flesh nor blood could ever contrive to grasp the message of salvation; and even if we had understanding, we could never be sure we were God's children or have any taste of our adoption, unless it were sealed in our hearts by the Holy Spirit. All the faithful, then, must together have the Holy Spirit, for by nature we are both blind and corrupt. In a word, our souls know only misery. The Spirit must, on the one hand, work in us to rescue us from the darkness of our ignorance; and on the other he must touch our hearts to the quick, and must put down all rebelliousness so that we yield to God.

Nevertheless, the Holy Spirit can fill us in a different way. It happens when someone is chosen and appointed to office. For example, when Saul was appointed king, he received, as we know, the Spirit of God (1 Sam. 10:10). Or when the prophets were called they received grace, without which they would have been useless. And when in former times God's servants and pastors were chosen, he endowed them with all that they needed to perform their duty. Paul therefore speaks of the grace given to Timothy by the laying on of hands, at the time of his commissioning (2 Tim. 1:6).

My point, then, is this. The Spirit of whom Isaiah speaks here is not what we call the Spirit of regeneration, by which God's children are made new. It is the Spirit of prophecy that is meant. Of course, as Paul says, there is only one Spirit. It is written that there is one God, one Lord, one Spirit (Eph. 4:4-6), but there is a variety of gifts, for God apportions the gifts of his Spirit as he pleases. The Spirit will equip one man for teaching, and will grant to another the gift of interpretation and exposition; to one he will give the gift of prophecy and to another the gift of writing. In promising these things, the prophet means that although all was in ruins when the Jews were deported to Babylon, God would nevertheless raise up prophets again, as was said in the fortieth chapter: 'God will say, "Comfort, comfort my people"' (Isa. 40:1). This shows that the punishment which God would send would only be temporary, and that he would yet have pity on the undeserving. Although they ought to rot and perish in their sin, God would again stretch forth his hand to them. Isaiah points also to the means God uses. Whatever riches our Lord pours out upon us, they can only do us good and we can only share in them, when we are taught by his word that he desires to be a Father to us.

Without faith, therefore, all of God's blessings fail to reach us, and we are like stones, so hardened that we find no profit in them which might lead us to salvation. As a result, Scripture says that God will send us prophets, but since this is beyond men's competence—for it is too high and difficult a task—the prophets are said to be clothed with heavenly strength and to be empowered by God. This is not a work in which men should meddle. Supposing I wished to testify to you concerning your salvation, would it matter much to you? Besides, as I said, no one can utter a single word unless the Holy Spirit controls his tongue (cf. 1 Cor. 12:3). Elsewhere Paul declares that no one can preach unless he is sent (Rom. 10:15). And to be sent implies that our sufficiency comes from above (2 Cor. 3:5); we cannot acquire it by our own hard work, our striving or by any other means. That is why Isaiah says that the Spirit of God is on Jesus Christ and on all who are his servants and instruments, and who, in his name and by his authority, proclaim the news of salvation.

Now many people boast of having God's Spirit. Moved only by recklessness and pride they worm their way in and disturb everything. That is why anointing is particularly mentioned here. There are many who picture God as a mere phantom; they are always carrying on about God, like those who call themselves 'Spirituals', but who are mad or simply senseless, or else downright arrogant.[1] The prophet Isaiah thus brings us back to the fact of God's anointing, as if to say that when God calls and commissions his prophets, this is no mere fiction. He stamps such marks upon them that we may know and judge that they have been sent by him. Anointing involves clear and present power, and gives us concrete proof that no one is claiming under false pretences to have been sent by God. Instead, he has all he needs and has God's full endorsement. That is the essence of what we are taught here.

It is clear, then, that because faith opens the way for us to share in God's blessings, we must make that our aim. We must

[1] The so-called Spirituals were a somewhat shadowy contemporary group with broadly mystical and pantheistic leanings, whose members laid claim to special revelation of the Spirit, and who were critical of a religion bound by the written word and a fixed creed. Cf. Calvin's treatise of 1545, *Against the Sect of the Libertines Called Spiritual*, IX-X, XV-XVI, XVIII-XIX.

not imagine that, apart from his word, God will allow us to enjoy the blessings promised to his children. It is by faith that we enter his church and are known and reckoned to be part of his flock. It is by faith that we are grafted into the body of our Lord Jesus Christ, and are thus made children of God, as we read in the first chapter of John (John 1:12). Since this is so, let us be all the more encouraged to hear God's word, for it is the key which opens the door by which we come to him, to be filled with every good and useful thing.

So that is one point. Without the preaching of God's word the world is completely lost. We must always remain accursed, having no hope of salvation. Is God willing to have pity on us and to demonstrate in a tangible way his mercy toward us? Then he sends us his word, so as to summon us to faith and to draw near to us; and not only to draw near but to enter in and dwell within us!

That said, it is important to note that when men have a certain gift for serving the church, it is not something they have acquired in their own strength or something they have inherited. It is a special gift, for as we know no one can even open his mouth to testify to God's grace or to propound wholesome doctrine, unless God's Spirit rests upon him—unless, that is, he has God's anointing. All of us, therefore, must humble ourselves, and those whom God has adorned and endowed and on whom he has poured his favours, must be aware that they are all the more indebted and beholden to God; they must walk in fear and trembling. When also we see that God sends us ministers of his word who so understand it that they can guide us along the path of salvation, let us recognize that we owe it to him, and let us gratefully give him the honour which is his due. That again is something to bear in mind.

We should now be able to see on what grounds the horned popish bishops call themselves prelates, pillars of the Catholic

Church, successors of the apostles and vicars of our Lord Jesus Christ.[2] There is nothing they do not claim for themselves. Yet where is the Spirit of God? One goes off to find him in the hunt, another at the gaming-table and another still in debauchery. What we see is awful ruin and profligacy, which defy not only God but nature itself. So it is that children are made bishops, or if of adult years they have hardly studied their ABC and can scarcely write their name; or else they will be warriors who always have a sword in their hand. Where, then, is the Spirit of God? Where is the mark of God's pastors and ministers which is spoken of here? For our part, let us learn to discriminate between those who call themselves pastors and those who really are, so that our Lord Jesus Christ may have sole dominion over us. This is the true obedience which we owe him. The papists speak well enough about humility, but in what does it consist? It is the kind which makes them answer God with scorn: in obeying men they openly defy God. They worship the pope's bulls, but what of Scripture? 'Oh,' they cry, 'it's a nose of wax, to be twisted any way you like!' Let us learn, then, to judge wisely and with discrimination, so that Jesus Christ always remains our teacher; and may all who teach and all who hear be scholars in his school. May nothing be done to diminish him in any way.

This passage from Isaiah contains the true sum and substance of the gospel. It is important that we remember this. It would not be enough to know that our Lord Jesus Christ is our chief teacher, whose instruction we must receive in all humility. We must also know what he brings to us, and for what task he was commissioned. If someone were to tell me: 'I have been sent by such-and-such a prince,' but if I then remained quite blank and simply said, 'Alright, come in,' that would be absurd. He might be a fraud or be set on committing a crime. We therefore

[2] 'Horned bishops', because the two points of the bishop's cap or mitre were called *cornua* (horns) in Latin.

need to test whoever it is who speaks, to discover whether or not God has sent him. If an edict is made public and the trumpet sounds, and if people run up but have no idea of what has been proclaimed, would that not be the height of foolishness? So it is not enough for us to know that Jesus Christ wishes to be heard, and that this is why he sends those he has made witnesses and ministers of the gospel. We must also know the substance of it.

Scripture says that Jesus Christ was anointed *to console the wretched and the afflicted, to heal the broken-hearted, to bind up their wounds* (for so Isaiah says), *to preach deliverance to the captives, to restore sight to the blind and to bring rest to the oppressed.* In short, there are many images here which all convey the same meaning, that the gospel is proclaimed because God has had pity on us and desires to lift us from the pit, out of the miseries in which we are plunged. The prophet could have said what he meant in one word, but he would not have so fully expressed the excellence of God's grace, nor would we have been moved enough to seek the blessing offered us.

How many are there who realize their plight? True, where our body is concerned we know how prone we are to sickness, how death threatens us on every hand, and that if today we have enough to eat and drink, famine tomorrow might press us hard. We are aware of these things, and according to how sensual we are we understand them to some degree. As for our souls, however, we are blinded by pride, and no one will admit to being a poor, sightless creature; no one feels his weakness and frailty; no one thinks that he is Satan's prisoner and is bound fast by the tyranny of death. And although we know in part—merely for form's sake—that we are poor and wretched, we are not so cut to the quick that we humble ourselves before God.

Pride and folly have always existed. Some people are puffed up with pride and will never admit that they are in the wrong. They want to be admired, despite the fact that they are rotten through and through; they want to be considered blameless, even though they deserve a hundred deaths. Where do our arrogance and pride come from, if not from those accursed passions which both excite and obsess us, from our ignorance of self, our lack of judgment, our sense of worth? This is how the proud knowingly deceive themselves. We might say the same about the foolish and the dull-witted. We might suppose indeed that they have some excuse. They are a poor and ignorant lot: if they fail, what can they do about it? Ah yes, but there is always an evil side to them. Even the most ignorant are capable of seeking material gain, and they never put a foot wrong. As to God's kingdom, however, as to the salvation of their souls, see how heedless they are, so that when they ought to be thinking about their plight their heads are empty. That is because they have deliberately chosen to be ignorant.

However that be, this is a fault which has prevailed in every age, just as it prevails today. Men cannot abase themselves because they do not know their misery. If they had some understanding of it, as they should, they would surely feel crushed. Not only would they be overcome with shame, they would be like men distraught. For anyone who asks, 'Alas, who am I?', when thinking of his condition, or who, when thinking of God, says, 'I must answer to my judge', will certainly reflect on these two things, and is bound to be chilled with fear. Truly, we can never think about God's grace without feeling that there is something amiss with us—much, in fact, which is worthy of rebuke.

For this very reason, Isaiah here lists so many kinds of misery and affliction. On the one hand he calls us prisoners and captives; on the other, he says that we are in extreme distress, poor and destitute of all good. Notice, then, that here God is extolling his grace in order to prepare us to receive it. It is only right that his grace should be clearly displayed to us, so that we may bless him for showing us such mercy. But to receive what he is offering, we must be empty of self-trust, for although we have nothing and are, in a manner of speaking, mere earthworms, we are still full to bursting—full, that is, of wind. Stupid ambition, pride and foolhardiness—that is what is in us, and the thought of these so fills us that God's grace finds no way in to us. We must thus be thoroughly purged and emptied, or else we cannot receive the blessing God wishes to give us.

Even so it is not enough to know that we are blind. We must also acknowledge that we are slaves of Satan, that he has his foot upon our throats, that he owns us and controls us; that we are in bondage to sin, wretched and poor, unable to lift a finger to do good or to think one good thought. We are destitute of goodness and have nothing in us which God commends. He condemns everything, since there is only corruption and rebelliousness in us. In a word, we must know that we are lost, and that we lack whatever is desirable for our salvation. We should therefore learn to put this teaching into practice, and when we fancy we are wise, or when some stray idea prompts us to ask, 'Would this not be right?', we should say, 'You poor blind soul, will you judge your own works?' Thus, believing ourselves to be blind, we must pray that God may enlighten us by his Holy Spirit, for up until now we have been in darkness.

Again, when we plan some undertaking, whereas the papists have their free will and various ways of preparing themselves for God's grace, how will we prepare ourselves, given that we are in shackles, bound hand and foot, and with a rope already around our necks? We who are prisoners of Satan and who, to use Paul's phrase, are sold under sin (Rom. 7:14), we who endure captivity worse than that of galley slaves who are tormented night and day, how could we find a way of escape? Let us acknowledge, then, our spiritual imprisonment, and turn to what is written in the eighth chapter of John: 'If the Son makes you free, you will be free indeed' (John 8:36). Our entire freedom lies in the fact that Jesus Christ is our deliverer. The same applies to everything else. Our wounds are fatal, and cannot be cured unless God is pleased to send us his word which brings us true health, for we are not merely sick, we are dead. Our Lord Jesus Christ refers to this in one of the images noted by John in his fifth chapter: 'The time is coming when the dead will hear my voice' (John 5:25). Paul makes the same point in the second chapter of Ephesians, a text we have already quoted (Eph. 2:1).

We must think hard about this passage and put it into practice, the more so as, in addition to God's word, the holy Supper will be ministered to us next Sunday.[3] May we know the purpose for which we gather at this holy table. If our Lord Jesus Christ is our food and drink, we should be hungry in ourselves. Remember that we cannot enjoy God's blessings, or any of the spiritual benefits in which our salvation, happiness and joy are found, unless we are brought low and earnestly feel our misery and affliction. That is how we must prepare ourselves.

Knowing, then, that we are captive to sin, that we are Satan's prisoners and mortally wounded, let us long for the deliverance which is offered to us, and to which the gospel daily testifies. Let us long for the blessing obtained for us by our Lord's death and passion. May he confirm the grace held out to us, and may we feel its reality and power. This he will do, providing we receive by faith the promises of salvation made to us, and may we not doubt that he, to whom God's Spirit has been given in all his fullness, will cause us to share in him, each according to his measure, and as he knows is fit and needful for our salvation.

Now let us cast ourselves down before the majesty of our good God, acknowledging our faults, and praying that he may help us so to feel them that we are brought back to him. May we at the same time know the deliverance which we have in Jesus Christ, so that we may give to him our full obedience.

[3] See above, p. 31, note 6.

12

SCRIPTURE IS FULFILLED

'The Spirit of the Lord is upon me, because he has anointed me to preach good news to the poor, to heal the broken-hearted, to proclaim deliverance to the captives and the recovering of sight to the blind, to set free those that are oppressed, [19] *and to preach the acceptable year of the Lord.'* [20] *He rolled up the book, handed it back to the attendant and sat down; and the eyes of all in the synagogue were fixed on him.* [21] *And he began to say to them, 'Today this Scripture has been fulfilled in your hearing.'* [22] *And all bore witness to him, and were astonished at the gracious words which came from his lips; and they said, 'Is not this the son of Joseph?'* (Luke 4:18-22).

WE have already explained how and why this passage from Isaiah is applied to the person of our Lord Jesus Christ. None of the prophets who ever lived could have set forth God's grace and mercy except in his name and by the power of his Holy Spirit. And although in their time he was not living on earth, it was nevertheless his right to testify to the will of God his Father, by which the world would be reconciled to him. At the present time, although our Lord has been raised to heavenly glory and is separated from us, we must accept the gospel message as coming from his own lips, for it is in his name that we proclaim the forgiveness of sins and invite those who were lost and condemned to become heirs of salvation, for God desires to be favourable to them.

Now because Jesus Christ has been sent to us *to give light to the blind, to comfort the oppressed and to free the captives*, it remains for us to acknowledge the evil within us. Otherwise we would not be able to accept the blessing which these words hold out to us: 'Come to me, you who labour and are heavy laden; I will relieve you, and you will find rest for your souls' (Matt. 11:28-29). So before we can receive light from our Lord Jesus Christ, we must know that we are poor blind souls, wandering in darkness and plunged into the depths of hell. We must know that there is no strength in us, only weakness, and that we are even more powerless than miserable cripples who cannot lift a finger. We must realize that we are not only in bondage to Satan's tyranny and to death, but that we are completely accursed. When we have examined all that is in us, and thoroughly considered what we are like, we will have every reason to condemn ourselves. Until we reach that point, we cannot possibly draw near to Jesus Christ, nor can we obtain access and entry to his grace.

To recognize these things means that we must first be brought low and humbled before God, and feel such distress that we find no rest but groan because of our misery—until, that is, God provides the remedy. For if evil is not displeasing to us, how can we seek the good? And if we are not repentant, how can we want God to receive us to himself? As long as we wallow in our filth, we flee from God as much as we can. This, then, is what we must remember.

We come now to the verse which says that Jesus Christ was sent *to preach the acceptable year of the Lord*. It is true that under the law there was the Jubilee, whose aim was to bring all things as it were to a new beginning. It was when slaves were freed (Lev. 25:39-40); in short it was a way of bringing order out of confusion. There is no doubt that the prophet meant to say two things here. First, the salvation which the gospel offers us comes from God's free grace; we are not to seek the reason for it. Second, it is not for us to hurry God along so that he might finish his work. He has determined his own time, and we must bow to his purpose and decree.

As to the first point, the Holy Spirit meant to rule out and deny any merits or worth which we might claim. The expression which the prophet uses implies pure goodwill, the generosity which God extends to us. He finds nothing in us deserving of acceptance, yet he does not fail to receive us in love. Indeed it is our wretchedness which has led and prompted him to show us mercy. His good pleasure is thus the cause on which our salvation depends, for if we ourselves could induce him to be good to us, if we had some inner disposition or if he could find some reason to treat us favourably, praise for our salvation would be half owed to us. Since, however, we are bare and empty of all goodness, since we are loathsome and accursed from the moment of our birth, that is why God's goodwill and free favour must prevail whenever he receives us in mercy.

Notice, however, that the faithful had always to be kept from going astray and from losing heart if, from the very first, God did not assist them. We remember how the fathers who lived under the law languished in the days when the church was wholly ruined and laid waste. They might well have been like men distraught. Hence the prophet reminds them of the year of God's goodwill. It is as if he said, 'Wait patiently, although it is hard for you to suffer such oppression. And if you suffered more than you do, and if every minute of the day it was as if a knife were held to your throat, you must nevertheless wait until the years have passed. And supposing, after living in such misery, you were to die without seeing how God planned to restore his church, know that he will finally have mercy on his people.'

In sum, the fathers who were living then are here exhorted to persevere, lest they be discouraged beyond measure, even though what God had promised them was not at once fulfilled, and even though they saw no sign of it.

What we are taught here is something that we too should apply today. While our Lord Jesus Christ has appeared, and while we have in him the very fullness of what is needed for our salvation—for as he said, when dying, 'It is finished' (John 19:30)—our salvation is, of necessity, hidden. We hope for it, as Paul writes in the eighth chapter of Romans: 'What we hope for, we do not visibly see' (Rom. 8:24). Experience amply shows that we must patiently await God's grace when it seems to be somehow withdrawn from us. Naturally we have sure and infallible proof of it in the gospel, but from the very first, reality does not always match God's word. We still have to groan on account of our present bondage; we drag our ropes and shackles after us; we are still plunged into darkness, and we see death assailing us on every hand. Faith must therefore do its work and keep us in check, until God speaks the word and solidly confirms what is told us in the gospel.

Isaiah makes this point more clearly in his forty-ninth chapter, when he says, 'God has answered his people at the acceptable time; he has helped them on the day of salvation' (Isa. 49:8). The prophet then goes on to urge the people to seek the Lord while he may be found, and to call upon him when he is near (Isa. 55:6). Let us put this teaching, therefore, into practice, and let us be sure that our Lord will answer us, not only when we believe in him, but because his grace goes before us. When he rescues us from perdition, we are like lost beasts which he takes and draws into his flock, all of his own free will. So since we know that out of pure grace he has brought us to himself, let us not be rebellious or ungrateful for the goodness that he shows us. May we reach out to it at the acceptable time. As Paul says, the day of salvation is when the gospel is preached (2 Cor. 6:2). Let us make sure we heed it. Again, in the fourth chapter of Galatians, Paul speaks of the fullness of time, meaning that God, having determined in his counsel to have mercy on wretched sinners, did not at first display his grace in the person of his only Son, but held it back until the appropriate time (Gal. 4:4). Now what is it that makes a time 'appropriate'? We must ascribe it to God's own counsel. He must be free to do as he chooses; his authority must prevail; he cannot behave according to our likes and dislikes. That is the lesson for us in this passage.

Isaiah, as well as speaking of God's good pleasure and free favour, also foretells the year of his vengeance, showing that God is mighty enough to crush and overthrow all our enemies (Isa. 61:2). He demonstrates, too, a most marvellous power when he brings us from death to life, and from condemnation to salvation. The devil, we know, is called the prince of this world (John 12:31). He rules over us and has us under his control. He is armed and equipped, for what else is sin? We ourselves know full well that the enemies we deal with are far too strong. Miserable men are forever struggling, unable to master their evil passions. Paul himself, who made so much progress in God's school, nevertheless exclaims: 'Wretched man that I am, who will deliver me from this body of death?' (Rom. 7:24). If such a man could not manage to serve God freely because he was hampered by weakness and by the sin still dwelling in his nature, must we not be completely senseless if we do not feel our limitations, and if we do not see that God must work to help us ponder heavenly things and the message of his kingdom?

The prophet therefore declares that although the devil, the world, sin and death conspire to destroy us, God will overcome them all, and the grace he shows us will always be victorious. It is as we read in the tenth chapter of John: 'The Father who has given you into my hand is mightier than all' (John 10:29). Accordingly, our Lord Jesus Christ teaches us to defy our enemies, for God will prove how strong he is—yes, infinitely strong—when it is a question of removing all that hinders our salvation.

Let us, however, take thought to ourselves, for without doubt God's vengeance is ready to fall on all the rebellious and unbelieving. The thanklessness of those who reject Jesus Christ cannot be left unpunished. When, therefore, our Lord threatens his enemies and ours with such terrible retribution, he intends that those who block their ears and refuse to be taught should tremble. That is why we should think hard about ourselves, lest we be among those he threatens. May we be conscious of God's power to protect us. Let this be our assurance, since we know that he is willing to display his power to uphold and defend us against all that would divert us from the way of salvation.

Observe what next the prophet has to say. Those who weep will be invited to rejoice; those with sackcloth on their backs and with dust in their hair will have cause to boast, for they will be made glad when they are lifted up again by the hand of God (cf. Isa. 61:3). Thus, to have light from our Lord Jesus Christ, to be set free once more, to be plucked from the deepest hell and to rise to the life of heaven, we must weep and seek life only in him. No one will ever rejoice as he should in Jesus Christ unless he gives him the tears and groans mentioned here, and acknowledges that he stands condemned. At the same time, consider Isaiah's aim in setting all this before us: we must be trees of righteousness planted by God's hand (Isa. 61:3). In using the word 'trees', the prophet means that we must be nurtured so that we hallow God's praises, dedicating our lives in obedience to him, and bringing our wills and works into conformity with his law, his commands and his wishes. So much, then, for that point.

Now because we cannot do these things by ourselves or by our own efforts, the prophet says that God must plant us, for from our mother's womb what else do we bring but defilement? And even if we had some guidance and direction, we would always be inclined to wickedness. Our heart is nothing but a flaming furnace which does not cease to send forth plumes of evil passion and endless greed. Until God provides us with roots and plants us with his hands, we can only produce the fruit of iniquity. That is the message of this text. We should take it in, not only by assenting to it—saying merely, 'That is so'—but by showing that we are truly touched, and that God has planted us that we might glorify him by living righteously.

In the verse that follows, Luke adds that *Jesus Christ sat down, and said, 'Today this prophecy has been fulfilled in your hearing.'* Nevertheless they did not fail to answer back. '*What*,' they said, '*this is Joseph's son!*'

The first thing to notice is that, in saying that the prophecy had been fulfilled in their hearing, our Lord rebukes them for their malice. Instead of being thrilled and aroused by God's priceless goodness, they remained drowsy; they gave no sign of excitement, emotion or zeal, but were like blocks of wood. They might have seen him a hundred times: they would never have recognized him as the Redeemer. It was not his physical appearance that might have brought them to that point. It would have taken the witness of the Holy Spirit to convince them, and to make this passage from Isaiah so clear to them that there was no longer any ambiguity which might have left them wavering or in doubt. They should have had assurance that the time had come when God would gladly gather them in and free them from all their misery. The time had come, I say again, when God would willingly restore them and bring them from death to life.

Thus, in telling them that what Isaiah had foretold had been fulfilled in their hearing, Jesus Christ upbraids them for their dullness and stupidity. Satan must indeed have possessed them, since nothing could induce them to desire God's grace and to accept it with fervent feeling. As we saw earlier, the Jews were like people in a wilderness: all was confusion in their midst. Their outward state clearly confirmed all that had been said about their bondage to sickness and affliction. They had been robbed and eaten up, devoured and trodden down; they had been disgraced. In a word, they were a people lost. If they had not been so unfeeling, so filled with the stench of their misery, they might have thought, 'Alas, what will become of us? If the promise which we have has come from God, should we not look to him? Should we not show him how sorry we are, that he may have mercy on us?' By reckoning up the days and years they might have had assurance of their redemption. But supposing they were forgiven for their slowness to comprehend, when our Lord Jesus Christ comes forward and shows that in him God makes his will known, not as in a picture but in actual fact; and when he declares that this is what God meant when he spoke by the mouth of the prophet—when this fails to either touch or move them, are they not like madmen, having no more sense or reason than brute beasts? Our Lord in any case is right to tell them that this prophecy has been fulfilled in their hearing.

Consider now whether the same charge may not be laid against us, to our deep shame. Every day the news that God's Son has come to bless us and to make us his heirs is drummed into our ears, so that we know with certainty that nothing will be denied us. So now that we have seen this evidence, not for one day only but by night and day, as often as we hear it, and now that God himself keeps giving us ever more assurance, if we continue to wallow in our filth, what excuse do we have? Must not such laziness provoke God's wrath? Since, therefore, the faithless are told that this prophecy has been fulfilled in their hearing, let us make sure that we know how to stand apart from them. Let us resolve, in other words, to be different. Moses explains how this is done, and Paul also cites the text to demonstrate how thankless we are if we do not profit from God's word. 'The word,' says Moses, 'which I give to you today will testify against you. I call heaven and earth as witness, that I have shown you the way of salvation' (cf. Deut. 30:14-15; Rom. 10:8). As Moses points out, we do not have to go over the seas or to climb above the clouds (Deut. 30:12-13). Why not? 'Because,' he says, 'the word is in your mouth and in your heart.' When God graciously instructs us and pierces our very ears so that we might hear his will, and when we also have his word in our mouth—that is, when we genuinely confess it—let us then reply, 'Amen!' May we accept it with willing hearts, showing that our delight, our happiness, is in possessing Jesus Christ and in enjoying the unfathomable blessings offered to us in him.

Since, however, hypocrites can also make confession with their mouth, the heart must go before, and may the things that we profess come from that root. So when God's word has its seat in our hearts and feelings, it will not only be in our ears to condemn us and to make us inexcusable before God. We should think even more carefully about this when we see the example which the Evangelist sets before us. It would seem that those who heard our Lord Jesus Christ really benefited, for what is said is worthy of praise: *They were astonished.* Not only did they recognize that he was speaking the truth, *they marvelled at the gracious words they heard.*

Be that as it may, this is not said in order to praise them, but rather to add to the gravity of their offence, and to show that they were even more guilty by not being cut to the quick, and by not willingly submitting to the gospel. They were stunned as if by a hammer blow. It was enough for them to bow their heads before a message which they should have savoured, and which, once savoured, should have fully satisfied them. It was merely a sound in their ears; it did not have the right taste which might have made them accept it as their spiritual food. Thus they are condemned by what may seem so commendable a thing, that is, their marvelling at our Lord's words.

For our part, to all this we must add such obedience that we persevere, seeking only to profit and to advance once we are on the right path. May God's word be sweeter to us than honey, as we read in Psalm 19 and again in Psalm 119 (Psa. 19:10; 119:103). For this to happen, remember what we said before: when God offers us his grace, he wants us to accept it every time the gospel is proclaimed.

It is true that when we read here of 'gracious words', Luke means those words in which the Holy Spirit's power was manifest. Jesus Christ possessed such skill that it was obvious none of this came from man, but openly revealed the power of God. We should, however, take the word 'gracious' in another sense, having a different resonance than it had for those there present. As Luke records both in the second and the fourteenth chapter of Acts, our Lord confirmed by signs and miracles the doctrine of grace (Acts 2:2-4; 14:3), namely that God is favourable to us, assisting us in time of need, loving us, not imputing our sins to us, wanting us to know him as our Father and blotting out all that might make us hateful in his sight, so that, at the judgment, he remembers it no more. In this sense the gospel is the word of grace. In the twentieth chapter of Acts, Paul, having spoken of his imminent death, commends his brethren 'to God and to the word of his grace' (Acts 20:32). He thus teaches us to commit ourselves to the protection of him who is mighty enough to support us, but at the same time he reveals the way and means by which we are preserved, and by which God maintains our salvation. It is by the word of grace, by which we have unfailing proof that God loves us and is merciful to us. He chooses not to call us to account or to impute our sins to us. In his pure mercy, his generosity and unmerited goodwill, he is reconciled to us, so that we are certain of his love and can flaunt our defiance of the devil, death and sin.

Now this is something we should take to heart. If we do, we will not be like those wretches who said, 'He is only Joseph's son.' Thus they shut the door through their ingratitude and ill-will. They ought to have thought, 'This is Joseph's son, but in what school was he brought up? He is, after all, a carpenter.' Yet, as we see, he was as it were an angel come from God, far above the prophets. Knowing this, they should have been led to exalt his authority even more, to give themselves to him more freely and to accept his teaching with greater zeal. Instead they say, 'This is Joseph's son.' They finally feel that all of God's grace which they have seen in him is nothing, and that the power of the Holy Spirit is only smoke and emptiness.

Must not those, then, of whom this passage speaks, have been dumb and brutish, possessed of devilish stupidity? This is nevertheless written for our sake, to teach us to overcome whatever might cause us to stumble, to turn aside and to prevent our giving God the obedience of faith, as is his due. One thing is sure: we will always meet similar stumbling blocks, for Scripture says that the message and preaching of the cross is an offence to the Jews and folly to the Gentiles (1 Cor. 1:23). God's word will be despised by many who pretend to be clever or who like to speculate about one thing or another. Scripture's style is not to their liking: they want something which gratifies the ear, as if listening to some pleasant melody. They therefore contrive to throw everything aside on the pretext that it is not to their taste. Then too, the proud and arrogant of this world will never allow God to have what is his. Some try to be wise in their own conceits; others have an inflated opinion of their rights and see themselves as equal partners with Jesus Christ; unwilling to trust God's mercy, they want to be important, though in fact they are nothing.

Such people are enemies of God's righteousness. They want to diminish it and to tread it down in order to elevate themselves.

That is how people come to stumble. The devil also has many means of troubling our sight in order to dazzle us, so that we fail to acknowledge Jesus Christ and to understand his powers and the gifts he seeks to share with us. To receive the good things which the gospel contains and the treasure of salvation offered to us there, let us first learn to overcome the things that make us stumble.

How should we begin? By humbling ourselves, so that we pay God homage and exalt him as is his right. For it is not enough to know that God exists, without knowing what is strictly his. So when we say that he alone is the fount of life, we should remember that we are in death. When we say that he alone is wise, we should remember that we are poor and blind, completely senseless. When we say that he alone is righteous, we should recognize that there is only sin in us. This is what we have to do if we do not want to be like those who are so sensitive that they cannot bear it when God scratches a sore spot, or puts them in a bad light in order to make them ashamed, both before him and before men. They cannot bear to let God condemn them, yet there is no other way for him to absolve us if we do not first condemn ourselves. Now since we have so benign a judge who only wants to settle differences with us, unless we are completely wayward we should have no trouble agreeing with what he says, and simply consenting to what might be hard and painful for us to stomach. We will therefore find that Scripture is so much to our taste that, while we may not understand many things which are too high or puzzling for us, we will surely grasp, in outline and in detail, all that is necessary for our salvation, to the extent that God knows is right and proper for us.

To conclude, let us now apply this to the Lord's Supper which is prepared for us here. We know that, in addition to the message of the gospel, God, in his unfathomable goodness, seeks to put our eyes to work, giving us firm assurance of what the gospel teaches. When the Supper is offered to us, it is as if our Lord Jesus Christ were present in our midst. If he condemned those to whom he showed his power for failing to benefit from it, what will he do today when he provides a further help? For it is his word I now proclaim, and it is by his command that we hear the promises which call us to himself. As well as our ears we have eyes, so we have no excuse if we are not disposed to receive him or to allow him to fulfil all that out text contains. Let us prove that he has not spoken in vain when he promises to free the captives, to comfort the broken-hearted, to bring light to those in darkness, to heal the sick and to cure all who are in anguish and distress. What will happen if we fail to benefit from this holy Supper as we should, since here we have God's word joined to the sacraments? Those to whom Luke refers were, as we see, condemned. With one word, our Lord disposes of all their tricks. 'It is enough,' he says, 'you have heard what I say.'

Now that we have heard him and have seen him as he is in his word and sacraments, how much fewer are the excuses that we have! True, all we have here is bread and wine. These are not things which can make us certain of the salvation of our souls: they are food which passes away—as Paul says, 'food for the belly' (1 Cor. 6:13). Nevertheless, we glimpse our salvation in them so far as is expedient and according to our frail means. If Jesus Christ had thought that it would help us, he would have opened the heavens and given us a clear view of his glory. He knows, however, what suits us best, and not without cause he has ordained this as a pledge for us. All we see is the bread, but let us be content to have the voice which says, 'This is my body.' All we see is the wine, yet Jesus Christ affirms that we receive, and share in, the blood he shed for our redemption. Of course the bread and wine are not our Lord's body and blood, as the papists foolishly imagine; but he did not bring us empty symbols in order to entertain us, as if some comedy were being acted on a stage.

Our Lord Jesus Christ thus accomplishes, in truth and by his own power, what surpasses our comprehension and our natural intelligence. He accomplishes, I say again, everything he promises and sets before us. So may his voice resound in our ears and in our hearts. Whenever we take the bread and wine, God's word testifies to us that Jesus Christ his Son gives himself to us. Let that be our sure and certain conviction. If that is not sufficient, do we think that if we clear ourselves we will be absolved by God, we who are guilty of such ingratitude?

Understand that when Jesus Christ gives himself to us to be our food, and when by these symbols he shows that he both nurtures us and brings us to maturity, he seeks to assure us that all his benefits are also bestowed on us. He does not come to us naked and empty-handed, nor does he come poor. For, as Paul says, he became poor once, so that we might become rich (2 Cor. 8:9). He was weak and lowly, so that we might be made strong by his invincible power. Therefore we must clothe our Lord Jesus Christ with all the graces which are wholly his, so that we may draw on him, confident that in him all things are ours, and that there is nothing else we could want.

For the rest, when the Supper is ministered to us, it is as if God were saying, 'Although you deserved to perish in hell where you lay before I drew you to myself, I wish to make you heirs of the kingdom of heaven. I offer it to you in the person of my Son, in whom the fullness of deity dwells.' Having, then, this testimony, must we not be worse than mad if we are not moved to dedicate ourselves to his service, and to honour him with all our strength and soul?

The holy Supper therefore provides not only a vivid picture for us, but an earnest and pledge that this very day God wills to free us from our captivity, to draw us from darkness to light, to give us healing instead of sickness and gladness instead of distress. Let us learn, as I said before, to rejoice amid our sadness, for we do not yet enjoy the things for which we wait and which our Lord has won for us. Nevertheless we find that in his death and passion all has been fulfilled, and has been so confirmed that we are led further on to the hope which, day by day, is set before us in the gospel.

Since we have these things, even though our enemies assail us on every side and although it seems that we must forever tremble, we should not doubt that our Lord is strong enough to aid us in time of need. And when we are hidden beneath his wings, we will be defended from all dangers which might fill us with alarm. What, after all, is the poor church? We are in the mouths of wolves! And what is our condition? Let us learn, then, to turn to him who promises to treat us kindly and with favour, as long as we allow him to protect us. On the other hand, he will terrify our enemies whom we may thus defy, having this testimony, that Jesus Christ lives in us by the power of God his Father. And although we can only receive it according to the measure of our faith, his power will always be complete. Whatever faults and weaknesses remain, they will not stop him guiding and upholding us until we reach the goal to which he calls us.

Now let us cast ourselves down before the majesty of our good God, acknowledging our faults and asking him so to touch us that they may cease to please us. May he bring us to such repentance that we feel thoroughly ashamed, until he clothes us with the gifts of his Holy Spirit; and being made new, may we conform to his will and righteousness.

13

CLOSING THE DOOR TO GOD

And he said to them, 'Surely you will quote to me this proverb, "Physician, heal yourself. What we have heard you did at Capernaum, do also in your own country."' [24]*And he said, 'Truly I say to you that no prophet is acceptable in his own country.* [25]*But in truth I tell you, there were many widows in Israel in the time of Elijah, when the heaven was shut up for three years and six months, when there was a great famine throughout the land;* [26]*and Elijah was sent to none of them except to Sarepta, in the land of Sidon, to a woman who was a widow.* [27]*And there were many lepers in Israel in the time of the prophet Elisha; and none of them was cleansed except Naaman the Syrian'* (Luke 4:23-27).

ALTHOUGH, as we have seen, God's majesty is clearly revealed in his word, many people try wickedly to obscure it. They scarcely discern it, and in the end, having scorned it, they are wholly alienated from it. This is a sin which has prevailed in every age, and would to God it were not so widespread as it is today! What the Evangelist tells us here is something we see with our own eyes. God gives such power to his word that even the most wicked are stupefied and dismayed. Yet they look for some reason to take offence, and to denigrate and vilify God's glory, however clearly it is displayed.

Accordingly, we are told here that Jesus Christ sought to deny the people of Nazareth every excuse, by quoting something they themselves might say, that the teaching which they had heard from his lips had not been confirmed by miracles. His fame had spread everywhere, and he had shown and proved in actual fact that he was an outstanding prophet. The Jews did not yet understand that he was God's Son: they had to advance gradually in their knowledge of him. Nevertheless the land of Judaea was filled with his fame, since he had performed many miracles.

Now the citizens of Nazareth might have said, 'We've seen none ourselves. Why don't you show yourself to us as well? If we had seen such evidence, we would be happy to accept you as a prophet—yes, even as Redeemer! But since we have only heard you speak, since we have your words with nothing to confirm them, we cannot believe in you.' Our Lord's reply is that it would not be right for God to cast his miracles to the ground where they can be trampled on. He wants them to be accepted as they deserve to be, with all reverence, that his power might be acknowledged and that he himself might therefore be worshipped and glorified. Yet the Nazarenes were not like that. Already we noted that they had been compelled to marvel at the teaching which came from Jesus Christ, revealing as it did the Holy Spirit's grace and power. Despite this, they simply said, 'This is Joseph's son.' Out of settled malice and ingratitude they closed the door to God. Our Lord Jesus Christ, then, reproaches them for making it impossible for God to work powerfully in them, because they shut their eyes to the light and would even have liked to veil the sun so that it ceased to shine. That is the gist of his reply.

In addition, however, he points to two examples in order to confirm his words, for those who scoff at God want miracles to happen on demand; they want God to entertain them. That is how they mock his majesty, which they ought to worship. Our

Lord thus tells them that *in Elijah's time there were many poor widows, for famine was everywhere in the land.* Not a drop of rain fell for three and a half years, since God wished to punish Israel for its idolatry. All was barren, so that everyone cried famine. Yet the prophet did not aid any of the widows in Israel, but did a miracle for a poor foreign woman, a pagan who did not belong to God's people, to the line of Abraham which of all nations boasted of being holy. What shall we say to that? So here is a poor widow who welcomes God's prophet and whom God feeds as long as the famine lasts (1 Kings 17:9-16). 'Thus,' says Jesus Christ, 'do not presume to bind God to yourselves so that he does his mighty works whenever you want him to.' It was the same when Naaman the Syrian came for healing (2 Kings 5:10-14). *There were at that time many lepers in Israel, yet none of them was healed.* 'But see,' he says, 'here is a heathen man who never knew anything about the living God, steeped in error and superstition, who was miraculously healed. Now go and tell God that he must serve you as you think fit, as if you had his power up your sleeve!' 'No, no,' he says, 'God must be free to display his power by means of miracles just as he pleases. It is not for us to bind him to our laws and wishes.'

To help us better understand this teaching and to get most benefit from it, see what our Lord says next: '*Physician, heal yourself.*' Imagine a doctor who claims to be able to heal all illnesses, but who is seen to languish and to be sickly in body. Supposing he is told, 'Why don't you look after yourself?', and he replies, 'I don't know what's wrong with me, I can't find a cure that helps', what will men say, except that he is an arrogant fool and a deceiver? Can he really diagnose a complaint which he does not feel, better than one he feels in his own body? So the proverb is to be taken as an analogy, showing that those who try to advise others but cannot help themselves in time of need are not worth welcoming.

It would be like a man who at home is either extravagant or foolish, and who goes away leaving everything to go to pot, as we say. His wife is a drunkard, and his serving men and women pilferers, so that one thieves and another robs. If a man who was so stupid in his own home were to say, 'I'm going to counsel my neighbours, telling them how to live properly, how to protect their wealth and how to run their households', would we not laugh at such an idiot, and would we not at once retort, 'What a fool he is to foist his advice on others, but not to follow it himself. He wants to lead others, yet don't we see how he rules his own house and what a mess it is?' The same might be said of the alchemists who promise to make everyone rich. 'Look, I have knowledge which will make the whole world wealthy, for in three months someone who invests fifty crowns will get ten thousand.' In short, if we listened to their bluster, the world would be awash with crowns and ducats! Yet they are no more than wretched ruffians, miserable rogues who do not have a penny in their purse; and if they ever have had sufficient, they will have spent it in their folly. They will try to make it up by huffing and puffing, and they will huff and puff every chance they get. Still, as I said, we always see them poor and badly dressed, yet they claim they can cover others with robes of gold cloth! They have nowhere they call home, yet they promise to create royal palaces for others!

That, then, is the point of the proverb, 'Physician, heal yourself.' It means that if someone wants to be considered influential and reliable as a counsellor of others, he must show that he has sense enough to behave properly. Paul therefore writes that if a man cannot manage his own household, how can he manage the church? (1 Tim. 3:5). If someone sets out to correct the faults of others by being their instructor, while he himself is as much or more at fault than anyone else; or if his wife, children and servants are known to be bad, it will doubtless be objected that he should look to himself and his family before looking to others. He himself will have none of it and is critical of everyone. 'Oh,' he will say, 'they sing rowdy songs in that house and lark about in the other.' In a word, he is so sharp in spying people's faults from afar that he misses none, whereas the offences committed in his own house are so shocking as to be plain to all, yet he sees nothing. This proverb is therefore right and proper; it conveys a sound lesson.

In any event, our Lord Jesus Christ informs the Nazarenes that they cannot ask him to perform some sign or to do in his own district what he did in other places. He rightly assumes that miracles are particular gifts of God which serve a specific purpose. They are not performed lightly, for no good reason. Given, then, that God displays his power by means of miracles so that he may be glorified and his word accepted, if a people is hardened in its wickedness and stubborn in its unbelief, is God obliged to do a miracle? He did do so among the heathen when he chose to, but it was to their greater condemnation. It was as if it were a final testimony to convince them that they were outright rebels against God. Nevertheless, here he did not observe quite the same measure, for Scripture says that Christ was not able to do miracles because of men's unbelief (Matt. 13:58; Mark 6:5-6). Not that he lacked power in himself, but it was not right that he should do them, which is why he refrained.

So the Nazarenes are silenced. They cannot criticize our Lord Jesus Christ for not confirming his message in their midst. Why was this, if not because they had closed the door to God, and had done all they could to resist the Holy Spirit's power? When that is the case, God cannot be impugned, nor can men claim any excuse, since they have refused to be humbled and to believe the gospel. They are to blame, and guilt is to be assigned entirely to them.

What was said about this people also applies to us today. There are many today who would like God to perform miracles, to show that he confirms the teaching of the gospel, which is widely disputed and about which there are many different views. Many people would like to settle matters by having God appear from heaven, raise the dead, heal the sick and calm the sea. But if we really think about these people, supposing they had all the miracles in the world, would they change on that account? Without a doubt all this would only serve to reveal their godlessness, to show that they are God's deadly enemies and that they conspire to disobey him. Shall we then say that the miracles which our Lord performed and which he commanded his apostles to do are useless to us? And that their power should not endure for ever? Their purpose was surely to confirm the truth of the teaching which is nowadays contested. These miracles, for all the good they do some people, lie buried and forgotten, as if nothing had been said of them. Nevertheless we preach them!

Thus we see that those who today want to force God to prove by miracles that the gospel comes from him, have no faith in it. Their thanklessness is clearly shown by the fact that they have every possible proof that God has endorsed the message that they resist. What is it, then, that explains their unbelief? Our Lord tells us through the prophet Isaiah, when he describes the Jews of his day as more senseless than the brute beasts: 'The ass knows its crib and the ox its stall, but God is not known by his people' (Isa. 1:3). The same is true of those who profess to be Christians and who boast of having been baptized, but who, when the message of Jesus Christ is put before them, will indeed bend the knee before the gospel and kiss it as they do with holy relics, but they refuse to taste and savour it. So because they are so stupid, having less intelligence and reason than oxen or asses, God should not be expected to display his miracles recklessly, or to allow these rogues to make fun of them and to criticize them at will.

We should thus think carefully about ourselves and follow this general rule: we must allow entry to all of God's gifts, otherwise we deserve to lose and forfeit them. If we did lose them it would be no use complaining to God that he had not been as kind, merciful and generous to us as to others, for whose fault would it be? That is the nub of the matter. What we would find is that we had tied God's hands as much as we were able and had pushed him far away, even though he was willing to draw near. In short, we must not want God to show himself to us by miracles, for it would be wrong to wish for them unless God inspired us to do this. And we know that he made an end of them because of men's ingratitude. We must not ask that the miracles done in former times be done again today. If, then, we want God to show himself to us, insofar as we may make a lawful request of him, let us resolve to give him a way in to us, as is said in the Psalm: 'Open your mouth, and I will fill it' (Psa. 81:10). The reason why the Lord withdraws his hand and does not give us his blessing as richly as we would like, is that our mouths are shut. Why? Because of our unfaithfulness. Through our ingratitude we scorn the good that he is ready to bestow on us. We scorn it, I say, and hold it in contempt. And what is worse, we cast it far away from us. That is one point.

As for the teaching which we find here, note that it was commonplace for the Jews to have this saying: *A prophet is not acceptable in his own country*. Now it often happens that an infant whom we first see at the breast, grows up to be stupid, so that at the age of fifteen he is scorned or admired a good deal less. Among the Jews, however, this saying has a different origin. It was meant to condemn their malice, in that the prophets were better received and enjoyed more respect among the heathen—among those who knew nothing of God—than among those who boasted that they belonged to the church and were of holy lineage. Thus although the heathen did not listen to the prophets, they did not murder them as happened in Judaea. In the days of Manasseh, Jerusalem flowed with blood (2 Kings 21:16). We know how furiously people persecuted God's true witnesses, and how hostile they were to their teaching. Inevitably there was open warfare, as God says to Jeremiah: 'They will fight against you' (Jer. 1:19). Among this people, then, God's servants were never heard in peace. But see how Jonah converts Nineveh, a city so large that it was like a nation. Its people never knew anything of God; they worshipped their idols. Yet when the prophet rebuked them they were immediately humbled; their only thought was to beg God for mercy. When they confessed their faults, they threw themselves down like guilty men and like poor miscreants around whose neck the noose already lay, beseeching God to have pity on them. So Jonah's preaching converted this very great people, who at that time were steeped in wealth, luxury and pleasures, and who possessed a whole empire in the east.

What, then, of Judaea? There the prophets were sometimes stoned, sometimes thrown into the fire and sometimes sawn in two (Heb. 11:37). In short, it is as if God's people had conspired with Satan to wage war on him and on his word. That, then, is why God willed this saying to be on everyone's lips: prophets were welcome everywhere except in their own country—that is, among those to whom they had been sent.

Now this has relevance also for us. The grace that God has shown us does not reach everybody. Many people, we know, are hungry for the message of salvation, but they are kept in such tight captivity that it is against the law for them to have sound and faithful teachers. Indeed, if it is merely rumoured that they are following true religion, it is a capital crime. There are many countries, therefore, which are deprived of God's truth which is freely available to us. Despite this, there are many here who have to be compelled to come and hear it; the church bell is rung, but there have to be edicts which prescribe punishment.[1] Even so, it is impossible to get people to come to church; and if they do come, they merely shrug it off. Some make fun of it, others engage in nit-picking arguments (for they do not come here to be taught), and others again pretend to prick up their ears and to listen attentively, but they still remain asses, as ignorant as on their first day.

Understand, then, that when God raises up people who purely proclaim his word, we are to welcome them, otherwise a curse on our rebelliousness! If we refuse this treasure or take no notice of it, God's word is too precious to be vilified. So when our Lord gives this privilege to us above other nations, when his word is purely expounded in our midst and proclaimed in its simplicity, we should be all the more moved to accept it. God makes us especially indebted to him by the grace he bestows on us, and when we show signs of spurning it, we can be sure that, supposing all the papists were saved and received God's forgiveness, we would perish wretchedly, for we would have offended God by rejecting so precious a thing which we should have valued. We ought to bear this in mind.

Let us consider now the two examples cited by our Lord Jesus Christ. *There were many widows in Israel during the famine, yet none was aided by the prophet except a poor woman from Sarepta in the land of Sidon*. Elijah visited her with such effect that a handful of flour and a little oil which she had, lasted until God caused it to rain. On the surface we might think that it was exceptionally harsh of God to allow so many poor widows and orphans to die of hunger. Of course! But we must consider why such barrenness had come about.

The prophets announced that the sky would become as brass and the earth as iron (Lev. 26:19). Now God gave the earth

[1] By Council ordinance, non-attendance at church services was punishable by a fine. Offenders might also be required to appear before the Consistory, the church court, to be admonished.

the power and task of conceiving and producing fruit, just as a woman conceives a child and after a time gives birth. Thus the earth conceives and feeds and nourishes us with its entrails, so to speak. The sun and sky must also play their part, for from them comes growth. The earth itself does not have sap or moisture to bring forth fruit unless it is helped. God, however, declares that he will make the earth and sky become hard, so that those who transgress his law will be caught, in a sense, between iron and steel. The earth will remain hard since they have rebelled against God and become hardened to his word. This was what had happened to Israel (1 Kings 16:29-33). The law of Moses contained ample advice that this would befall them, for although the other prophets had not yet written or said these things, the law gave them more than enough warning. Nevertheless, they threw off all restraint and forsook the living God. They worshipped idols, yet this was the land that God had set apart for his service and where he wished to dwell. On that account no one could claim to be innocent. What happened was what the prophet Jeremiah reproached his own contemporaries for: the men cut down trees, the women bundled them up and the children gathered them to make sacrifice to idols (Jer. 7:18). There was no one, great or small, who was not defiled by idolatry and superstition.

God cannot be accused of being too severe, even though he sent such affliction upon the earth, and even though there was the awful sight of widows and children dying of hunger. All were guilty. Since that was so, anyone wanting to lay a charge against God would be doubly—no, triply—at fault. We cannot see it, but do we have the eyes to contemplate God's perfect righteousness? Alas, far from it! Let us learn, then, that when God sends plagues, famine and other such things, we must tremble before his majesty and acknowledge him to be our judge, so that he who regards himself as perfectly innocent must humble himself, knowing that he and all his house must be called to account.

When God chooses to be strict, no one deserves to be spared, although he is always just and fair.

This is what we should remember when we read in the story of Elijah how all the widows in Israel were passed over. God did not come to their aid, but showed mercy instead to a poor woman who had lived among idolaters, had never been taught the law and who, dwelling in Sidon, had only heard of the prophets by hearsay, from her neighbours. When we read about this, let us learn not to lay down the law to God, as I said before, and let us not be driven by our arrogance to think that he should first be gracious to us rather than to someone else. The Israelites might indeed have claimed a certain eminence conferred on them by God. They had been circumcised and they bore the mark of God's adoption, having been set apart from all the rest. Accordingly, since God had by this external sign reckoned them to be his people, should he not also have blessed them instead of those who were considered outcasts? Yes, he should. But what are we to think when he bestows his grace on us more than on others, yet does so freely, without constraint? Everything which comes to us from him is undeserved. Hence the very best of men may say, 'God must begin his work in me, and must keep on working. And because he has begun, he will surely be mindful of the benefits I have already received from him.' That may be so, but, as I said, since God acts entirely out of generosity, we are in his debt, and he always remains completely free.

When we use God's gifts as we should, and not in a way contrary to his intention—ah then, he will certainly fulfil what is said in the twenty-fifth chapter of Matthew: 'There now, my good and faithful servant,' says our Lord, 'I set you over a little, which now will be made much greater, for to him who has, more will be given' (Matt. 25:23, 29). God will certainly ensure that his gifts endure forever, and that he will finish the work he has begun. He has bound himself to do it, but on this condition, that we refer everything we have received from him to his glory alone, and that we put it to good use.

In short, just as all of God's gifts are pure and holy when we hallow them by using them well and by our obedient service, so we profane and defile what he has dedicated to our salvation when we misuse it, and make it serve a purpose other than his glory. Is it right, after all, for us to enjoy God's gifts and graces if we mock him and spit on the good things he gives us? And should we presume to keep him, as it were, up our sleeve, telling him how to act? That is what this passage teaches us.

Now if we think of what God did, we might say that the people of Sidon were punished because of Israel's fault. If we ask why the land of Sidon was barren, it was because it was adjacent to Israel. Elijah had told the Israelites that because of their sins there would be neither dew nor rain for all those years. See how God's wrath burned so hot against the people that their neighbours also felt it! We should not be surprised, then, if God did not have mercy on Israel's widows or look with friendly eye to help them in their need. In the same way, if we today suffer ten times more than the ignorant and the blind who have never tasted the gospel message, can we really protest and hit back at God? Let us instead compare the ignorant with us who, knowing God's will, have nevertheless deliberately fought against him. We have resisted his righteousness, for there is so much evil in us, so much disdain, ingratitude and hellish obstinacy toward God. Do we think that we have anything to gain by hitting back at him?

Let us recognize, then, that it is we who are wrong, and if we suffer more than the ignorant do, God is judging us justly and fairly, because although we knew his will, we did not obey it as we should. Moreover, when we see God doing good to this one or that, but not in equal measure to us, let us not grumble. All our grumbling will serve only to aggravate our plight, and we will end up more shame-faced than ever. We should learn to receive calmly all that God sends us, and allow him when he chooses to bless others more than ourselves and to deal more generously with them. Let us not be upset by that, but let us glorify him, confessing that he does everything according to his righteousness, goodness, power and wisdom, and that he does nothing deserving our reproach.

Nor should we feel upset that we do not see the miracles done by God in former times, for he has given us gifts different to those he gave our fathers. Admittedly, we think he treated them with greater kindness, but if we recall what he has done for us, we will see that our lot is no worse, or is even better. Supposing, for example, that God was mean toward us: so far as his simple generosity goes, he is not bound by any rule. And as our Lord Jesus Christ reminds us, if someone treats one person more favourably than another, should the one who has received less look on it with an evil eye (Matt. 20:15-16)? As if people could not dispose of their goods any way they liked! Do we expect God not to enjoy the rights we accord to mortal men? Do we want him to have less authority? To be inferior to his creatures, so that he may not dispense his favours as and when he pleases? We must therefore let God allot his blessings just as he wills, and each of us must receive his given share, whether large or small.

This is the point to which we must return: it is we who prevent God, as much as we can, from treating us as kindly as we would like. We refuse his mercy, we close the door to him and we block out his power. So let us learn to attribute everything to our failings, and not only confess it with our lips but amend our lives, so that from now on we cease our opposition and receive what has been denied us.

We also read here of Naaman the Syrian. *Israel*, it is said, *had many lepers, but none was healed*. Naaman, the king of Syria's general, was afflicted with the disease. God sends him into Israel to be cured, thus choosing to display his power in a poor idolater. How, then, can God forget all about his people, to whom he shows no signs of his goodness or favour? To our way of thinking God is certainly to be condemned. We would regard him as wrong-headed and as acting for no good reason. But whatever we did or said, our arrogance would bring shame upon us. Let us learn to humble ourselves when God makes judgments that to our mind seem odd. It is not for us to lay down the law to him: his judgments are beyond our understanding. We should worship them in all humility and be sober lest we go astray. It would be to our everlasting loss if we judged God's works unthinkingly.

A second point to which we should always return is this: when God deprives men of his grace, it is with good cause. They cannot cope with it, and the fault is entirely theirs. Thus the king of Syria sent a letter concerning his general, saying that he had been informed that he should go to Israel to be healed (2 Kings 5:5). When Naaman arrived, the king of Israel was far from giving glory to God who had willed by this means to confirm the true religion. The king ought to have thought: 'Here, then, God seeks to be exalted. The king of Syria has his idols in which he trusts, but they can effect no cure. This man who has come for healing has called upon them a hundred thousand times, but has gained nothing. Now he has come to the living God whom Israel worships, though all around is superstition.' Now in Israel there still remained traces of the law, and Abraham's God was still renowned. It is as if God meant genuinely to seal his law to prove that this was the only pure and true religion in the world. But what does Israel's king do? 'Oh,' he says, 'I see that my neighbour is looking to catch me unawares (for the king of Syria was strong and powerful). He is looking for a chance to wage war on me, as if I had refused to heal his general. It will be a bad day if he does that to me' (cf. 2 Kings 5:7).

Here the king reveals his unbelief, and all his people were no better. Their filth and corruption had made them senseless, so that God's name was buried in the place where it should have been loudly proclaimed. They had, so to speak, stripped him of all his power; they thought that he was helpless, unable to defend his honour and to display his majesty in such a way that even the faithless would be convinced. Were the Israelites not thankless where God was concerned? Judge, then, whether he was not right to fight against their wickedness and to perform a miracle, since they had banished themselves by their rebellion and had veiled his grace. Even so, they still thought that God was tied and bound to them.

We should put this lesson into practice whenever God does good to those who do not know him. What possible objection could we make to him? It would be as if we raised our horns against him, to stop him handing out his gifts according as he chooses. Where would that get us? We are like devils who rise up against God whenever we grumble that he bestows his favours where he wills. We should therefore understand that when we have got so little from the many good things that God has done for us, and when today we make such ill use of them; when we cannot fruitfully employ the splendid gifts he has poured upon us—we should understand, I say, that we are rightly deprived of them, and that God cuts off our share because we do not acknowledge him as our Father, and because we cannot reckon up his benefits toward us, which should rouse us to bless him and to give ourselves to his service.

These are the things that we should gather from this passage. We must not be like those who thoughtlessly look for miracles, without knowing how or why, and who, as the saying goes, love to have God dancing to their tune. Let us not be so reckless, but let us learn from the miracles which God has done. And although they may not have been done to us, we should know that they belong to our salvation. We should allow God to enter in. 'Open your mouth,' he says, 'and I will fill it' (Psa. 81:10). Let us not refuse the blessings he is ready to give us, for we know that he is their ever-flowing source which never runs dry. So if he is pleased to prefer others to ourselves, let us not be jealous of them or begin to grumble as a result. Let us all be content with our portion, with our measure and our share. May we all, both great and small, glorify him together, knowing that if some receive more than others, it is to be employed for the common good, for the whole body of the church. Those who have less should know that this should give them cause to humble themselves, and to yield peaceably to those who show them the way that leads to God. Be assured, then, that God knows why he dispenses his temporal and spiritual gifts in varied measure. Let us allow him to work according to his purposes, and let us concede, without dissent, that all that he does is good, just and well-ordered.

Now let us cast ourselves down before the majesty of our good God, acknowledging our faults and begging him so to touch us that, more and more, we may rid ourselves of evil and come ever closer to him. May we be enriched with the gifts and graces that today we lack, and since we have strayed far from the right path, may he bring us back to it, and grant us to continue on until he draws us wholly to himself.

14

LIGHT AFTER DARKNESS

And leaving Nazareth he came and dwelt in Capernaum, a town close to the sea, on the borders of Zebulun and Naphtali, [14]*so that what had been spoken by the prophet Isaiah might be fulfilled:* [15]*'The land of Zebulun and the land of Naphtali, toward the sea, beyond the Jordan, Galilee of the Gentiles—*[16]*the people who lay in darkness have seen a great light, and on those who lay in the region and shadow of death, light has risen'* (Matt. 4:13-16).

When they heard this, all in the synagogue were filled with anger. [29]*And they rose up and put him out of the town, and led him to the edge of the mountain on which their town was built, in order to throw him down to the bottom.* [30]*But he passed through the midst of them and went away* (Luke 4:28-30).

WE saw last Sunday how, through their malice, men close the door to God when he is prepared to let them taste all of his goodness. It is true that he often uses a different method when he fights against their thanklessness and unbelief. He does good to them, unworthy though they are. Sometimes, however, we prevent him from doing good to us because we are gripped either by hypocrisy or rebelliousness. At any rate, we do not want to accept the benefits he generously bestows. It was for this fault that Jesus Christ reproached the Nazarenes.

Thus it is now said that *they were all filled with anger*, because he had unmasked the evil which they thought was well hidden. Their anger, so the Evangelist tells us, reached such a pitch that they were ready to *hurl him from the top to the bottom of the mountain on which their town stood*. So although he was known to be a native of that place, they so forgot themselves that they were prepared to commit murder, simply because of one word which they did not like. What this shows us is that those who are most guilty, those who most need to be rebuked for their faults and to be severely reprimanded, cannot bear to be touched. In the same way it often happens that the worse a sick person is, the more he rejects all remedies. If he has an inflammation, he trembles as soon as he sees someone coming near, and without anyone touching him he becomes so distressed that he takes vengeance on those who try to bring him relief and health.

This is how it is with those who are so controlled by the devil that they reject God, spurn his word and refuse all correction. We see all this as in a mirror, but not in order to condemn the Nazarenes. The Holy Spirit instead reveals to us the kind of people we are, before God gives us so meek a disposition that we allow ourselves not only to be taught by his word but to be rebuked and condemned, according as God thinks it necessary to tame us, and to make us teachable and pliant. This incident, however, will serve us best if we note that we will never be good scholars for God unless, as James reminds us, we are easy-going. 'Receive God's implanted word,' he says (James 1:21). How? 'With meekness', for it cannot find room in our souls until we are led to this consideration. Without doubt all men are, by nature, full of arrogance and faithlessness; they are also full of hypocrisy and are blinded by self-love; they shut their eyes to their own failings and wish to be indulged.

Do we want the gospel, therefore, to take root in us and to bear fruit to the glory of God? Here is where we must begin: we must hate being so ill-tempered, so completely intractable that God does not know, as it were, what to make of us. Let us learn to feel our affliction and to turn to the cure, praying that God may graciously master us, so that we bow beneath his hand and willingly accept his yoke. May we also ask him to treat us roughly if he should choose, by pointing out our sins and by threatening us. May this not make us worse as a result; may we not lose heart or depart from his word which is food for our souls. His word serves as medicine for our spiritual illnesses, and if it is somehow bitter to the taste, let us nevertheless submit to it. When we are sick, in order to save our life and obtain healing, necessity will surely force us to take really bitter potions, to be bled and to allow ourselves to be seared by cauteries or by other things still worse. Now if, for the sake of this fleeting life, we bring force to bear on our feelings, why, when our eternal salvation is at stake, cannot we make room for God's word? Will we, as I said, find God's word hard and harsh? Will the chastisements which it contains be bitter and painful to us? Will we try to object to it as much as we are able, in order to give our greedy passions free rein? That, in brief, is what this passage teaches.

The fact that the Nazarenes were hostile to our Lord Jesus Christ should serve to strengthen us against every obstacle which prevents us from pursuing the right path. When we see the majority of people resisting God and warring against his truth, we are appalled, and we start to think, 'How is it that men will not do homage to him who created and fashioned them? How can those who are no more than frail creatures dare to rise up against God on whom they depend, and by whose power they are sustained?' We find this horrifying, which is why many weak people abandon the gospel and begin to doubt whether or not it is the word of God. 'For,' they say, 'how can God allow people to resist him in this way?'

Now we should realize that we are not the first to experience this evil. We see how Jesus Christ provoked not only the wrath but the fierce cruelty of those among whom he had been raised. They would not spare his life even though he had come in order to obtain salvation for them. So when we learn that this is what happened to the Son of God, we should not be shocked when we see the wicked rounding on God and engaging in conflict with him. Although we see so much resistance, so much dissent and so much agitation, that whenever the gospel is preached all seems to be in turmoil and confusion, we must remain steadfast. Since God has spoken, let us listen to him, and let us leave those who cannot or will not yield, to perish. This is the way to arm and defend ourselves when today we see men who are deadly enemies of the message of salvation.

Rest assured in any case that there is power contained in God's word, though men would love to scorn it if they could. The authority of God's word is far from being diminished by being everywhere rejected and foolishly withstood. We perceive it to be full of divine majesty and might. People would dearly love to mock, if they could, everything they are told in God's name. In their contempt they would like to trample on it, but for all their efforts they cannot. They are bound to feel pangs of conscience: God's word will transfix them, probing their hidden dispositions and uncovering their godlessness. So hot with indignation will they be that they will lash out and completely lose control. Those, then, who despise God become furious, and senselessly rage against his word when it cuts them to the quick. This proves that it has more than human power. We ought therefore to receive it with utmost reverence, defying the resistance and objections of the wicked and the scornful. That is the lesson for us here.

Next, it is said that *Jesus Christ passed through the midst of them.* We learn that under God's protection he was kept from harm. There is no need to suppose that he became invisible in order to escape. Rather, we should assume that, as often happens, God covered the eyes of those intent on murder. At all events God took special care of his only Son, for in him all the promises made to the body of the church are perfectly fulfilled, since he is its Head. For our part, we know that we are made to share in everything that is his, and that by faith we are clothed with him, being grafted into his body. That is why he calls us his members. Observe, then, that just as the life of our Lord Jesus was miraculously saved by his Father's protection, the same will happen to us, providing we can say with a tranquil heart, 'Lord, into your hands I commit my spirit' (Psa. 31:5). When we are able to rest thus in God, we can be confident that since he is the guardian of our life, he will uphold and defend it by his power according to our need, and until he wills to gather us to himself. We will most certainly experience what is written here: we will pass through the midst of all the faithless.

This in fact is what we see, unless we wilfully close our eyes. For how is it possible that the church, which God was pleased to restore fifty years ago, should have been upheld and have grown in numbers, as we know to be the case? For at the time when there were only one or two hundred in it, the world was against it. There were no emperors or potentates on earth who did not seek to destroy these few people. And who preserved them? The gospel was proclaimed, but only in one small corner. How did it not come to be crushed a hundred times over? It is impossible to tell, and even harder to explain how it came about, except that those whom God first called simply passed through. In the meantime the seed spread far and wide. Still, thirty or more times we have seen how likely it was that all would be destroyed and ruined, with no remedy in sight. Nevertheless God worked in such a way that those who had no means of repelling their enemies passed through their midst, though scattered on all sides, and though none could help his comrade. Poor believers were dispersed: in a town or village there might be only ten or twelve, or thirty or forty. Yet supposing there were three thousand of them, behold three hundred thousand men who come against so small a handful of people! They are singled out, so that each one cries that he is being crushed, while all men rise against him. There is often indeed such brutality that a father will not spare his son, or a son his father; brothers and sisters will betray each other.

Nevertheless God retains some seed after he permits such great and awful persecution. In a large city a small group will remain, and in a village, half a dozen, so that there will always be some to raise up seed in God's church, to worship him purely and to glorify his name, in spite of unbelievers and regardless of their efforts. So when we see this with our own eyes, we can be sure that, even today, God shows that what he began in his Son he continues in the body of the church. He causes us to pass through the midst of our enemies, and so covers their eyes that they do not know what to make of it. Although they devise one thing after another, all their efforts are in vain, because God does not allow them to achieve their goal. It is no use their taking counsel, deliberating and settling on some plan. God accomplishes what he says through Isaiah, his prophet: 'Take counsel, deliberate, consider and decide: nothing will come of it' (Isa. 8:10).

Today, therefore, let us apply what we have learned. When we see that we are like a poor lamb or sheep in the mouth not of one but of many wolves who surround us and who are filled with rage and cruelty, let us not doubt that God will still be merciful to us, and that his power is as great as ever to help us pass through the midst of our enemies. How he delivers us we cannot know, for as to our safety we can see no way out. God, then, must act by letting us pass through our enemies without their harming us, for when we are half-devoured he desires to add lustre to his grace by preserving us. When this occurs, when, that is, he is pleased to allow us to pass through so many dangers, we will be much better preserved than if we had every possible means of getting help from elsewhere. That is what we need to remember here.

When our Lord Jesus Christ was driven out of Nazareth where he had been brought up, it looked as if the progress of the gospel was at an end. He withdrew as if into a place of hiding. Jerusalem could not tolerate him: there lived the scribes and Pharisees who had completely debased religion and who could not bear to hear one word of truth. It is the same today: if we tried to preach the gospel in Rome, there would be uproar and clashes everywhere. Our Lord, then, had only Nazareth as his small retreat. It was but a hamlet of little reputation; it was not a populous town, nor did any of its people have any standing or authority. But for a short time he retired there, having performed miracles in other places but not in Nazareth. As we saw, he found no openings or welcome there because of unbelief. Nazareth was thus no more than a refuge for him, but because he was driven out, we might think that all was lost.

Matthew records that *he left Nazareth and withdrew toward the sea, to the border region of Galilee of the Gentiles*, since there Gentiles had mingled with God's people. We know indeed that in that area Solomon had ceded certain towns to Hiram king of Tyre (1 Kings 9:11). It was to there that Jesus Christ withdrew. There, says Matthew, *on the borders of Naphtali and Zebulun*, and up against the frontier of Judah, the prophecy of Isaiah was fulfilled. In the land of Zebulun and Naphtali there had been much affliction; but at length light would shine on those who were in darkness and who lay in death's dark shadow (Isa. 9:1-2).

Let us remember that when God's edifice seems ready to collapse and to be totally destroyed, his work will nevertheless proceed in a strange and unknown way. By 'God's edifice' I mean all of his works in general, but especially the state of his church. We may often see turmoil which threatens to throw down all that has been built and to bury God's name. Those whom he has gathered as his people to serve and worship him risk being wiped from the face of the earth. Confusion reigns, yet God turns this evil into good, into a much greater good than if affairs had gone exactly as we wished. Certainly we would take little notice if the church were sustained by ordinary means, and if God proceeded naturally, employing men to do the work according to his usual order. We would take little notice if this was the way he set out to obtain salvation for his church and brought it to conclusion.

It is the same as when we see the sun shining every day, and the moon by night: we become hardened to it. Who feels moved by the miracle—which it is—of seeing the sun shedding light on the world and circling it each day at a well-measured pace? We also see the moon and stars doing their duty to perfection, yet we do not spare a thought for them. Familiarity, as I say, makes us quite obtuse. So we should consider with greater care what we are told here, that God works in so strange and incomprehensible a way that we are forced, whether we like it or not, to recognize that it is his hand and power which are at work, and that he does not have to act according to our wishes and ideas.

Here, then, we see our Lord Jesus Christ cast out of Nazareth. If we were to speculate, we might think that all was lost. Indeed all would have been, had not the prophet Isaiah foretold that God would bring extreme suffering upon his people, but that the darkness would not be so great as in earlier times, when the lands of Zebulun and Naphtali were laid waste by their enemies, and when God had so worked as to make death easier to bear than sickness. In this way God confirmed the authority of his

Son, our Lord Jesus Christ, who came to heal the sick, to give life to the dead and to restore those who had been totally oppressed.

Before moving on, however, we should pause to consider this passage from Isaiah. In the eighth chapter, which mixes promises with threats, the prophet concludes that nothing but adversity and disaster will come upon all the people. So great will be the turmoil that they will dash against each other and break their necks; they will be driven by force into darkness and obscurity (Isa. 8:7-8). How wretched will their condition be, and how frightful! Although the prophet had formerly announced that God would dwell in the land of Judaea and would be called Immanuel, 'God with us' (Isa. 7:14), this did not stop everything from being taken from them, looted, practically ruined and made desolate. True, the prophet comforts the faithful, but he declares that they are so few that God must treat his promises as sealed letters (Isa. 8:16). 'Take care,' says God, 'that you do not walk with this people, for they and their fathers have risen up against me. To overcome their unbelief and their rebelliousness, I must bring great distress upon them so that all will be laid waste. You and my disciples have my promises as in letters closed and sealed.' To which the prophet replies, 'Here I am with the children you have given me, but they are portents and objects of hate among the people who claim your name' (Isa. 8:18).

God is thus said to be a stumbling block to both houses of Israel, that is, to all the chosen people, for there were two kingdoms, one called Israel, the other Judah. In short, here we see God's wrath poured out on all, and even weighing on the remnant who were left. Nevertheless, Isaiah adds that although all was in darkness, the gloom would not be so deep as it was when Naphtali and Zebulun were destroyed by their enemies the Assyrians, who devastated the territory of four tribes, driving their inhabitants into exile. For the kingdom of Israel was conquered on two separate occasions. Tiglath-Pileser first began the conquest and Shalmaneser completed it (2 Kings 15:29; 17:5-6; 18:9-12). The wretched people were deported to a foreign land and the rest were left behind, abandoned. Among these, rebellion broke out, so that Shalmaneser returned a second time and conquered the other tribes, taking them off into captivity. The country was more or less a wilderness. God had so vented his anger that the place was hideous to behold. The body of the former king had been thrown to the crows, and had decayed so that the stench infected all around. That is what happened to the kingdom of Israel, which had been so prosperous in wealth, in worldly power and in population.[1]

Now the prophet declared that the final conquest and calamity with which he threatened the people in general would not be as severe as the earlier two. How could that be? When we think of what occurred we seem to find the opposite. The city of Jerusalem, God's sanctuary, was razed, the temple was thrown down and abuse heaped upon it. The Jews, the nation from which Jesus Christ was to come, were carted off to a distant land (2 Kings 24:10-14; 25:8-12). The name 'Israel', which before had been blessed, now seemed cursed and abhorrent to God and men. Not a single grain of seed was left. How, then, could the prophet say that this disaster, which he calls darkness, would not be as great as when Zebulun and Naphtali were afflicted?

The basic principle we need to remember is this: when Israel was conquered, God had made no sure promise that he would restore what he had destroyed. While overall his promises applied to both Israel and Judah, the promises given to the ten

[1] In explaining the historical background to Isa. 9:1, Calvin refers to the two Assyrian campaigns of 734–33 (under Tiglath-Pileser III) and 724–21 (under Shalmaneser V and his successor, Sargon II), which ended Israel's existence as a nation state. The preacher goes on to speak of the 'final conquest' as foretold by Isaiah, that is, Nebuchadnezzar's invasion of Judah in 588, which resulted in the destruction of Jerusalem and its temple, and the deportation of large sections of its population to Babylon. Appalling as the disaster was, it did not prevent the eventual restoration, foretold by the prophets, of the people and their worship.

tribes—that is, to Israel—depended on the special promise that the tribe of Judah would be restored (Gen. 49:10). The prophet declares that Israel's double calamity was absolutely fatal, but that through the tribe of Judah the people would again rise to their feet. So when Isaiah goes on to say that God will afflict Judah in turn, the disaster will be easier to bear because the Jews have something on which they may rely. God had assigned a term of sixty or seventy years (Jer. 25:11; 29:10), after which they would return in freedom, the temple would be rebuilt, and the edifice of the second temple, at the coming of our Lord Jesus Christ, would be even more glorious than the first (Hag. 2:6-9). When the prophets speak of the people returning from captivity in Babylon, they have in mind the purpose of God's ingathering—that the Son of God should bring them to salvation, and that the sceptre once belonging to Mount Sion should be everywhere made known, holding sway from east to west, as we read particularly in the Psalms (Psa. 72:8; 89:25; 110:2).

We may better understand what Isaiah says by means of an illustration. Imagine a poor man who falls into a small stream but remains face down, because he has no strength to get up. It takes only a foot of water to drown him, yet the water covers less than half his body. If he had strength enough to get back on his feet, he could easily escape, but because he is impossibly weak, he must suffocate. Imagine, on the other hand, a boat which sinks at sea. A man grasps a piece of wood or throws himself onto a plank, thus saving his life. Yet the sea could easily swallow a whole world, let alone a man! But this man has something to rely on, and has enough strength to hold tight until he reaches port.

This was how it was with the ten tribes which we mentioned earlier: they so wickedly mocked God's word that the prophets were, so to speak, pilloried. 'These loud-mouths,' they would say, 'are forever bawling in our ears. If we took them at their word, no one would ever have fun.' Then they would threaten the prophets, and when it was obvious that they would keep on sharply rebuking the people and speaking in grim earnest, fires would be lit on every hand and there was talk only of killing and murdering these true servants of God. 'Look, these men are nothing but trouble. We should get rid of them, otherwise we will never be at peace.'

Now when God witnesses such rebelliousness and wild obstinacy in this people, he determines to sweep the lot away. It is true that he declares that, in the end, he will have mercy on them, but he points them toward Judah, since this was the kingdom chosen by him to represent and symbolize the rule of our Lord Jesus Christ. The Israelites, however, took no notice of this, so that when they were afflicted (though less harshly than the others), they had nothing to support them; it took a mere half-foot of water to drown them! On the other hand, when God makes a firm promise to the inhabitants of Judah, he tells them that though their enemies will overwhelm them and though all memory of them may seem to perish, he will nevertheless sustain and protect them. And although they may be banished to every foreign land, and blown here and there as if by wind, he will finally gather them in. He will sound the trumpet and summon them to a greater triumph than when he brought their fathers out of Egypt. When God fulfils his promise, his people will return with banners flying; they will be full of joy and gladness. That is their support when on the sea and amid earth's yawning pits. They cannot drown, for they stand firm upon the promises which can help them overcome all the world's obstacles, impediments and deaths.

Hence what Isaiah foretold was in fact fulfilled. As we said before, when the prophets declared that the people, being freed from the hand and tyranny of the Chaldeans, would return and be restored by God's grace, they were referring to the redemption obtained by our Lord Jesus Christ. See, then, just how well this verse applies to the person of God's Son, who visited Zebulun and Naphtali and the whole coastal tract, together with Galilee of the Gentiles. For it is clear that Isaiah was speaking not only of the kingdom of Judaea; he also included all of Israel. We thus infer that what the prophet foretold could only be attested and fulfilled by the coming of God's Son, the Redeemer of the world.

Matthew, in keeping with the tenor of the text (although he does not strictly follow its wording), points to Isaiah's final words: *The people who sat in the shadow of death have seen a great light, and on those who sat in darkness, light has come.* Notice that what the prophet says readily confirms the explanation which I have given. The third calamity would not be so severe as the first two, for although it appeared to be more serious, it would be easier and more bearable. The double defeat of the ten tribes began what would be a long, drawn-out night. No one knew when day would dawn, yet the night contained a better hope which might sustain poor souls who, in the midst of hell, found more consolation and joy than did those who had earlier suffered only ordinary affliction. These, I say, although deep in death, were quickened by God and had cause to rejoice in their misery and distress, however great their suffering, because they had something firm on which they could rely. This, as I said before, is related to the promises—promises which could have effect only at the coming of our Lord Jesus Christ.

Bear this in mind: although Isaiah speaks of those who at that time were God's chosen people, the whole world may see its own condition in theirs. When he comes to us, our Lord Jesus Christ finds us sunk in darkness and in the shadow of death, although we do not know it. The darkness from which our Lord delivers us is quite contrary to his kingdom, for the light of his kingdom is not for seeing things that benefit the body and this transitory life; it is for the eternal salvation of our souls. The darkness mentioned here is that dreadful blindness which means that we know nothing about God and are given to futility, lies and errors. In a word, Satan owns us; we are mindless and incapable of goodness, not one drop of which we can call our own. Such is the awful darkness in which we remain plunged, until our Lord Jesus Christ comes to our rescue. By nature we are utterly ruined. Let us learn, then, to recognize the wretchedness into which we are born, so that we feel shame and dismay before God, and sigh and groan. May we be roused to praise still more the boundless goodness of our God, and the unfathomable benefits which he brought us at the coming of our Lord Jesus Christ.

Now Jesus Christ, while still living in this world, already fulfilled what had been promised through Isaiah. Nevertheless every time the gospel is preached, grace is renewed for us. Let us open our eyes, then, when today light is offered to us, and let us know that our Lord has come so that we may no longer dwell in deepest hell, where we lie crushed. Let us also respond to Paul's appeal, which shows us what our Lord's office was: 'Sleeper, rise up; and awake, you who are in the grave' (Eph. 5:14). The object of the gospel, says Paul, is that Jesus Christ, who is the Sun of righteousness, should come to give us light, and to show us the path to follow if we would reach him. It is as when the morning sun begins to rise: we wake up and rejoice. Our Lord Jesus Christ, the Sun of righteousness, calls us to him and invites us to come, that we might be glad. By what name does he call us? 'All you who sleep,' he says. It is no natural or ordinary sleep that is meant. He means that we have perished and are dead, because we are estranged from God, who is the fount of life.

Remember, then, that our Lord Jesus Christ has always had this light in himself, to lead us to the heavenly life, above all when the gospel is proclaimed. Hence he declares, in the fifth chapter of John: 'The time is coming, and now is, when the dead who are in the grave will hear the voice of the Son of man; they will rise and live' (John 5:25). We are in death, therefore, until our Lord Jesus Christ brings us forth. We should learn to commit ourselves wholly to him and to give him true obedience, until we come to enjoy to the full the good things which he has promised us.

> *Now let us cast ourselves down before the majesty of our good God, acknowledging our faults and beseeching him to make us feel them more and more. May we be brought to true repentance, and may we be so strengthened that, rid of all our sins, we are clothed with his righteousness for which we ought now to long. And may he so uphold us in our weaknesses that, although we do not draw as near to our goal as we should, we may nevertheless be counted and reckoned as his children.*

15

FISHERS OF MEN

As he walked by the Sea of Galilee, he saw two brothers, Simon
who is called Peter and Andrew his brother, casting a net into the
sea, for they were fishermen. [19]*And he said to them, 'Come after me,*
and I will make you fishers of men.' [20]*Immediately they left their*
nets and followed him. [21]*And going on from there he saw two other*
brothers, James the son of Zebedee and John his brother, in the boat
with Zebedee their father, mending their nets, and he called them.
[22]*Immediately they left the boat and their father, and followed him*
(Matt. 4:18-22).

And walking along by the Sea of Galilee, he saw Simon and An-
drew, the brother of Simon, casting a net into the sea, for they were
fishermen. [17]*And Jesus said to them, 'Come after me and I will make*
you fishers of men.' [18]*And at once they left their nets and followed*
him. [19]*And going on a little further, he saw James the son of Zebe-*
dee and John his brother, who were mending the nets in their boat.
[20]*And immediately he called them, and they left their father Zebedee*
in the boat with the workmen, and followed him (Mark 1:16-20).

It happened that as he was standing by the lake of Gennesaret, the
people pressed upon him. [2]*And he saw two boats, for the fishermen*
had left them and were washing their nets. [3]*He got into one of the*
boats, which belonged to Simon, and asked him to put out a little

from the land. Then sitting down he taught the people from the boat. [4]And when he had ceased speaking, he said to Simon, 'Put out into the deep and let down your nets and fish.' [5]And Simon answered, 'Master, we toiled all night and took nothing. But at your word I will let down the nets.' [6]That being done, they enclosed a great number of fish, so as to break their nets. [7]They signalled to their companions in the other boat to come and help them. And they came and filled both the boats, so that they began to sink. [8]But when Simon Peter saw it, he fell down at Jesus' knees, saying, 'Master, depart from me, for I am a sinful man.' [9]Fear had overcome him and all who were with him, because of the catch of fish which had been taken; [10]likewise James and John, the sons of Zebedee, who were Simon's companions. And Jesus said to Simon, 'Do not be afraid; henceforth you will be catching men.' [11]And when they had brought their boats to land, they left everything and followed him (Luke 5:1-11).

IT is most necessary for us to know by what means the door of heaven has been opened to us, and how the gospel, which is called the key to the door, was proclaimed, so that we who were condemned to everlasting death might share in heaven's victory. This knowledge, I repeat, is most necessary, for we must be certain that the teaching on which our salvation rests is not derived from men, but that God is seen to be its author, and that he has given unerring proof that it comes from him.

This is the chief point which we must grasp in the story told to us here. Luke, it is true, recounts much more than Matthew or Mark, who provide a brief narrative of how our Lord called Peter, James, Andrew and John. Luke records the circumstances in which this happened, and he inserts details of a miracle which neither Mark nor Matthew mentions.

To understand all of this better, we should note that Peter had already come to our Lord Jesus Christ to be taught by him.

When he called him 'Master', this does not mean that he did not already hold him in reverence and regard him as a teacher sent by God. John makes this point in the first chapter of his Gospel, where he tells us that Andrew was a disciple of John the Baptist, and having met Jesus Christ, he said to Peter, his brother, 'I have found the Redeemer of the world, the Messiah promised in the law.' So he brought Peter to him (John 1:40-42). Not that Peter was retained as our Lord's servant at that time. The calling of which we are told here was more particular. Here Jesus Christ desires to place them in his service and to entrust them with the tasks he would later have for them. He does not yet make them apostles, but he seeks to prepare them so that they will be fit and ready for duty when the time comes. We should thus bear in mind that Andrew and Peter had already some inkling of the fact that Jesus Christ had come to bring order out of chaos, and that God was having mercy on his people, so that they should honour and revere him, and hold his teaching to be holy and divine. As yet, however, they had not committed themselves to him.

What we have here is a second phase, when our Lord Jesus Christ chooses them, meaning to employ them, as we will see, in the role of apostles. When it is said that *they were fishermen*, that is, ignorant men who had had no schooling, we perceive that God must certainly have changed them, as if suddenly making new creatures of them. Otherwise their teaching would not have met with full approval, supposing they had been the greatest and cleverest scholars in the world. Knowledge would not have been enough—unless it was the knowledge of philosophers or of those from whom we readily seek instruction! We tend to weigh men's teaching to see whether they have spoken well or ill. We accept nothing as certain except what pleases us and what we think is reasonable.

Our faith, however, must be founded on far greater certainty, which is only when we know that it is grounded in God and in his everlasting truth, so that it cannot be bent in any way at all. The apostles, then, had to be so shaped by the hand of our Lord Jesus Christ that there was nothing about them which men normally possessed. In a word, everything in them had to be superior to nature. This happened when these poor fishermen were called, and when their coarseness was so corrected that they became as angels handling God's marvellous secrets, and in a way which takes our breath away. They had to become instruments of God's Spirit.

Yet we learn that, after three and a half years or thereabouts, our Lord Jesus Christ left them as dull as they had ever been. Even after his resurrection, they imagined that he would restore the kingdom to Israel and that they would triumph in this world, as if the only benefits our Lord had brought were earthly and transitory (Acts 1:6). How foolish was that? And after the resurrection too! So as Matthew, Mark and Luke record, our Lord Jesus Christ most certainly took these men exactly as they were—poor fishermen, having neither skill nor knowledge apart from the ability to cast their nets into the sea and to catch fish—and made apostles of them. This shows that all the wisdom they possessed could not have come from their own excellence, that they had not had the benefit of human education or had themselves achieved what was given to them. Instead, God spoke by their mouths as if he had sent messengers from heaven—or something even better! For the kind of renewal which we see in the apostles is rather like God creating a world in miniature. That is one point.

It is said next that our Lord Jesus Christ *was walking along by the lake of Gennesaret* (called 'sea', as is the custom in Hebrew), and that *he first called Simon* (whom our Lord nicknamed Peter) *and Andrew his brother*. As we saw, it was Andrew who had already brought Peter to Jesus Christ, although later Peter ranked above him, and while both were apostles, Peter was the more outstanding because God used him in a more prominent way. In the beginning, however, Andrew was the one who directed him to our Lord. From this we learn that God makes use of those he calls to him, just as he chooses. As Paul says, our Lord Jesus Christ apportions his gifts according to the measure he determines, and not as we prefer (Eph. 4:7).

Furthermore, when we see that Jesus Christ called poor fishermen, poor ignorant folk, and made them his messengers to reveal things hidden from the start of time, things beyond our comprehension—when we see this, let us all learn to humble ourselves. Without doubt we should learn from their example to live as Paul exhorts the Corinthians. When the church began, there were not many noble, not many wise and not many rich (1 Cor. 1:26). Why? Because God wished to abase all loftiness in men, who are so prone to be puffed up with pride and to rob God of his glory. God sought to sweep all arrogance aside, and to demonstrate that what appears to be weak and foolish surpasses all the world's might and wisdom.

That is not to say that this is a rule, or a rule equal for all, as in our own time there have been madmen who fancied they were all the more learned for being ignorant—yes, stupid even! They tried to become apostles without having to be taught. 'For my part,' they would say, 'I had no education, and I have no use for it. It is revelations that we need!' And on the strength of that they made themselves not only teachers but apostles. How did they do it? As I said, by proudly asserting themselves, believing that, in their foolishness, they resembled the apostles and were so much closer to the kingdom of heaven. Well now, he who chose Peter and Andrew, James and John, later chose Paul, who from childhood had been brought up in Jerusalem and had been so thoroughly instructed in the law that he was among the very greatest teachers.

It is obvious, then, that our Lord Jesus Christ did not commit himself to something binding, nor did he rule out human means when he took the apostles from such a setting, finding them, as it were, in a cowshed and turning them all at once into teachers. I repeat, he did not intend to make a general rule, but it happened this once as I have said. The apostles brought nothing of their own; their message was not hatched in their own brains; they did not acquire it in any earthly school. It came from heaven, as our Lord desired. On the other hand, he desired also to test our obedience and humility. It would not be surprising if we had had as our teachers certain of the philosophers forever celebrated among the pagans. When, however, we come to be taught by these poor, ignorant fishermen, and when we know that Peter and John were far more learned than all whom the world counts great, and whom it regards as the cleverest, loftiest and deepest thinkers imaginable—when we thus give God our obedience and accept his word in all reverence, although he conveys it to us through these messengers who, in human eyes, are beneath contempt, we glorify God by believing their teaching. This is what the word 'fishermen' should mean to us.

Observe what Luke says regarding the circumstances of their calling: *Jesus Christ was busy teaching the people, but because of the crowd he was forced to withdraw to a boat*. This shows that he was already known to Peter, for as we mentioned he calls him 'Master' or 'Teacher' and defers to him. Nor would Peter have been so ready to oblige him, if he had not been in some way certain about him, regarding him as a person of some worth. For as Luke goes on to say, *they had toiled all night, but their efforts had been wasted*. They might have become cross or resentful. Our Lord would not have been heard so readily and with such prompt obedience if they had not recognized him as a man sent by God. To acknowledge him as the Son of God, of course, was as yet out of the question. Peter, his brother and the other two were rough men: it was not easy for them to have savoured a word or two about the coming of Christ, who would proclaim

God's mercy to his people. Yet while they had grasped nothing very clearly, something had prepared them, so that Peter was disposed to do as Jesus Christ commanded.

Our Lord does not yet ask him to leave the boat and his nets, but *to put out from the land*, in order to have a more convenient place from which he may be heard and understood by the crowd. We see here that while Jesus Christ was living in this world, he did not cease to do what God his Father had commanded him, which was to recall to the way of salvation poor lost souls, to comfort the afflicted, to bring light to the blind and to those who sat in darkness, and to proclaim God's grace to all who were in despair. As John says, his food was to obey God his Father, and to fulfil his appointed duty (John 4:34). The word 'food' is a metaphor. It is as if he said, 'My whole joy and pleasure is to be busy about the tasks which my Father has set for me.' Remember, as we saw before, that he had been anointed by the Holy Spirit on this condition, that he should proclaim forgiveness and deliverance to the captives, and the other things announced by the prophet Isaiah (Isa. 61:1-2). Here, then, was the substance of our Lord's message; he now assembled the people in order to teach them.

For the rest, we clearly see the kind of hearers he had—people of little consequence. For the most part he kept to places which were out of the way, as when he walked by the lake of Gennesaret and hardly ever went to Jerusalem, except when crowds had gathered so that now and then he might be heard by all. Still, he did not disdain people who were of no account. This confirms the verse of Paul which I cited earlier (1 Cor. 1:26-27): he began with the lowly who had no standing or honour or worth, thus showing that it is out of sheer generosity that God calls us.

If the news of the birth of our Lord had been brought only to the high priests who were of Aaron's line, and to the rulers of the people, we might think that God was only concerned with men of eminence: his grace would then have been obscured. But since he began with the shepherds in the fields, we who follow them should say to ourselves, 'God is plainly showing us, in these first fruits whom he has chosen, that we must humble ourselves, forgetting all loftiness and putting aside all arrogance, for we know that we owe our salvation to his pure mercy.' Indeed, both kings and princes, if there are any among Jesus Christ's disciples, must follow the shepherds and do homage to the Son of God. Let there be neither sceptre nor crown nor anything else which men esteem. Let all be brought low when homage is paid to our Lord Jesus Christ.

Next, Luke relates that *Jesus Christ ordered Peter to put out into the deep, to cast his nets and to fish*. Peter, whose efforts had been unavailing, replied, '*Master, we toiled all night long*,' for night is a better time for fishing than day. He is saying, in effect: 'It's a waste of time. There is nothing to catch; we have no hope of getting anything. Let's wait for another time.' Now our Lord Jesus Christ wants Peter to realize this for himself, so that he will later acclaim his power all the more. Nevertheless Peter says, '*At your word I will let down the nets*.'

To be sure this is all about a petty, mundane thing—fishing! Still, it teaches us a most useful lesson. This verse gives us a rule for right belief and action. We are not to follow our own wisdom and reason; we must prefer God's will and the authority of Jesus Christ, our supreme teacher, to any ideas which we might have. Until we are firmly resolved on this, we will simply drift through life, and whatever abilities we may have, however great they are, will be nothing but smoke which melts away. Where, then, do we begin, when we want our lives to pass God's test? Once he has spoken, once we know what he approves and finds pleasing, we should not argue and adopt a contrary position. Even though we may not see why and to what end he bids us do a certain thing, we should say, 'Your word is enough for us.' Accordingly, although Peter had scarcely made any progress in the school of Jesus Christ, he nevertheless, unintentionally, gives us a lesson which we must practise as long as we live. We may try to keep to it for thirty or forty years, but still not quite succeed; but we will have done well, and gained much, if only we remember the words, 'At the Lord's command, we must do all.' This is regardless of the fact that we will find reasons to object, to answer one way or another and to resist; we may even think that we have every cause to fancy we have won, since we are easily entangled in our own conceits. There never was a time when, having to give an answer, we did not shut our mouths, believing that we knew better and blaming God for acting inconsiderately. Not that we voice our objections out loud, but God knows that what he requires of us is more than just and reasonable. We, however, are always disposed to argue against him whenever we let our ideas run free.

We should take careful note, in any case, of this: although we seem to have wasted our time, although our toil appears unending and although troubles are so great that we never manage to do as God commands, we should nevertheless, at his word, press on, dismissing whatever considerations might deter us from doing what he reveals is pleasing to him. This is worth remembering, for it is teaching which has wide implications. If some poor soul is bereft of help, and feels that he is only beating the air, going backward rather than forward, he should learn to say, 'Lord, fierce storms have come upon me and winds swirl round about me. However much I toil, I suffer lack. All vanishes like smoke, and though I walk uprightly and in sincerity, I am swallowed up by evil men on every hand. Much of me has already been consumed, my trials are great indeed. Nevertheless I will obey your word, and since you bid me labour on and act justly toward everyone, Lord, I will do according to your word.' This is the way that unhappy souls should strengthen themselves whenever they feel that what they do is fruitless.

We must thus prefer God's will to our own whims and expectations, so that when he orders us to act, we should follow him, not doing as we like but according to what he knows is right. He is wise enough to lead us to our proper goal, even though at times we may appear to drift.

We are further told that there was such a catch of fish that all could see it was a miracle. *So many fish were caught that the nets began to break*, and the two boats had to come together to take on board this one catch. Could that have happened if our Lord Jesus Christ had not performed a miracle? Here, then, is sure and certain evidence that he was not simply a mortal or ordinary man, but that there was divine majesty in him. Peter therefore knelt before him, saying, '*Depart from me, Lord, for I am a sinful man*.' What this shows is that Peter, like his brother Andrew, was ignorant. Both of them vaguely discerned that Jesus Christ was worthy of men's reverence, but as to thinking that he was in some way heavenly or divine—no, nothing like that. Peter is overwhelmed by the miracle he has witnessed and asks to move away, for he cannot abide God's presence which the miracle has revealed. We see from this how inconsistent our wishes are and how confused: we do not know what to wish for; we shun what is good rather than seek it out. True, when people are conscious of their plight they generally want God to draw near to them. Think of the most ungodly people who know nothing of Scripture, the law or the gospel. When they suffer some affliction, we will hear them cry: 'Alas, God, have mercy on me!' That was how the heathen spoke: it is a plea which nature teaches men. Not that their knowledge is either true or clear, but God chose to grant it to them so that, quite unthinkingly, they might say, 'May God have mercy on us. May he help us.' There is no one, then, who does not want to draw close to God; even the wicked call upon God to visit them and to make himself known to them.

Yet when God does come, and when men sense his presence, they would rather push him far away from them, for their plight grows even worse! The wicked feel even greater pain, and cry, 'Must I suffer so? What will happen if God does not have mercy when he shows himself to me? My suffering will be twice as bad!' That, I say, is how an evil man will pass judgment on himself, whether he likes it or not. Whereas at first his pain was hard to bear, now that God presses him hard and makes him conscious of his presence, the mental anguish he feels on seeing God's vengeance prepared for him exceeds every torment imaginable. That is the inconsistency of which I spoke. When God is absent and withdrawn from us, but gives no sign that he intends to punish, we ask him to visit us; but when it comes to an actual encounter, we want him to leave us alone! This happened in the case of Job. 'Would to God,' he cried, 'that he had left me as I am, without pursuing me so hard' (Job 7:16-19). The same was true of David, who said, 'Lord, remove your hand from me, that I may breathe; then let me go and die' (cf. Psa. 39:13). Peter, as we see, was in the same position: 'Depart from me, for I am a sinful man.' Of course he had cause to speak this way. He recognized that he was not fit to be in the company of Jesus Christ, in whom he saw God's glory and majesty, while he himself was but a sinner, a man depraved, wretched and corrupt. From one point of view he made a sound confession.

Now what are sinners to do, except ask our Lord Jesus Christ to have mercy on them? He did not come into the world, or live here, for those who, as he later says, were holy and righteous; he came to heal the sick (Matt. 9:12-13). According, then, as we each acknowledge our sins, we must ask Jesus Christ to accept us, so that we may look to him and press toward him. This is what Peter should have done. Observe, however, that he simply recognized God's majesty in him, and thus perceived him as his judge. He failed to see the grace he has brought us. This is a truth we do well to note: it will help us make sure that the sum total of all that we know about God is made to serve our salvation.

If we imagine God only in his power and justice, we will feel only terror. There is no man living who would not choose to hide under rocks or throw himself into the deepest chasm or pit, if he felt that God would not be kind or merciful to him. In sum, when we perceive that God is almighty and righteous, and that he cannot bear iniquity but loves justice—when we perceive only this, we not only mean to rob him of his infinite power, but we seek in fact our own immediate destruction. What then ought we to do? If we want God's presence to be sweet and pleasant to us, he must show himself to us in the person of Jesus Christ. We must know why he came into the world and what it is he brings us. Yes, he is called our Judge, yet he comes to reconcile us to God his Father because he is our Advocate. When we call upon the Father in his name, he makes it possible for us to obtain pardon and mercy. If we know this about him, we can say, in contrast to Peter and much more wisely, 'Lord, I am a wretched sinner. I am therefore here to ask you to make me your own, to dwell even in me, and to clothe me with yourself.'

Knowing what our Lord's work is, we thus draw near to him, and he will draw near to us. Admittedly we will need to recognize that he possesses the Father's power, and that his majesty might crush us and everyone else besides. Why? So that he may truly master us, and rid us of those foolish ideas which make us think that we can come before him with heads held high; and so that, knowing that we are lost without his grace, we should look for it in him. It is to this point, I say, that knowledge of his majesty should take us. We must, however, be careful not to lapse into sorrow which leads to despair. When we are cast down, let us learn to rise up again and to speak in the way I indicated earlier: 'Lord, because I am a wretched sinner, draw near to me, keep me in fellowship with you, and may I never cease to remember your kindness. May I feel that you are always present and will continue with me, whether in life or death.' Let us bear this in mind.

As our Lord's answer shows, Peter did not need to flee from his presence or to withdraw, even though he saw from the miracle that here was no mortal man. '*Do not be afraid*,' he was told, '*from now on you will catch men*.' The same thing is said to all four of them. We thus learn something which we touched on earlier, that Jesus Christ does not call them to be only his disciples, but appoints them to be teachers and instructors in his church. This is clear from the fact that not all to whom our Lord preached followed in his steps wherever he went. They did not remain in his company; indeed, as we know, he refused some who offered themselves. 'Master,' said one, 'I am ready to join and follow you.' 'No,' he replied, 'depart' (cf. Matt. 8:19-20). Not that he sought to exclude him from his church: he merely refused to have him as a close servant. Why? That was for him to know. We should not enquire about the reason. In any event, as I said, everything comes from the generosity of him who is on high.

Therefore the four who are mentioned here were set apart by Jesus Christ to be finally his apostles and to announce the gospel. He is speaking figuratively when he says that *they will be fishers of men*. Let us not waste our time, as many do, on speculating why fishing and the bringing of men to salvation should be compared. Jesus Christ spoke simply of the purpose he had in view. He was addressing fishermen who had their nets ready, and he adapted his words to the scene before him. Just as fish swim in the sea which resembles a million chasms, and are gathered and brought to the surface, so until God gathers us in we are in such dire straits that chasms are all around; by the power of his word we are drawn back to him and brought together. There is no point in pressing the image further, and it would be childish to sift through every detail. It should be enough to know that the gospel is preached so that, being led back to God, we might offer ourselves to him as a sacrifice, instead of being, as before, scattered over the earth and hopelessly confused.

Let us learn, then, to return to God whenever he graciously calls us into his church to share in the unity we have. Let us not err and stray as we once did, and as the children of darkness and all unbelievers still do. Let us also copy the example of the disciples and follow our Lord Jesus Christ. True, he does not want us all to leave our occupation and station in life: that would be a reckless thing to do. Instead, we should consider what he asks of each of us. Thus those who are called to positions of honour should realize that they must perform their tasks all the more earnestly, and must toil so as to render a good account to God. Let them not be so entangled in this world's cares as to be in any way diverted from their duties. Each of us should have due regard to his place and calling.

For example, as Christians we are all required to deny ourselves. But the one who is called to proclaim God's word should understand that his vocation lays a stricter obligation on him—to refrain from many things which are allowed a private person. However that be, let each, according to his calling and condition, know that when Jesus Christ summons him, he must move, forgetting everything which might hold him back. All must be trodden underfoot, and all the bonds by which Satan tries to tie us down must be broken, allowing God's word to have its powerful effect in us. We are to do all that he commands without dissent. And because none of this comes from us, and because God's word cannot readily enter our hearts, change our disposition, make us teachable and kindle our love so that we conform to God's will, let us ask our Lord Jesus Christ, when his word touches our ears, to help us also open our hearts to it, that it may guide us. May it give us power to overcome all our earthly affections, and may we be quick and alert, as were the disciples who left mother, father, and all that they had.

Now let us cast ourselves down before the majesty of our good God, acknowledging our faults and begging him so to make us feel them that we may turn back to him with true repentance. Let us ask him not only to pardon our past sins, but to lead us by his Holy Spirit, so that our one desire may be to obey his holy will. May we follow wherever Jesus Christ, our good Shepherd, calls us to go, for only on these terms are we given to him by God his Father.

16

A TEACHER WITH AUTHORITY

And he went about all Galilee, teaching in their synagogues and preaching the gospel of the kingdom and healing every sort of illness and infirmity among the people. [24]*So his fame spread throughout all Syria, and they brought to him all who were afflicted and stricken with various diseases and pains, the demon-possessed, epileptics and paralytics, and he healed them.* [25]*And large crowds followed him from Galilee, from the Decapolis, from Jerusalem and Judaea and from beyond the Jordan* (Matt. 4:23-25).

Then they came to Capernaum, and soon after on the Sabbath he entered the synagogue and taught. [22]*And they were astonished at his teaching, for he taught them as one who had authority, and not as the scribes* (Mark 1:21-22).

And he went down to Capernaum, a city of Galilee. And he taught them on the Sabbath; [32]*and they were astonished at his teaching, for his word was with authority* (Luke 4:31-32).

THERE are three points which these narratives contain. The first is that our Lord Jesus Christ confirmed his teaching and backed it up by means of miracles. In each case the hand of God was joined to the word which Jesus Christ proclaimed. It was as if God was attesting the fact that he had sent him. Thus it is expressly said that *his fame spread everywhere, as far even as Syria*.

Now we know that the Syrians had in every age been enemies of the Israelites, and that there had been many wars between them. Although everything at that time was subject to the rule of Rome—Syria being a province under Roman control, having the same head, and belonging to the one all-embracing empire—the quarrels of the past and present had not abated to the point that the Syrians would not have liked to see the Jews destroyed. Nevertheless, the fame of Jesus Christ had reached their land, though not in a way that would have drawn them to the gospel. That time had not yet come. No, the point of this was that it made the Jews inexcusable for remaining muddled by their unbelief and rebellion. God does indeed allow poor blind souls to discover things which do them no good, but which allow them to judge us who claim to see clearly and to have assured truth. For once we harden our hearts against God, once God can get nothing by way of obedience from us, he must open the eyes of the blind who sit in darkness, so that it is they who condemn us. That is what happened in this instance.

Be that as it may, notice how the teaching of the gospel was confirmed by the miracles which are mentioned here. Notice, too, how our Lord Jesus Christ performed the task which God his Father had entrusted to him: he taught everywhere.[1] Again, he shows us just how his teaching was received: it astonished his hearers, so that many people followed him—people of poor standing, common people, people, as we say, of little means or rank. This is what these verses have to tell us.

Overall, it is most useful to observe that the real purpose of the miracles, their main thrust, was to corroborate the truth

[1] This is the second of Calvin's three summary points. The third point follows immediately.

of the gospel, so that it might be accepted without reserve as coming from God. For the devil has always attempted to separate these two things, which should always go together. We know that in popery so-called miracles are lies, delusions, witchcraft. They serve ends which are contrary to God's intentions; they are meant to prove the truth of their superstitions and idolatry. The devil therefore uses the delusions which he works to make us believe that they have God's approval. We should be all the more mindful, then, of what I said a moment ago, that God put forth his arm and demonstrated his power in the miracles that were done, not only by our Lord but by the prophets and apostles, so that he might be obeyed and his word received in all humility. When people do not willingly accept the yoke which they find hard and wearisome, God must intervene to show that it is pointless to resist him and to argue about whether or not his word is acceptable. We should ignore all of that and consider whatever is said in his name as sure and unfailing truth, and as teaching which cannot lawfully be denied. Since, however, we will discuss this point elsewhere, I merely touch on it here.

Now Jesus Christ was not only his Father's ambassador, sent to bear witness to his will; by his actual deeds he gave firm proof of what he said, showing that it came not from men but had God as its author. It remains for us, therefore, quietly to accept and embrace the gospel message, otherwise we wilfully fight against God. How will that help us? Rather, let us regard the teaching of the gospel as genuine, for when we see a seal on some official document we make no difficulty about accepting its contents. What shall we say, then, when God has sealed his word not with wax, lead, gold or silver, but has fully disclosed his power in it, and when his glory shines forth from it and is etched deep upon it?

Let us learn to make the most of God's witness to the truth of the gospel, so that our faith may be all the more assured. May

God train us to accept the yoke and to cleanse our emotions, for experience shows us all too well that we can never quietly submit to him without feeling some reluctance. To put an end to all resistance, we should lift our eyes on high and fix our minds on the power by which God has chosen to enhance and authenticate the teaching of his word. That is one thing.

Next it is said that our Lord Jesus Christ did not heal one kind of illness only, but many: *he healed every sort of illness among the people*. He healed not by normal remedies, but in a way which revealed the hand of God. No one who is demon-possessed can be cured by means of potions or bleedings. As for epileptics who from time to time fall down, although their affliction can sometimes be relieved, it is very hard to effect a cure by means of some particular skill. With paralytics, their suffering goes back a long way. Where is the doctor who can restore strength to ligaments grown weak and wasted? That would be a kind of resurrection!

Moreover, given the diversity of afflictions, we see even more clearly how much our Lord Jesus Christ had to work in the power of the Spirit of God his Father, and not through lesser, earthly means. Later we will discuss how our Lord's miracles were also meant to bring relief, for these had to harmonize with and match his teaching. The gospel is not preached in order to terrify people, but to soothe their sorrow and to call them to Jesus Christ, so that they receive healing from him if they are sick and quickening for their souls, dead though they are. Miracles, as we will soon see, had to encompass all these things.

We might, however, wonder how there could be so many paralytics, epileptics and the demon-possessed, which is not something we normally find. We should first reflect that the devil was extremely active when he discovered that the Son of God had come to put the world to rights. In addition, God had given him greater freedom, as if loosening the reins on his neck. Hence we see people more afflicted and troubled both in body and mind, and experiencing extreme distress. Why was that? Because, as I already said, Satan's nature is to resist God as much as possible. His rule is wrecked when the Son of God appears for men's salvation. He was thus beside himself, fiercely aggressive. Nevertheless without God's leave and permission he can attempt or do nothing. He acts, as it were, under compulsion. His firm aim is to withstand God, and in doing this he is bent on ruining everything and wreaking havoc. Yet God uses him in order to exalt his glory all the more, which is what happened.

The devil sought to make our Lord's presence hateful to men who were suffering illness: they would be conscious only of the rods and scourges—signs of God's wrath and retribution. It might be thought that our Lord Jesus Christ had come only to inflict hardship on men, so that they would shun and loathe him. That was what the devil had in mind. God, on the other hand, found a way to enhance the grace brought by his only-begotten Son. So just as we might pile up wood to make a blazing fire, all that the devil did to torment men, to make them despise the gospel, to inflame them and to distance them from their salvation—God in his providence used all of this to provide Jesus Christ with targets in whom he might display the treasures of his grace and mercy.

See, then, just when the devil lashes out and thinks he has won the day, how God shames and defeats him. However much Satan contrives to fill the world with darkness, so that no one knows which way to turn, God makes everything work for good. He brings light out of darkness, as Paul declares in Second Corinthians (2 Cor. 4:6). That is what we must remember.

If today we do not see as many epileptics and paralytics as in earlier days, and even fewer who are demon-possessed, it is because God willed these conditions to prevail at the coming of his Son. That too is why, when our Lord speaks of the man born blind but who regained his sight, we read in John that God meant him to bear this affliction from birth, in order to exalt his glory in him (John 9:1–3). This is a rule we should often observe when we read about the paralysed who are only half alive and who languish in this world; or when we read of epileptics afflicted with what we call *grand mal*, or of the demon-possessed and the insane. God's intention was to give lustre to the grace of which Jesus Christ was both servant and giver. Such is the meaning of our first point.

The following verse tells us that *Jesus Christ went about the country and preached in their synagogues.* This shows us that things were not yet so debased among the Jews that there was not still some trace of the order which God had formerly established. He did not intend that people should visit the temple only for sacrifice and for the ceremonies of the law. Teaching had to be combined with these, for without God's word we have no guidance or direction. He must therefore teach us with his own lips, otherwise everything we think of as religion will be nonsense—in a word, monkey-tricks! That is why in popery there are endless ritual devotions, all show and gorgeous spectacle. Anyone entering their church will be struck with wonder: here the organ will be singing, and there statuettes will pout or grin. As well there is the farcical display of one Mass after another, together with all the rest. But once you get back home, what good will it have done you? Remember, then, that we need the word in order to enlighten us and to give us guidance, or else whatever we hope to do by serving and worshipping God is mere superstition and folly. Under the law, teaching had to come first.

Thus, although in the time of Jesus Christ everything had become debased, and although the scribes and Pharisees especially had added to the law so many of their own ideas that hardly anyone could tell black from white; although they held tyrannical sway and were caught up in their own word-games, we see from this and other passages that there was still a place for teaching.

As we noted earlier, before he began to preach, our Lord Jesus Christ was in a synagogue and was presented with the book of Isaiah. If we compare popery today with the confusion which then reigned in Judaea, there is no doubt that the devil holds a much more powerful sway over the papists than he did over the Jews. True, if you ask the papists what they think of Annas, Caiaphas and their followers, they detest them outright. Even so these still allowed room for God's law and the prophets. The scrolls were there, and whenever the people assembled they were read and expounded if someone was present who could explain them. At present, however, in popery, it is absolutely forbidden for God's word to be made known; instead it is turned into a holy relic! If those humbugs hint at it, it is only the merest whiff, as we say, and they would have us believe that it says whatever they like.

And what about ourselves? If in those days the Jews assembled without really knowing why, but kept the custom of hearing some teaching or other, when we come here, when the bell is rung and when the church is set up to receive us all as one, we should recognize that the main thing we must do is call upon God and pray that he may lead and govern us by his word, and thus learn how we may truly and lawfully obey him. Our gatherings will meet with God's approval when we give priority to his word. It is in this that the church's beauty (for so David calls it) consists (Psa. 27:4); not in statuettes or in stupid goings-on, which are merely childish games, but in God's appearing face to face, which he now does in the gospel, so that we are transformed into his glory (2 Cor. 3:18). Let us, I say, take particular note that Masses, matins, vespers and compline are simply a worldly muddle, abhorrent to God. When they shout, howl and chant in an unknown tongue, know that there is not one word of teaching which is of benefit to the people. Enough said, however, on that point.

The news that our Lord preached in his own times is meant to assure us that the message which today is proclaimed to us does not come from men, and that its contents have not been hatched in anyone's brain. We derive it from Jesus Christ. Those appointed to teach the people are, it is true, his deputies and servants, but he has no intention of surrendering his office to them or of ceasing to be the supreme Shepherd, teacher and instructor. He will remain so to the end of the world. When, therefore, we see a mere man up in the pulpit, as long as he does his duty, faithfully preaching what he has received from his teacher, be sure that our Lord Jesus Christ is in our midst and that we are under his rule.

Let us look now at what is said about those who heard, and at what our Lord gained by his teaching. We read that *many were astonished, because his teaching was with power*; or as Mark writes, *he taught with authority, and not as the scribes and Pharisees.* Here we are reminded that not all profited equally from God's message. Earlier on we learned that Peter, Andrew, James and John immediately left their nets, their work and even their parents. Why? To follow Jesus Christ. They did more than accept his teaching as true, trust it and get ready to be his disciples. Instead of keeping them occupied at home, he wished to use them in a much nobler calling. They therefore forgot their former work and trampled it down in order to follow our Lord Jesus Christ. Nevertheless Peter, as we will shortly see, had a wife, as perhaps the others also had. Yet our Lord chooses to make them his close pupils, so that, in time, he should prepare them to be apostles. No earthly sentiment, then, holds them back or prevents them from joining Jesus Christ. It might have occurred to them that they would get no pay, since, as he said elsewhere, he had nowhere to lay his head, and his lot was worse than that of the birds of the air: they find a place to nest in the branches of a tree, but he had not a foot of ground on which to rest (Matt. 8:20; Luke 9:58). He was thus poor and despised by all, and his disciples had to be ready to face much conflict, since the gospel was bound to have many enemies. Despite that they left everything. They were not of course great lords, but their work had been enough to support them day by day. Yet off they went, not knowing what might happen, but swept up by the power of our Lord's words, for God had touched them by his Holy Spirit.

See, too, how other hearers were drawn to Peter, Andrew, James and John. We are told that *many came from Galilee, from the region of the Ten Towns, and even from Jerusalem.* They ran after our Lord Jesus Christ to be filled with this heavenly food, the message of the gospel. Such zeal deserves high praise, for here were poor souls who came in haste, abandoning their homes and occupations in order to be taught by the mouth of the Son of God, whom they judged to be only a prophet. Many groups are said to have come, showing that these were not people of high repute or noble standing.

It was necessary for God to begin with the lowly of this world, in order to abase all pride, as we said before. We must understand that this world's honours, pleasures and wealth are like thorns which twine around us, taking away our freedom to give ourselves to God and to yield to his word. That was how the great of this world took no account of our Lord Jesus Christ. True, they were obliged to hear of his fame as an outstanding teacher, which the common people had spread abroad; but it faded away, due to their contempt and ingratitude. What, then, prevented them from coming to our Lord Jesus Christ? They were simply wallowing in their ease, in delights and sensual pleasures, in their titles and their transitory possessions. These things, I say, are what held them back.

The poor, by contrast, were like hungry men who, ignoring their bodily needs, ran to receive spiritual refreshment for their souls. We should therefore learn to have more love for God's word, since we know that Jesus Christ was not only a prophet sent by God but was the sovereign head of the house, as the apostle says in Hebrews (Heb. 3:6). He is over all; he has fulfilled all revelation and in him is all fullness of wisdom. When we read that he is seated at God's right hand, we should do him homage in all humility, as is our due. We must bow the knee to him, not by way of some external rite but by giving him sincere obedience, not only as our teacher but as our king. And if we find it necessary to go to one place or another to receive teaching and instruction, let us not spare our steps, and let us not think that we are wasting our time by seeking after Jesus Christ. This is something else to bear in mind.

If we do this, we will be armed to meet those things that cause the weak to stumble and to go awry. When they see the great of this world mocking our simplicity, and so caught up by pride and arrogance that they will not yield to Jesus Christ, these poor souls will say: 'What's this? If the gospel were God's truth, shouldn't it change those who follow it? We see prelates and pillars of the Catholic faith, kings, great lords and magistrates who are used to governing, yet none of them will move an inch to follow this religion.' These people think that the gospel cannot have authority because in men's eyes it has no prestige or respect. Now as I said, we should be armed to meet this stumbling block, seeing that although God's Son preached in person, only humble, ordinary folk were sympathetic and zealous enough to accept his message.

So let us today allow God to call us and to forsake the great who brag and boast. They are as men cast out by God, however much they admire themselves and however much men marvel at their greatness and are dazzled by their ostentation. Be sure of this: in God's eyes they are merely rogues, filth and rubbish. For our part, let us treasure the grace and special privilege which

God has given us by adopting us as his children. May our faith be robust enough to look with disdain upon what the world holds dear. One thing is sure, God's children should be meek enough to bear with the humblest of men; but their faith should rise above the world and defy all godless arrogance when confronted with the enemies of the gospel, who would obscure the glory of God's Son and snatch him from his seat.

When Scripture speaks of 'those who were amazed at his teaching', it describes a third class of hearer. Although many thought highly of his teaching, they were not moved or changed enough to give themselves completely to him. There were quite a few who did, but others grasped his teaching for a time and were overcome with amazement. It soon, however, disappeared; it had neither solidity nor staying power. We should beware lest we are like them. They were not, it is true, absolutely hopeless, since they were touched by the majesty of God. There was some good seed in them, but it was, in a way, smothered: it could not grow or ripen, still less produce its fruit. That is why I said that they had grasped enough to be amazed, but there they stopped. There were of course others who jeered and who put out their tongues, as is the case today with those who speak of God's truth only in jest and with disparagement.

Nevertheless, such people cannot avoid being touched, despite themselves. If they do not obey willingly, God stokes a fire within them which little by little burns them—a worm which continually gnaws at them. That is how it is with all enemies of the gospel, and above all with those zealots for the papacy who are so frenzied in their opposition, and who would rather turn the world upside down than submit to God's truth. They are, to be sure, touched with a feeling for God's majesty, which drives them to distraction though they do not know its source. Of course they are scoffers who only want to laugh and jeer, but when they are alone, all by themselves, they cannot quite deaden their conscience or silence their inner misgivings. God's word is thus rightly described as a sharp, two-edged sword, which penetrates the heart and pierces to the very marrow of our bones (Heb. 4:12). There is nothing which it cannot fathom, since it has this power and quality from God from whom it comes.

Just as it is God's privilege to plumb our deepest thoughts, so must the word test us one from the other, but not in equal measure. Some people are so moved that their only wish is to conform to God's righteousness; that is their one desire and purpose. Others for a time show signs of zeal, but it is only a grass fire which soon dies down. Again, others are seized by fear, but they have no proper will or disposition to yield to God. Still others (the very worst!) fly into a rage; intoxicated by the devil, they nevertheless feel the power of God, which makes them confess: 'Yes, all this is true.' Yet that does not stop them lashing out at him. Such majesty, however, is found in God's word that even the most brazen and those so drunk with arrogance that they no longer think of themselves as mortal—even these, I say, cannot avoid being impressed.

Hence Paul, when speaking of the purpose and usefulness of prophecy, says that when an unbeliever enters a place where Scripture is being purely expounded and rightly applied, he will look within and examine himself, even though he has no inkling of who God is and has wandered in as if on a whim. He will see himself as under judgment and, being convinced, will be compelled to condemn himself. He will have to fall on his face and worship God with fear and with humility (1 Cor. 14:23-25). Furthermore, Scripture says that God's word consists not in talk but in power (cf. 1 Cor. 4:20). The readiest explanation of this is provided by Luke, when he declares that 'his word was with power'. Mark tells us that he did not preach like the scribes, but that 'he spoke with authority'.

Now in those times the scribes, and above all the Pharisees, had most influence. Men were expected to abide by their determinations, just as nowadays in popery it is the holy councils of 'our holy mother church' that are cited. This is meant to shut the mouths of everyone—yes, and to bury the law of God, the prophets and the gospel! The same was true in those times: all further enquiry was forbidden beyond what 'our venerable masters' had decreed. This was the title given to the scribes and Pharisees, since they expounded Scripture. So although the scribes were pre-eminent among the people, and although everyone trembled at their every word, the Evangelists note that Jesus Christ did not teach as they did. He taught with authority or, as Luke says, with power.

How could that be? Although the scribes—the word means 'teachers' in Hebrew—were highly regarded and so much esteemed that no one dared object to their explanations, they were cold when it came to handling holy Scripture. They went in for obscure, hidden interpretations and glosses; there was no really useful teaching, so that what they taught was incapable of moving people. On the other hand, when Jesus Christ spoke, they realized that he taught with the authority of God his Father. Even though he was not of great repute or influence, and was considered ignorant since he had been a carpenter all his life, they were nevertheless astonished by his teaching. Why? It is as I said earlier, the kingdom of God—that is, the proclamation of the gospel—does not consist in words or talk, or in some kind of eloquence or splendid oratory which we find agreeable and which tickles our ears. Talk like that is useless. No, it consists in power, which is worth far more than all the eloquence in the world.

Because, therefore, that same power is offered to us today in the gospel—that same power and more, and in much truer measure—let us learn not only to be astonished for a time, but to be renewed and made obedient to our God. May there be zeal which burns within us and which drives us on, and may it last so that we persevere throughout our lives. May we learn also to stand apart from those whom Paul describes as hearers who never benefit from teaching, however hard they try (2 Tim. 3:7). It is the same in popery. There are those who spend their lives in endless speculation. A doctor of theology will have spent ten years in pointless debate! Now how could anyone spend so much time and yet learn nothing? The fact is, they concentrate on silly trifles and on more gross absurdities than anyone could imagine. And having spent their whole life at it, they still will not have grasped the ABC of faith! They have no concept of faith, repentance or of prayer to God; they have no idea how they can be justified or saved; they know nothing of the remission of sins, or of the nature and purpose of the sacraments. The busier they are with their nonsense, the stupider they become, so that, to their shame, mere children, beginners in the catechism, are able to instruct them. And when they go up into the pulpit, all they do is entertain the people, or pose such crazy, half-baked questions as is dreadful to relate. Their preaching makes a mockery of holy Scripture, or else is so far-fetched that it buries it completely.

Occasionally, it is true, there will be some who preach sound doctrine. They seem to work wonders, but at the slightest sign of persecution we find that it is all a matter of form. They have never had a real fear of God, nor any true religion. When we see such cold and lifeless teaching, we should realize how good God has been to us in choosing to reveal himself through the law, the prophets and the gospel. Let us recognize his majesty and power, since he teaches us with power, and since our Lord Jesus Christ holds the royal sceptre in his hand, so that we might give obedience to him. May he have dominion over us, as is his right, and may we be for him a people peaceful and submissive.

Now let us cast ourselves down before the majesty of our good God, acknowledging our faults and praying that he may touch us to the quick, so that we may more and more detest them. May we not only seek pardon for them, but may he so correct us by his Holy Spirit that we are drawn ever closer to him, to the end that, being made new, we may serve him as he demands, not only by outward show but with true affection of heart.

17

THE HOLY ONE OF GOD

And there was in their synagogue a man with an unclean spirit; [24]and he cried out, 'What is there between you and us, Jesus of Nazareth? Have you come to destroy us? I know who you are, the Holy One of God.' [25]But Jesus rebuked him, saying, 'Be silent, and come out of him.' [26]And the unclean spirit, convulsing him and crying with a loud voice, came out of him. [27]They were all amazed, so that they questioned among themselves, saying, 'What new teaching is this? With authority he commands even the unclean spirits, and they obey him' (Mark 1:23-27).

And in the synagogue there was a man who had the spirit of an unclean demon; and he cried out with a loud voice, [34]'Ah, what is there between you and us, Jesus of Nazareth? Have you come to destroy us? I know who you are, the Holy One of God.' [35]But Jesus rebuked him, saying, 'Be silent, and come out of him.' And when the demon had thrown him down in the midst, he came out of him and did him no harm. [36]Then amazement came over all of them, and they said to one another, 'What is this new word, that with authority and power he commands the unclean spirits, and they come out?' (Luke 4:33-36).

IN THE POWER OF THE SPIRIT

We have seen in general how our Lord Jesus Christ healed many who were demon-possessed. Now Mark and Luke tell the story of a man who was healed in the synagogue at Capernaum, for there are certain events here which are worth noting. This miracle is out of the ordinary and stands apart from the rest.

We must always remember that miracles were not performed without teaching being added. They were related to a specific purpose, as was explained earlier in some detail. Thus if our Lord had simply cured the man possessed by the devil without showing that he was a teacher and prophet sent by God, it would not have achieved much. As it was, the gospel was confirmed, so that all were made aware that the one who spoke did so by virtue of a heavenly gift, that God acknowledged him as his servant and that he had authority.

The people of Capernaum clearly recognized this, for we are told at the end that they were astonished by his teaching. Moreover it is said that the demon spoke through the lips of this poor man, asking, 'Have you come to destroy us? We know that you are the Holy One of God. Let that be enough!' See, on the one hand, how the demons were compelled to do homage to the Son of God, for as Scripture says, 'Every knee must bow before him' (Phil. 2:10). However rebellious the demons are, and however hard they war against God, they must nevertheless kneel before his majesty. The end result is not that they accept the yoke in a peaceable spirit: they always remain proud and wage frenzied war upon God. Even so, they are brought to the point of confessing that God keeps them in check and tightly bound, and that they can do nothing without his leave.

This shows that they are beings created by God. Not that they were like this originally: it was their own wickedness which corrupted them. Just as our father Adam by his fall made us full of sin and iniquity, so too the devil estranged himself from God.

He was stripped of uprightness and integrity, so that all that was left to him was utter evil and damnation. There was, however, one difference. God took pity on men and sought to repair our sin by rescuing us from death through our Lord Jesus Christ. The demons, on the other hand, remained irretrievably lost.

This ought to make us prize God's goodness all the more, because while those he created to be his angels remained damned and ruined, he stretched out his hand to us to bring us back to life—life from which we had been banished. This, then, is one point. The devils are forced, one way or another, to confess that God holds them in check; they are subject to him and under his power. Naturally they would dearly love to escape his hand and control. They are like an offender who appears before his judge to receive a guilty verdict, one that leads to death. It is not as if he does not rebel and gnash his teeth. He would love to sweep all social and civil order away if he could. It is the same with the demons: they indeed bow before God, the sovereign judge, but they bow unwillingly, by force. For all that, as I said, they are by no means mollified; they will not curb their wilfulness or correct their rebelliousness.

This is why the demon says, '*What have you to do with us, Jesus of Nazareth? We know who you are, the Holy One of God!*' The demon admittedly confesses who Jesus Christ is, but our Lord does not accept his confession. He demands that he be silent, and commands him to come out of the man. His confession is clearly reluctant and unwilling. We conclude, however, that in calling Jesus Christ the Holy One of God, the demon sees him as his judge, as the one who has come to strip him of the fatal tyranny and dominion he holds over Adam's children. Jesus Christ is not simply in himself the Holy One of God: he has come to fill the world with his holiness, but this can only happen when the devil is defeated. So it is only because he is constrained that the demon says, 'You have nothing to do with us, for you are the Holy One of God.' This, then, is the type of homage which the unclean spirits pay to the Son of God, to him who is sovereign over every creature. It is forced homage. The demons would gladly take back what they gave, and would willingly destroy his power if they could.

Before continuing, however, we might ask how the demon knew that Jesus Christ was the world's Redeemer. True, this is a special revelation given by God to his elect, but we should understand that there are many levels of knowledge. Faith implies that we know that God holds all things in his hand, that as the Creator of the world he must also preserve it, and that we therefore owe him honour and obedience. Believers, however, know both this and more besides. They know that God is their Father and Saviour, that they must rely entirely on his goodness and be certain of their salvation, since he receives them in his grace and mercy. Yet to know that there is a God who rules the world is a confused sort of knowledge, which is what the devil has. If he were not convinced of it, he would never tremble before God's judgment seat. Hence we see in Job the devil along with the angels begging leave to do his work, and God issuing commands just as he wills (Job 1:6-12; 2:1-6). This demonstrates that in the demons as in men, there is a general awareness of God's majesty. Believers, however, have much more, as I said. They know that God is favourable to them, and that in pardoning their sins he reckons them as righteous; when they call upon him, he is ready to answer them. Thus it is that James mocks those who think of faith as fickle belief in God's existence, and declares that the devils have something more. 'They tremble,' he says (James 2:19).

Evildoers will glibly concede that it is right that God be honoured, yet they despise him and deride his word and worship. So as we see, the demons have much more knowledge than the worldly and the faithless who have stifled all religion in their hearts. Instead of trembling before God's awful majesty, they merely scoff; they are drowsy like brute beasts. The devil, on the other hand, is compelled to quake! It is not surprising, then, that he acknowledges God's majesty whenever it appears.

As for our Lord Jesus Christ, the demons, as we see, knew that he had been sent to save the world, to condemn them and to rouse them to fury all the more, since God had had mercy on the human race, while leaving them defeated and dismayed. Furthermore, because God wished to display more openly the riches of his grace and to reveal his glory, the devils strove all the more to oppose and to thwart it. This was bound to happen.

Now the popish theologians in their folly and stupidity have never been able to distinguish real faith from what the devil knows and believes about God. James indeed uses the word 'faith', but in the sense understood by those he is addressing (James 2:19). He does so ironically, saying to them, 'You believe, but you are worse than the devils.' Popish theology regards faith simply as awareness which has God as its object, as knowledge that Jesus Christ is his only-begotten Son, and as certainty concerning the truth of Scripture. That is what the papists hold faith to be. They think, however, that we can come to it thanks to our own natural ability, with just a small addition supplied by God through his Holy Spirit. At all events, they consider faith to be a vague kind of understanding. That is why they say that faith is without shape or form. It is like a disordered mass; only with the help of love does it begin to become formed.[1] They fail to see the principle I touched on earlier, which is that God's children do not merely comprehend God's majesty so that it fills

[1] Calvin identifies two kinds of faith as defined by the mediaeval Schoolmen: faith as bare assent to Christian doctrine ('unformed faith'), and faith supplemented by love ('formed faith'). He argues that unformed faith is an illusion, tantamount to ignorance, and that to regard love as an accessory to faith is to misunderstand faith's true nature: faith places the believer in an immediate relationship of trust and love toward God in Christ. Cf. *Inst.* III.2.8-10.

them with awe, nor do they view him only in his eternal essence and in the power by which he upholds and rules all things. They go much further, for they are led to see that he is their Father, and that Jesus Christ came to unite them to himself in a life that never ends, so that by this means he might deliver them from everlasting death.

The devil, however, knows nothing of this. Here we see him trying to escape from the hands of our Lord Jesus Christ and choosing to push him far away. Believers, by contrast, are taught to draw near to God by faith. Faith, therefore, is the means by which we are united with God, whereas the knowledge which the demons and unbelievers have inflames them all the more, so that they loathe God, shun him and drive him far from them. The knowledge that God exists continually terrifies both men and demons. They abhor the thought that God might draw near to them; instead, as I said, they want to get as far away from him as possible.

There is thus a world of difference between faith as given to us by God, and the knowledge which the godless and unbelieving possess. We cannot believe in God unless we are enlightened by his Holy Spirit. This is not something common to everyone. In any case, how absurd it is to call faith unformed, when God has given us the Spirit of adoption, by whom we cry aloud that he is our Father and recognize him as such (Rom. 8:15; Gal. 4:6)! How absurd, when we have the earnest of our inheritance and of the life which has been promised to us, and when, assured of the mercy and goodness of our God, we are reconciled to him and are reckoned to be his children! How can this be called faith without shape or form?

It is plain, then, that the devil has so blinded the papists that they are blinder than the prince of darkness. This is God's just judgment on them for having rejected his word in favour of idle speculation, which keeps them in error and in devilish superstition. When we see these things, we ought to praise God all the more for his grace, for we would be the same as they are if he had forsaken us as he has them.

Let us be assured of this: the demons know that they are God's creation, and that they should therefore yield to his dominion. This does not stop them resisting him and making frenzied attempts to diminish his power, but they can do nothing. Although awareness of God's supreme power and knowledge of their own powerlessness are two contrasting things, we see both of them at work here. The demon confesses that Jesus Christ has been sent by God his Father, yet he tries to push him far away and to stop him doing his appointed work. Such, however, is the devil's fury that, in knowing, he does not know. The same can be said of all unbelievers.

The phrase 'the Holy One of God' reveals that our Lord Jesus Christ was, of necessity, set apart as Mediator from the ranks of ordinary men. The faithful, it is true, are also called holy, but it is because they are counted as God's children. There is a vast difference between the Head and the body! Scripture calls the whole of Israel 'the sons of God', and even 'God's first-born', as Hosea says (cf. Hos. 11:1). Yet the title only applies to Jesus Christ, who is the true Son of God. Thus, in our Creed, we say that he is God's only-begotten Son. Although we are called children of God, it is he who is God's proper Son; we are children by adoption, since being united to him we are made to share in all his benefits. The privilege of being God's children does not belong to us: we enjoy it because of God's free gift. Thus when we are called holy, holiness is not something we bring from our mother's womb. We are filthy and corrupt; all of us are defiled in God's sight. So in Psalm 51 David declares that he was begotten in iniquity and conceived by his mother in sin (Psa. 51:5). He does not mean to accuse his mother, but expresses the condemnation which he himself deserves. It is as if he says, 'Lord, I had not yet emerged from my mother's womb, but I was already a vile, loathsome creature, unclean through and through.'

While the title 'holy' cannot in any way be ascribed to us, our Lord Jesus Christ was conceived, as we know, by the Holy Spirit, that he might be without spot. Then too he was sanctified, so that grace in all its fullness might dwell in him. From him we must draw all the goodness we have, for, as we read in the first chapter of John, he has it to perfection (John 1:16). However wonderfully endowed with grace we may be, not one of us has it except in part and to a limited degree. Our Lord Jesus Christ has it totally, in himself. If, then, we all come thirstily to drink at this spring, we will be fully satisfied, but we cannot look within ourselves for what comes to us from somewhere else.

To sum up, our Lord's holiness differs in three ways from the holiness of believers. First, his holiness is natural, while we are cursed from our mother's womb. Second, he has it in its fullness, but we only to the extent that God judges is expedient for us. Third, his holiness is such that it is given to all of us; ours is sufficient only for our salvation. His is a holiness which sanctifies. As for ourselves, we are holy because we draw upon his holiness, which is complete and perfect, and which we have in part, according as God apportions, and then only as we are cleansed from sin and are allied with him, being engrafted into his body so that, as members of him, we may also share in his Spirit.

We are thus able to understand the sense in which our Lord Jesus Christ is called the Holy One of God. This expression was without doubt popular among the people, for the devil adapted his words to what was then generally understood. The Jews were well aware that the Redeemer who was to be sent would be the Holy One of God, for God would sign and mark him not by some outward mark but by anointing him with every perfection. We ourselves are called 'Christs', God's anointed, but only in order to show that we have it through him who is called the Christ. As Simeon had earlier said, 'Now that I have seen the Lord's anointed, I am content for God to take me to himself whenever he pleases' (cf. Luke 2:29-30). So now we have a name which derives from him, demonstrating that our Lord Jesus Christ is the source of that spiritual anointing, and thus of the holiness of which this verse speaks.

As the world's Redeemer who has brought us salvation, Jesus Christ stands apart from the ranks of ordinary men. How is that? It is because he was pure and clear of every fault and blemish. That is one point. A second is that he received the Holy Spirit's gifts in all their fullness. As Isaiah says, God's Spirit rested on him (Isa. 11:2; 61:1). In the third place, he was richly endowed not for his own sake and purpose—he needed nothing—but for ours. Accordingly his riches are meant to help and remedy our poverty and indigence, for we are empty of all goodness. We must, however, receive them through him alone.

Now if we take an overall view of things, what more do we have that the devil does not? We can go much further. We know that our Lord Jesus Christ was sanctified to cleanse us by his grace of all defilement. He was set apart from men to make us partners with the angels and heirs of the kingdom of heaven; to bring us to new birth that we might serve God and walk in righteousness of life, instead of in our sinful passions and desires. He was set apart so that when we appear before God our transgressions should no longer be imputed to us, and so that we might be certain that God will accept us as if we were blameless. In any event, only in God's Son, and when we are joined to him by faith, do we have all that is necessary for our salvation. This, then, is what we need if we are rightly and sincerely to confess that Jesus Christ is the Holy One of God.

That was why the demon was compelled to say no more, and why our Lord said to him, '*Be silent.*' For although the demon confessed the essence of the gospel in one word, he intended to convey the very opposite. His aim, as we see, was to rob Jesus Christ of what belonged to him and to maintain his own tyranny. The devil is the king and prince of darkness; his one aim is to draw into it everyone on earth and to keep them there. On the other hand, our Lord Jesus Christ is the light of the world; he is life and resurrection, righteousness and sanctification, as is so often said in Scripture. He cannot be the Holy One of God without the devil being vanquished, for darkness must become light, death must cease, life must be restored and iniquity blotted out. As John says in his first letter, Jesus Christ came to take away sin and to establish God's righteousness (1 John 3:5). Our Lord had thus every reason to command silence, but he also had something else in mind. The devil resorted to this ruse in order to give the impression that he had some connection with the Son of God. This was meant to diminish confidence in the gospel. Nor did it happen only once. Satan has continued to follow this strategy, so that, under the guise of Christianity, there has been so much falsity and fiction—all of it completely absurd. On this pretext false teaching has been introduced.

For example, the gospel simply and plainly sets Jesus Christ before us, but the devil will have none of it. What, then, does he do? He will try of course to trample sound teaching underfoot, and will arm everyone to combat it. If, however, he cannot openly succeed, he stirs up bigots and rogues to write stories about our Lord's childhood, books so full of idiocy and nonsense that stories like those of Melusine are not nearly so silly.[2] Others again write tales where there is only falsehood and deceit. The devil pretends to honour the Son of God, but his purpose is to make us think that the gospel is full of lies. How, then, could

[2] Melusine (Melusina) appears in European folklore as a water-spirit, half-woman, half-serpent or fish. Jean d'Arras popularized her legend in a series of fourteenth-century tales. Calvin's point is that miracle stories concerning the holy family and those worshipped as saints belong to the same realm of myth.

anyone tell the difference between it and all that nonsense once it makes its way into the world? In this indirect and underhand way, Satan has sought to destroy the authority of the gospel so that we are left in suspense, not knowing what we should hold to. The same is true of the miracle stories which have been written, crediting our Lord with any number of magic tricks.

Since then worse has happened. In our own day madmen have followed suit by pretending that, like us, they adhere to sound teaching; but in publishing the first part of Mark's Gospel they have composed a book which is good only for a laugh, for there is no one, Turk, Jew or pagan, who cannot see how shocking it is, with all its lies and deceptions. Yet they make out that these are all miracles wrought by God during the childhood of Jesus Christ![3] So the devil has continued to employ his guile, as is clear from Mark and Luke's accounts, and as later became so popular among the papists.

The devil does not deny that Jesus Christ is God's only-begotten Son, and that there is but one God. He says the same today through the mouths of these charlatans and liars. But instead of honouring our Lord by declaring him to be the way, the truth and the life (John 14:6), they insist that we must worship Mary his mother, the saints and angels—idols and statuettes! They preach endlessly about free will, argue about merits and works of supererogation, about how paradise can be won, about intercessions and spiritual devotions—that is, about how they have perverted, degraded and falsified God's worship! When we see how the devil has made a false confession and by mixing in his poison has made it impossible to tell truth from error—when we see this, we must follow our Lord's example and drive all such fantasies away. We must keep the gospel pure

[3] The book has not been identified. A spurious Gospel of Mark, perhaps, designed to appeal to a popular readership? The reference is in any case puzzling, since of the three Synoptists, Mark is the only one not to speak of Jesus' birth and childhood.

and whole. When, therefore, we confess Jesus Christ to be the Son of God, let us be sure we know why God sent him. It was so that we should make him our only teacher and instructor, and should close our ears to all other teachings, showing that we no more agree with them than we do with Satan and Belial.

For the rest, let this miracle be an image of our own experience. While Satan may not possess us visibly, he is the prince of this world; we are in bondage to him. Hence it is said in the eighth chapter of John that if we would be free, it is Jesus Christ who must deliver us (John 8:31-32). In the story recorded for us here, we have a mirror which shows us what we are and in what condition God finds us. Let us, then, make that our boast, and vaunt our free will, our works of merit, our ready disposition, all the favours we return to God and all the worship we pay him! Even so, the devil will most surely be our master until our Lord Jesus Christ receives us in his mercy.

We read that when this poor man was freed from Satan, *he was convulsed; the demon threw him down upon the ground, but did not harm him.* In the same way, when Jesus Christ delivers us, we should not be surprised if we feel some violent agitation. No harm will come to us and we will be preserved by the power of God's Son. True, we cannot turn and believe unless we deny ourselves. This is in itself a hard fight, and the devil more than ever strives to stir up our resentment against God. We will be severely troubled and tested. Yet we should bear this patiently and be content to know that it will all work for our good and for our salvation. Inwardly we will suffer much strain, and may even go so far as to gnash our teeth, as it were. All this can be put behind us, provided we reach the goal to which this story points.

Our passage concludes this way: *Amazement came over those who saw the miracle.* To this Luke adds: *They were overcome with fear, and said, 'What is this new word? For with authority and power he commands the unclean spirits; they obey him and come out.'* Here we see, as I said before, that those who witnessed this evidence of Jesus Christ's power knew that it confirmed his teaching. Earlier they had shown caution by calling him a great man. Now they started to say, 'This man possesses more than human power. God, we must admit, has given proof of his authority.' Why? Because his message had to bear God's seal, showing that God was its author. That was the thought which ran through their minds. So at the very least (though, as we will see, they remained only on the threshold)—at the very least, I say, we must discern the end to which our Lord's miracles were directed. For who are these people speaking here? Poor folk, who have some grasp of who God is, and who are moved by feelings of reverence. Yet they do not enter the church; they remain uncommitted—only dabbling, we might say.

We must go further than they did if we would be disciples of Jesus Christ. We must progress to the point where his teaching becomes thoroughly familiar to us. Here we find poor folk who always remained ignorant, but who nevertheless perceived that miracles are evidence that the gospel is God's truth. In popery, the only effect of miracles is to abolish all real teaching, so that they worship some saint or other, go off on pilgrimages, pray for the dead, canonize the body of this one or that, or bring in some petty devotion. The truth of the gospel is meant to be sealed by genuine miracles. Yet what have they done? They have made sure that the gospel message perishes, that we ignore its contents, that we throw ashes on the fire to damp it down, or even a bucketful of water to put it completely out! Meanwhile they waste their time over a lamp lit at high noon, but refuse the light of the sun! And what are they on about today? There is no chance that they will say, 'It is written. This is what holy Scripture teaches, and we must stick to it.' No, 'Scripture is a nose of wax,' they cry. 'There is no certainty in it, but miracles are infallible.' So what do these miracles say? The very opposite to what the gospel says. They set the creature upon the throne of God, so that, to quote their own proverb, God is lost in the crowd.[4]

That is one thing to note. A second concerns the fact that 'fear came upon them'. What this shows is that every time we witness signs of God's glory, we should tremble before him and humble ourselves. This is different from how these folk behaved. They were moved by feelings of awe; indeed it is almost as if they were overwhelmed. Yet they remained confused. We too should be overwhelmed, but we should control our feelings, not forgetting that there is a God who wants us to revere him, to love him and to be united with him so that he dwells in us, for we are temples of his Holy Spirit and members of the body of his only Son (1 Cor. 3:16; 6:19).

When, in addition, they say, 'What is this new word?', they do not mean to rebuke our Lord's teaching, as some have wrongly understood. They are showing that in our Lord Jesus Christ they find something unaccustomed. We should not regard the message of the gospel as in any way new, for Jesus Christ is the end of the law; he is its soul. He is also the pattern which Moses saw on the mountain, and to which all the symbols of the law point (Exod. 25:9, 40). In short, the gospel must not be separated from the law. This is why we are called children of Abraham (Rom. 4:16; Gal. 3:7, 29). If the faith we have did not agree with his, how could he be the father of all believers? In terms of their basic teaching, the gospel and the law agree.[5]

The fact remains, however, that this is a new teaching, for as Isaiah says, with the coming of the Son of God and the restoration of the church, all will be renewed (Isa. 65:17). The

[4] On the 'nose of wax' image, see above, p. 111, note 3; and on the saying, 'God is lost in the crowd', p. 42, note 2.

[5] Unlike Luther, who contrasts the law (which condemns) with the gospel (which acquits), Calvin holds that both law and gospel belong to the one covenant of grace, which locates salvation only in God's mercy and makes Jesus Christ its sole Mediator. See further *Inst.* II.10.2-4.

gospel is both an old and new message. Thus, although our Lord Jesus Christ, in thinking of the evils of the past, said, 'I bring you a new commandment, that you should love one another' (John 13:34), John, in his first letter, calls it both an old and new commandment (1 John 2:7). In saying this he makes it clear that the gospel contains nothing which is not also in the law, but because our reason cannot grasp this commandment, he calls it new.

There is another, more weighty reason, why the gospel is a new message. The law was a matter of symbols and shadows, but in the gospel God appears to us as if face to face. The veil which was in front of Moses' face has now been removed (2 Cor. 3:15). God's will is that we know him intimately in the person of our Lord Jesus Christ. That is why he says that he will no longer call his disciples servants, but close friends (John 15:15). The message of the gospel can thus be said to be not old, but neither is it new. Its authority is timeless.

Although, then, these poor folk had been badly taught, they showed no contempt when they called the gospel 'new teaching'. Nevertheless they got only half-way along the road, and remained standing outside the door. They ought to have enquired much more in order to strengthen their faith and to receive what Jesus Christ was bringing them. They were left awe-struck. For our part, we should learn to feel such awe as will dispose us to humility and make us bow our necks to accept the yoke, to kneel in worship and to abase ourselves, so that he, in his grace, may lift us up. That is the final point we need to bear in mind.

It remains for me to inform you that Master Jean Raimond Merlin has been chosen and accepted by our city fathers and, God willing, will be inducted next Sunday. If anyone knows of any objection to him, either to his life or doctrine, let him tell it to the authorities.[6]

[6] Previously professor of Hebrew in Lausanne, Merlin was pastor of a rural parish

Now let us cast ourselves down before the majesty of our good God, acknowledging our faults and praying that he may so touch us that we cease to love them, and ask forgiveness for them. And since by nature we are under the devil's tyranny and in bondage to him, and must remain so until delivered by our Lord Jesus Christ, may he be pleased to draw us to himself and to bring us to the glory into which he entered for our sake.

at the time of his transfer to Geneva (1560). Between 1561 and 1564 he was entrusted with important missions in France. While ministers were nominated by the Genevan pastorate, it was the City Council which appointed and paid them.

18

BEARER OF OUR INFIRMITIES

And coming into Peter's house, Jesus saw his mother-in-law lying in bed with a fever. [15]*He touched her hand and the fever left her, and she rose and served them.* [16]*When evening had come, they brought many who were demon-possessed, from whom he cast out spirits with his word, and healed all who were sick,* [17]*so that what was said by the prophet Isaiah was fulfilled, 'He took our infirmities and bore our diseases.'* [18]*Then, seeing great crowds of people around him, he gave orders to go over to the other side* (Matt. 8:14-18).

Soon after, leaving the synagogue, they came with John and James into the house of Simon and Andrew. [30]*Now Simon's mother-in-law lay in bed with a fever, and immediately they told him about her.* [31]*Then, drawing near, he took her by the hand and lifted her up, and immediately the fever left her, and she served them.* [32]*When evening had come, as the sun was setting, they brought to him all who were sick or demon-possessed.* [33]*The whole town was gathered at the door.* [34]*And he healed many who were sick with various diseases and cast out many demons; and he would not allow the demons to say that they knew him.* [35]*Then, in the morning, while it was still quite dark, he got up and went out to a lonely place, and there he prayed.* [36]*And Simon and those who were with him followed him;* [37]*and when they found him, they said, 'Everyone is looking for you.'* [38]*Then he said to*

them, 'Let us go on to the next towns, that I may preach there also,
for that is why I have come.' 39 *Thus he preached in their synagogues*
throughout Galilee, casting out demons (Mark 1:29-39).

When Jesus arose and left the synagogue, he entered Simon's house.
Now Simon's mother-in-law was ill with a high fever, and they
pleaded with him for her. 39 *And leaning over her he rebuked the*
fever and it left her; and immediately she got up and served them.
40 *And as the sun was setting, all who had any who were sick with*
various diseases brought them to him, and laying his hands on each
of them he healed them. 41 *Demons also came out of many, crying,*
'You are the Son of God.' But he rebuked them, and would not allow
them to say that they knew he was the Christ. 42 *And when it was*
day, he departed and went into a lonely place; the crowd looked for
him and came to him, restraining him in case he should leave them.
43 *But he said to them, 'I must go and preach the good news of the*
kingdom of God to the other towns also, for this is why I was sent'
(Luke 4:38-43).

ALTHOUGH the Evangelists give us a general account of how our Lord Jesus Christ gave proof of his divine majesty and power, by healing the sick and casting out demons, we have a striking illustration here in the case of Peter's mother-in-law, whom our Lord cured of a fever. It is true that to cast out demons was a much more miraculous work, more memorable than the act of curing a fever. In the same way, to restore paralytics to health, and to give light to the blind and hearing to the deaf, are much more impressive than healing a common illness. This story, however, is expressly told because of the person it concerns.

Here, then, we see Peter who has already been called to be a disciple of Jesus Christ. *His mother-in-law lies ill.* We should note from this that those who follow the Son of God are not so privileged that they never suffer affliction, they, their friends or relatives. Our Lord does not accept us as his disciples on the understanding that we will live in pleasure, to our heart's content, as if in some earthly paradise. We have to be trained by many afflictions, if only because we need to be humbled and to be made aware of our misery. These prompt us to call upon God and are meant to test our endurance.

Nevertheless, we learn that our Lord Jesus Christ cured the woman. There is no doubt that by this means he sought to support Peter in his weakness, and also the household who may have felt upset. We know that poor folk who live from hand to mouth are anxious when all work ceases and when money does not come in as usual. In the past, Peter and his brother had earned a living by fishing, but in following Jesus Christ they had taken a backward step. It seemed as if they had given up work and become mere idlers! No one at home was immediately aware of the zeal which had motivated them. There might easily have been grumbling, for we all think about ourselves and about our daily food. Poor people find it harder to manage than the rich, because all at once they have nothing left. Any savings they may have do not amount to much, and only a week or month is needed before everything is exhausted. Our Lord thus sought to forestall all this and to make amends by healing Peter's mother-in-law.

Because, then, the disciples were still very ignorant—novices, really—they needed to be strengthened and to be convinced that it was not for nothing that they had given themselves to the one who had called them to be partners with him, and to leave home, at least in part. This miracle was thus of benefit to Peter and his brother Andrew, as it was to John and James. It also benefited the whole family. The mother-in-law was cured by the hand of God's Son and had cause for satisfaction, even though her son-in-law was now following one who had previously been despised. In sum, we see that our Lord Jesus Christ took pity on this woman and on all who were with her, not only by restoring her to health and by relieving her of her illness, but by enabling them all to consent calmly to Peter's being called, so that neither his wife nor his friends stopped him, or quarrelled or reproached him for giving up his occupation. That is the significance of this particular miracle.

Again, we read that those who were in the house *pleaded with him for her, and spoke to him about her*. The papists immediately take this verse to mean that we should pray to the saints, and that Jesus Christ's disciples were acting here as intercessors and advocates! In distorting holy Scripture this way and in tearing it to pieces, they merely display their folly and, with it, their impudence. They shamelessly trot out such passages but make them say the very opposite of what was intended. The fact that the disciples were concerned for this poor woman and tried to help her in her need, teaches us that we should feel compassion for those who suffer, so that we pray for them and ask God to look with favour on them.

This verse speaks of the living, and this is how we should practise love, with each of us thinking not simply of ourselves when we pray. Let us remember that God has hallowed fellowship among us and that we should unite with all our neighbours, praying as one to God. So if we see someone who is suffering illness or some other adversity, this should rouse and spur us to pray all the more intensely. That is the lesson for us here.

We discover also that our prayers are not in vain. In granting their requests concerning Peter's mother-in-law, our Lord demonstrates that our hopes will not be disappointed when we address our prayers to God—our prayers, that is, not just for ourselves but for those to whom we are attached, and whose welfare and safety we ought to ensure as much as we can.

Our Lord Jesus Christ could well have healed this woman beforehand, for that was what he had decided to do. He wished, however, to be asked. Why was that? It was meant for our instruction, as will shortly be explained. Now when Scripture says that *he rebuked the fever*, there is no suggestion that the illness understood what was said to it. What it means is that although illnesses have neither sense nor reason, they nevertheless obey God one way or another. They are messengers of his wrath when he sends us sickness, famine, plague, war or other afflictions. In this way illnesses obey God; they therefore obey our Lord Jesus Christ who is true God, manifest in the flesh (1 Tim. 3:16). They obey him whenever, according to his good pleasure, he chastises us for our faults. In short, just as Scripture calls afflictions rods in God's hand by which he tames our pride and rebelliousness, reminds us of the sins we have committed or tests our faith and obedience, so too they can be rightly called God's messengers.[1] Accordingly, although illnesses are devoid of feeling and understanding, God works through them so that they appear to convey a lesson, for he says to them, 'This is the work I now have for you. You will go thus far but no further. Such-and-such a one will suffer this much, but not more.' We note, then, from the fact that Jesus Christ rebuked the fever, that afflictions do a secret work which is beyond our understanding; but this is to show that he rules over everything and orders all things in such a way that there is nothing which is not subject to him.

We are taught a double lesson here. First, when we are buffeted by illness or some other misfortune, if we complain and become most upset and impatient, we are really battling against God. Admittedly, we find illness painful and we are bound to feel regret. Even so we should bow our heads and accept the yoke which is placed on our necks, knowing that illnesses do not come of their own accord but are sent by God, who tells them to what extent they may afflict us.

[1] A classic statement of the threefold 'uses' of adversity: punishment, humility and testing. Cf. *Inst.* III.8.4-6.

The second lesson is that we must turn to God, not doubting that although illnesses are hard to bear and may even seem fatal, so that they overwhelm us to the point that we can hardly breathe, when God is pleased to grant us relief and a happy outcome—when, I say, he is disposed to do this, and when we know these things are in his hand, then we should learn to look to him for aid and to be sure that he will have compassion on us. And if he delays, we should understand that it is not for us to lay down dates and times; we must wait for the right moment, when his work is done.

That said, Matthew comments that in healing the demon-possessed and others who were ill, our Lord Jesus Christ fulfilled the prophecy of Isaiah: *He took our infirmities and bore our diseases* (Isa. 53:4). At first glance we might think this passage was inappropriately cited, and that its natural meaning had been twisted. Isaiah was not referring to bodily diseases, and he made no mention of things to do with this world's transitory life. He was referring to the sins which lead us to death, and which are portents of death itself. Scripture says that our Lord bore them all. This, then, is Isaiah's starting point: our Lord Jesus Christ was so bruised that all turned their faces from him; he was so horribly disfigured that his face was scarcely human; everyone considered him to be past all hope (Isa. 53:2-3). In short, Isaiah is referring to the fact not only that our Lord became a mortal man, subject to all our misery, but that he finally suffered a shameful death in the eyes of men, a death cursed by the mouth of God himself. It was as if he were the worst criminal who ever lived, on whom God poured such vengeance as to make the hairs of our head stand on end whenever we hear of it.

Despite this, however, Isaiah tells us not to turn our eyes away from Jesus Christ, not to despise him or shrink in horror from him. Instead, we are to seek from him not only healing but everlasting salvation. The prophet thus points us to the fruit which comes to us from the death and passion of God's Son. He took our infirmities and bore our diseases—our spiritual diseases. Yet in this passage Matthew is describing paralysis, fevers and similar things. How do these agree with what Isaiah says?

It is true that Jesus Christ's kingdom is spiritual, but while reconciling us to God his Father he nevertheless causes us, even in this perishable life, to be blessed. Still, we must always remember the main point, which is that our Lord's task is to call us out of this world to the life of heaven. And how does that happen? It is only when our sins are pardoned and when, being born again by the Holy Spirit, we receive the sign of adoption and the assurance that God reckons us as his children. It is absolutely certain, then, that in our Lord Jesus Christ we must seek healing for our sins, which make us not only sick and feeble in God's sight but completely dead, for we have transgressed God's law and are accursed. Further, we are estranged from him who is the source of life: we are therefore lost. However, when our Lord Jesus Christ offered himself as a sacrifice, it was to blot out our offences, and to make us guiltless in God's sight. Our sins will not be held to our account.

This is what we must seek in Jesus Christ. Once we are washed and cleansed by his blood, we must ask to be healed of our spiritual diseases, so that, being born of his Holy Spirit, we may dwell in God and he in us, and may belong to him. The devil, on the other hand, holds sway over all who do not belong to our Lord Jesus Christ.

Such is the prophet's meaning. Had he said only that Jesus Christ would be crucified, we would all surely have turned away from him, for, as Scripture says, 'Cursed is he who hangs on the tree' (Deut. 21:23). Again, we see Jesus Christ hanging between two thieves and everyone spitting in his face. We see him burdened with shame, as if he were suffering for his own crimes. If all we had was the simple story of our Lord's death and passion, it would be enough to make us turn our backs on him and walk away, instead of drawing nearer. When, however, we are shown the fruit of his death and passion and the priceless benefit he has obtained, we will no longer be ashamed of him, as Paul says (cf. Gal. 6:14). Rather, we will boast that we find life in his death and God's grace in the condemnation which he bore. It is as Isaiah says, 'The punishment that brings us peace was laid upon him' (Isa. 53:5). His punishment was our peace, for God could not be reconciled to us or show us favour until we had given him satisfaction. We were answerable to him. In us there is only iniquity, but in him is full and complete righteousness. We ourselves cannot give him satisfaction. Our Lord Jesus Christ took that burden on himself and freed us from it. In this way our debt has been discharged, thanks to the payment he made by his death and passion.

We can see, however, that Matthew made apt use of Isaiah's testimony, consistent with his purpose. All that our Lord did was, in a sense, an image or representation adapted to men's ignorance. Things concerning his office and kingdom had to be represented by external means. There is a principle which we see at work here. Jesus Christ healed bodily diseases in order to show that he was the spiritual physician of our souls. In restoring strength and energy to paralytics, he showed that all power comes to us from him. In giving sight to the blind, he showed that we are all blind, not in our bodies but in our souls, and that it is only in him that we can have light. He has unstopped our ears so that we may hear his word and the message of life. In raising the dead, he testified that we are like poor decaying corpses whom he must pluck from the grave, not visibly but in a more excellent way, for he has to rescue us who are in Satan's bonds from the pit of everlasting death.

In all the visible miracles which Jesus Christ performed, we have a token of the work he does spiritually in our souls. What

Matthew therefore does is provide a good and fitting image of what our Lord was seen to do, an image which points to the essential thing that we must seek in him. It is as if Matthew were saying, 'Our Lord healed the sick in order to show that all that the world counts as health comes from his pure grace; he gave sight to the blind to show that we can hardly see a thing until he opens the eyes of our soul; and we are deaf until he unstops our ears so that we hear what he has to say.' In a word, we are powerless, with no strength even in a finger unless it is given to us by him. We are immersed in death until he comes to save us, according as he said, 'I am the resurrection and the life' (John 11:25).

So now we have a key to understanding all the miracles which are later recorded for us. Though we may not explain them in detail, we should each have wisdom to see that, when we read that Jesus Christ caused the lame to walk, we must tell ourselves, 'We could not walk one step unless our Lord supported us, or move an inch to accomplish some good work without his enabling power.' All the other miracles of bodily healing which we will see should be similarly interpreted. We should apply them to our souls, for our Lord was not sent to bring us earthly bliss, to give us victory in this world and to let us live a life of ease and comfort. Instead, he told us that we should have persecution and affliction in this world, and be mocked, abused, spat upon and vilified by all (Matt. 5:11; John 16:33). Scripture also says that we must be conformed to his image and suffer every hardship, so that, being gathered in by him, we may share the glory of his resurrection (Phil. 3:10-11).

When, therefore, we think of why our Lord was sent and of his appointed work, we must conclude that his miracles of bodily healing were simply images and types of what we must seek in him. He must be our physician, not only healing our diseases but raising us again to life.

The Gospels next relate that *he drew apart by himself to pray, and the crowd looked for him*. We will discuss prayer at another time, as the opportunity presents itself. For the moment, let us consider the closing verse, where we learn that our Lord Jesus Christ did not wish to stop in any one place, since he had to proclaim the gospel which, as we noted earlier, he calls the kingdom of God. He tells us why: '*For this reason I came out*, (or *was sent*).' We must remember that our Lord was to be the church's chief and supreme teacher. His duty and calling were to preach the gospel, not just in one place but in all Judaea. His role was not to be a shepherd in one place only, but throughout the land, until he had done all that pertained to our salvation. It was not enough for him to offer himself as a sacrifice to reconcile us to God; he had also to gather together God's elect by his teaching, and to grant them possession of their heavenly inheritance. When we think of how carefully he fulfilled his task, we should ponder the great concern he had for our salvation and the depth of his love for us. For although he was obedient to the one who sent him, he never lost sight of his goal, which was to take pity on his poor, wayward sheep, and, more widely, to have mercy on the human race by delivering it from perdition.

In the beginning, it is true, he preached only to the Jews, for as he later declares, he came for the lost sheep of the house of Israel (Matt. 15:24). Afterwards, however, it was necessary for the message which now calls all to the hope of salvation to be proclaimed to Gentiles and Jews without distinction. Our Lord's will is that he should permanently teach the church through those whom he appoints as ministers and pastors of his word. The voice from heaven which commanded us to listen to him (Matt. 17:5) teaches us not only to hear what he says with his own lips, but to accord his teaching authority to the very end of time. It teaches us also to see that the only way we can be united with God is by being quickened by faith in the gospel. This also is why Paul says, when speaking of our Lord's infinite power, that he ascended to heaven in order to fill all things (Eph. 4:10). So although Jesus Christ is absent from us in the body, and although here on earth we crawl about in dust and slime, he is not so absent from us that he does not show us how he fills all things by his power. How, then, does he do that? By giving us, says Paul, prophets, apostles, evangelists, pastors and teachers (Eph. 4:11). This is how our Lord Jesus Christ is today present among us. His voice is heard through those whom he chooses to be his organs and instruments.

Let us submit, therefore, to the order which he has established among us, and let us remember the zeal and love shown by these poor folk. They were ready to hear him, hanging as it were on his every word. They wanted him never to part from them, yet because of his responsibilities he could not satisfy them, for he was not appointed to be shepherd in one place only. Today, however, his will is that there should be shepherds in every church who represent him personally, and who should be heard in his name. They are, we might say, his deputies, commissioned for this very purpose. That being so, how ungrateful would we be if we refused to listen to the teaching which we know comes from God, and if we treat it with contempt!

That is the lesson for us here, and we must put it into practice. Whenever there are ministers to be inducted, it is vital that we know in whose name they come. For who are we, that we should be witnesses for God, and should promise the kingdom of heaven, the forgiveness of sins and, in a word, blessing in all its fullness? Do we have power and authority unless we receive it from on high? And when people listen to us, will not our teaching be cold and bare indeed unless they know that it is Jesus Christ who speaks? We should all remember that to hear those who bring us Jesus Christ's word is to hear Jesus Christ himself; and conversely, to reject or disparage the gospel message is to offend him, as if he did not deserve to be heard.

It was announced earlier that, since our Lord has withdrawn some by death and others by leave of absence, provision must be made for the good order of this church. Following the notice which you have received, our brother here present has been chosen and accepted by the city fathers.[2] What, then, remains to be done? Since a minister is to be inducted, we should reflect on what our Lord has said. He came down to earth once and once only to save our souls from hell, and he fulfilled the office of teacher for three and a half years. Nevertheless, he desires to continue his work until the end of the world. So day by day he summons us. God has not only shown us such intimacy as to reveal himself fully in his word; but, as Scripture says, he rises early to follow closely after us (Jer. 7:13, 25; 25:4; 35:15; 44:4). Now if this was said well before our Lord appeared in the flesh, and when he was known only in dark and shadowy form; and if God in another place is said to stretch out his arms all day long to a thankless and rebellious people (Isa. 65:2), let us make sure that such rebukes are not addressed to us, and that whenever the gospel is preached we come to God, believing that he is calling us and will always welcome us.

When we baptize a child, therefore, we should each recall the fruit that comes to us from our baptism—that is, our spiritual washing, so that this seal may be more deeply engraved on our hearts. I say 'seal', because the effect of baptism is to seal our adoption by which we are made children of God. It is the same when ministers are ordained: this is God's way of showing, visibly as it were, that he desires to lead and shepherd us.

When God uses men in this way, he surrenders nothing of his power or of his right to rule as sovereign over us. He does so only to demonstrate that he can use men as his instruments and can

[2] See above, p. 271, note 6.

make them do as he wishes. So it is only right that those who bring the message of salvation should be instituted and be clearly seen to have God's sanction. God is not the God of confusion, to use Paul's words (1 Cor. 14:33): there must be order. Elsewhere we read that even our Lord Jesus Christ did not intrude, but waited for the Father's solemn commission, when he said, 'You are a priest forever after the order of Melchizedek' (Heb. 5:6). We are not of course appointed to make sacrifice, unlike the papists who seek to replace God's Son. Our work is to offer a different sacrifice, which Paul describes as a holy offering of all the souls brought to God by our preaching, kept obedient in the faith and preserved to the very end (cf. Rom. 15:16). Thus those who are appointed to the task of teaching and of leading the church should be formally instituted in God's name.

The papists, it is true, make such a spectacle of things that God is plainly mocked. Their priests are instituted just like the Levites, thus smothering the light of the gospel. Yet this does not stop the church from observing order and from lawfully appointing men to office. Those who are to be messengers of Jesus Christ and ministers of his secrets should be stewards in his house. Let those who manage his household and share out the good gifts that he apportions among his elect be properly installed in office, so that they know their own role, and the people know theirs. Ministers, then, must resolve to dedicate themselves to God: they are no longer their own masters but are under a heavy obligation, and if they fail in their duty they will be severely punished, for they are answerable to God. That is their role. The people, equally, have theirs. When a man goes up into the pulpit, we should recognize that he has been appointed in our Lord's name and has been ordained by the church over which Jesus Christ presides. Scripture itself says that where two or three are gathered together in his name, he will be in their midst to sanction whatever is done in fear and in obedience to his word (Matt. 18:20).

Now our brother here has already served our Lord, but because he was not inducted into this church he is once again presented. What we must do is pray to God that he may work in him so as to make him a faithful minister, for we know that we are not competent in ourselves; as Paul says, no one is fit for this purpose (2 Cor. 3:5). We will, however, be competent once God supplies our need and once we are equipped with the necessary gifts. Our Lord Jesus Christ possesses the fullness of the Holy Spirit, and apportions him to any he chooses to use for spiritual leadership in his church. If we thought carefully about how gracious God is in giving us people who will guide us day by day along the path of salvation, we would most certainly set a higher value on prayer. If we ask God to make the wheat and the vine grow in order to give us food, should we not care for our souls even more? From this we see how ignorant and mindless we are, since we benefit and prosper by praying for our magistrates, asking God to rule and lead them by his Holy Spirit, so that justice may prevail and so that those who sit in this seat may know that, as God's deputies, they must deny themselves. When this happens, it is the highest blessing there is.

The same may be said about the teaching we receive, for good order and purity of doctrine are like the two eyes of the church. Let us learn, then, that when a minister is presented, he must offer himself to God as well as being offered and given to the church. May we each also present him in prayer and supplication, begging God to use him so that fruit from his preaching should come to all of us, and that we should have cause to thank God for it.

Now let us cast ourselves down before the majesty of our good God, acknowledging our faults and beseeching him so to make us feel them that we may be humbled before him and may sigh for our sins. Above all, may he deliver us from our bondage to Satan and cleanse us from all our filth, clothing us with the purity of his righteousness. And may we endeavour to glorify his holy name as long as we live, and to obey his holy commandments by which he is pleased to rule over us.

INDEX OF SCRIPTURE REFERENCES

Index of Scripture References

INDEX OF SUBJECTS

The Banner of Truth Trust originated in 1957 in London. The founders believed that much of the best literature of historic Christianity had been allowed to fall into oblivion and that, under God, its recovery could well lead not only to a strengthening of the church, but to true revival.

Interdenominational in vision, this publishing work is now international, and our lists include a number of contemporary authors, together with classics from the past. The translation of these books into many languages is encouraged.

A monthly magazine, *The Banner of Truth*, is also published, and further information about this, and all our other publications, may be found on our website, banneroftruth.org, or by contacting the offices below:

Head Office:
3 Murrayfield Road
Edinburgh
EH12 6EL
United Kingdom
Email: info@banneroftruth.co.uk

North America Office:
610 Alexander Spring Road
Carlisle, PA 17015
United States of America
Email: info@banneroftruth.org